Gulf of
Mexico

Siboney sailed
April 19, 1989

Nassau

George Town, Exuma

Great Inagua
Haiti St. Domingo

Puerto Rico

Jamaica

Morant Cays

Caribbean Sea

Nicaragua

Sailed
May 25, 1989

Panama
Canal

Rescued
Aug 19. 1989

Costa Rica

Venezuela

Isla de Cocos

Isla de
Malpelo

Colombia

Voyage of *Siboney*

Galapagos Islands

OUR LAST CHANCE

THE CREW OF THE SAILING VESSEL

SIBONEY

INVITE YOU TO JOIN US FOR

A TOAST

AS WE SET SAIL FOR THE PACIFIC AND INDIAN OCEANS

EN ROUTE TO THE START OF THE "AMERICAS 500" REGATTA

DEPARTING PALOS, SPAIN, AUGUST 1992 FOR MIAMI, FLORIDA

APRIL 9, 1989 - 11:00 HOURS   BILL BUTLER, CAPTAIN
PIER "I", MATHESON HAMMOCK MARINA   SIMONNE BUTLER, PILOT
CORAL GABLES, FLORIDA

OUR LAST CHANCE

SIXTY-SIX DEADLY DAYS ADRIFT

by

Bill and Simonne Butler

FIRST EDITION

LIBRARY OF CONGRESS CATALOGING-IN-PUBLICATION DATA

BUTLER, WILLIAM A.,   1929-
BUTLER, SIMONNE S.,   1937-

OUR LAST CHANCE / SIXTY-SIX DEADLY DAYS ADRIFT /
WILLIAM AND SIMONNE BUTLER. - 1st. ed.

ISBN 0-9632519-0-2 (hard) - ISBN 0-9632519-2-9 (soft)

92-81605
CIP

PRINTED IN THE UNITED STATES OF AMERICA

PUBLISHED BY:

EXMART PRESS
P. O. BOX 432140
MIAMI, FL 33243-2140

0 9 8 7 6 5 4 3 2 1

INDUSTRIAL CODE NO: 662856-10032 (hard)
662856-10034 (soft)

We once were lost, but now we're found.
We were blind, but now can see.

Thanks be to God.

His amazing grace
made this story possible.

foreword

This story begins in the far reaches of a dark and very desolate Pacific Ocean after dozens of maddened whales hammered through the hull of *Siboney*, our boat and home. *Siboney* quickly filled with water, the weight of its lead keel drawing it towards the bottom two miles below. Moments before my ever faithful vessel sunk, Simonne and I boarded a six foot plastic liferaft. In pounding seas propelled by a fierce southerly wind, 1200 miles from shore, lost in every sense of the word, our lives depended entirely on our fragile vessel. On the second day adrift, with two drops of brandy, we christened it *Last Chance*. She was truly to become *Our Last Chance*.

Simonne and I venture to use this Foreword at the outset of our tale as a vehicle for conveying to the reader who we are and why we sailed into the Pacific Ocean. The Introduction that follows carries the story from Miami through the Caribbean Sea and the Pacific Ocean to moments before destiny drove us alongside a dense pod of pilot whales. A chart on the front cover end-leaf outlines this passage. In Chapter One, we begin to tell the story of how we survived sixty-six days in our miniscule "deflatable" craft. A chart on the back cover end-leaf pictures this voyage together with various milestones while adrift. I have superimposed on the same chart the tracks of the Bailey's and the Robertson's, both sunk by whales in the early seventies. Aside from our three tracks crossing in the far reaches of the Pacific Ocean, we are fascinated to note that the Robertson's sank on June 15, 1972. We sank June 15, 1989, obviously not a good day for full keeled sailboats to be sailing in those waters.

At the end of our story, in a chapter labeled SURVIVAL, we pass on to readers who someday may venture offshore some facets on the subject learned the hard way. Later we include a chapter labeled

LIFE AMIDST THE WORLD OF SHARKS, written for those of you who have interest in that direction. Following SHARKS, we include a LIST OF ITEMS SAVED from *Siboney* in the few minutes before *Siboney* sank. Even we remain surprised with the amount of supplies we gathered in so few minutes. READINGS contains prayers, psalms, and parables found by Simonne among belongings rescued from the sinking boat. Beginning with Day 1, she read each every evening, usually in the order listed. On days when mountainous waves and stinging rain prevented us from taking the small cards out from their protective plastic, we recited from memory.

We maintained a written account of our daily activities until day 52 when sharks and dolphins, wild and maddened, damaged our raft. Sea water soaked the Log Book and made further entries impossible. Once safely ashore in the Golfito hospital, long-nailed nurses helped us separate and dry the pages. To our amazement, the Log remained fully legible, and we have reproduced it at the end of our story.

For reasons of clarity, I tell the story. However, in an experience such as ours, where our lives dangled daily from the thinnest of threads, where we fought constantly for our lives, inches apart, ever on the edge of death, Simonne's voice cannot be but an equal part of mine. When our thoughts are not collective or when we engage in action that separates us, such as when *Siboney* filled with water, voice shifts directly to Simonne.

This story begins in the late 1930's, in Cuba, when I was eleven. My mother, exhausted with my mischievous energy, surrendered me to the care of a sailboat captain. "Take him as crew," my mother insisted. From that moment on, the sea had me.

Later, when my father took notice in my interest in the sea and that it kept me out of trouble, he bought me a 15 foot Snipe. In it, I took my first high seas cruise: to Varadero and back to Havana...more than two hundred miles...with my faithful crew, Bob Harras, a 5 gallon jug of water, a large can of crackers, four cans of sardines, a bar of guava paste, and $10. We were gone two weeks and had a great time.

In the late forties, I met world renowned Argentinean solo sailor, Vito Dumas, as he passed through Havana. It was then that I began to dream of circling the globe in a sailboat. Forty years would pass before I converted my dream into reality.

My engineering degree from Purdue led me to a job with General Electric in Cuba. When Castro closed GE, we moved to Manila. In 1960, on my first visit to the Manila Yacht Club, I saw my dream boat and fell in love. Her name was *Mysterious* and she wasn't for sale. Anyway, I couldn't afford her, so I bought a Star boat.

Two years later, I owned a 26 foot sailboat with a five foot bowsprit called *Monsoon*. She'd passed the War years sunk up the river from Hong Kong. Still, whenever I sailed out of the yacht basin, my eyes were always on the beautiful lines of the 38 foot cutter. Finally, in 1966, *Mysterious* was mine.

She was one of more than thirty boats of the Mystery Class designed in England by Robert Clark. Sussex Yacht Works in Shoreham built her in 1938, and she sailed British waters until 1956 when a new owner shipped her to Manila. I changed her name to *Siboney*, a Cuban love song, and with friends raced her every weekend. In 1968, we sailed to Hong Kong and joined the China Sea Race to Manila. When GE moved me to Caracas, *Siboney* followed atop a bulk sugar carrier. Through the next eight years with my sons and friends, I sailed her to just about every Island in the Caribbean.

Simonne is French who, as a young girl, escaped the worse of the war years on a farm in the hills northwest of Nice. Later her family moved alongside the beach in Menton, a small town five miles east of Monte Carlo, near the Italian border. There, with her sister and brother, she came to know and love the sea. After completing secondary school, she travelled to England, Germany, and Spain where she studied and worked and added three languages to her native French and the Italian learned from her mother.

Sim and I met in Venezuela during our first marriages. When GE reassigned me to Miami in early 1977, she helped sail *Siboney* up in 20 days. I left GE in 1979 to open an export business in partnership with Simonne. We married in 1983 and worked side by side shipping heavy electrical equipment to Venezuela. Business was good until exchange controls froze new orders. We then closed down our sales operation and prepared to travel...aboard *Siboney*.

Simonne knew how much my dream of circumnavigating meant to me, but she was also reluctant to leave her children. She insisted we wait a year or two. This was the moment to go, I argued. At last, she broke down and agreed to cast-off all ties to shore and sail away. I made *Siboney* ready for sea while Sim attended to all of the shoreside activities connected with relocating children and closing a home. Sim did all the packing and moving under a tight schedule which she carried out resolutely.

With all shoreside burdens in order, we began our or, better said, my dream voyage. I longed for the sense of freedom and the daily challenges that crossing great expanses of ocean under sail provides. Simonne is a hearty sailor and good crew, but she made it clear that going on this cruise was one hundred percent love for me. Sim enjoys short sails between sandy beaches. Fifty day passages were not meant for her. Alone, in the depths of the ocean, we would face countless hazards, all of which we would have to solve on our own. Storms would try our seamanship; mechanical and electrical emergencies would arise as the boat sailed across unmarked expanses of water to a precise spot on a paper chart.

All the same, we prepared to sail away.

introduction

Siboney became a beauty as we approached our scheduled departure date in early April, 1989. Months earlier, I had emptied the entire cabin, then painted and varnished every nook. The Awl-Grip on the topsides was bright, and the bottom paint was barely a year old. Varnished topsides gleamed. New sails, a new Bimini sunshade, new fuel and water tanks would help make our trip safer and more comfortable. A Fleming self steering gear built in New Zealand replaced my trusty Hasler. It should steer us effortlessly around-the - world.

Simonne's petite sister Michele flew in from her home in Menton, France and spent more than 30 hours in a bosun's chair refastening the mast track. While she rested, friends heaved me up to inspect the wire and every tang, clevis, and cotter pin. We grounded the masthead lighting rod solidly to two Dynaplates alongside the mast that also served as boat ground. A new Profurl jib-reefing system went on the forestay while we fitted the old genoa furler to the staysail. These two sail furling devices coupled with boom furling should take much of the work out of sail handling.

Dodge Morgan's *American Promise* became the inspiration for a stern-mounted, four legged aluminum tower. A 12x24 inch platform at the head of the tower supported the Windbugger wind generator and a Furuno radar, my Hustler SSB, VHF, and SATNAV antennas, wind instrument sensors, and the wind sensor for the Autohelm autopilot. The radar was easily adjustable from the deck to any angle of heel with a device I designed. All wiring ran through two of the tower legs and into plastic conduit. By April 1, all systems checked out perfectly.

Everything necessary for a four year voyage found its place on board. Two new gel batteries plus a year old large Starrett battery totalled more than 500 ampere hours of stored power, a solid backbone on which to operate all our creature comforts. A 600 watt inverter gave us the 110 volt power we needed to run the computer and for power tools. The engine driven alternator, the wind driven generator, and two large solar panels would keep the batteries charged. A new electrical panel with three main switches would supply power to loads with any combination of batteries.

My old boat slowly became an electronic wonder. A Satellite Navigator would provide navigational fixes worldwide. Data from the speed sensor and the electronic compass fed to the SATNAV would update our position between satellite fixes. A PAK-RAT data controller could process radio signals and send them to my IBM laptop for conversion into weather charts. I could look at the charts on the screen or print them out. Wind speed and boat speed, displayed on a swinging panel, would be visible either from the cockpit or cabin. Radar would help spot ships and land. The single sideband radio could also work the ham bands. With both my FCC ship radio license and Novice Ham ticket, I planned to stay in close contact with our family.

A new Perkins 4.108 replaced the eight year old Westerbeke for main propulsion. However, the three new sails would provide the real power to drive *Siboney*. One sail, a jib to replace the roller furling genoa for heavy weather work to windward, was our only spare. *Siboney* was ready for the world and her ultimate cruise.

The new cabinets in the bow increased our storage capabilities two fold and held medicine for the entire trip. A large dry shelf held charts for the entire first leg to Manila together with all my navigation books. Individual plastic wrappers covered each against the inevitable rough weather. An extra dry nitch held my sextant.

More than a hundred close friends and well-wishers showed up for our departure party at high tide, April 9. We had champagne, blessings, balloons, kisses, and sunshine. It was a memorable event for all..most probably because we didn't sail off. The boat wasn't ready; our business was far from closed, and the house wasn't empty. Our original plan called for us to leave Miami in mid-March, three weeks before our farewell party, which would have brought us into Hawaii before the beginning of the hurricane season. I sailed away on April twenty first with my good friend Gus, who goes back to my sailing days in Cuba. Simonne remained behind to wrap up myriads of loose ends and would meet us in Nassau.

With Cuba blocking our way to Panama, we had to head west for the straights of Yucatan or east to the Windward Passage. If we sailed west, we would have to fight wind and strong currents south of Cuba for a hundred or more miles. We opted to sail upwind across the Gulf Stream to Cat Cay and over the bank to Nassau. In Nassau, we pulled *Siboney* into the fuel dock and called Sim to meet us. She still couldn't make it, so we refueled and headed to the Exumas. Days later, Sim flew to Georgetown and joined the boat. Gus flew back to Miami as we swung the bow south.

In a tight beat against a howling southeasterly, we approached Great Inagua late in the afternoon of May 5. Spray flew. *Siboney* leaped over the waves as I raced her towards shore in the waning light. Night was nearly upon us when a young man waved *Siboney* into the island's minute basin, then helped secure our lines. When Saturday dawned, the constable roused us to announce that the Mail Boat was about to arrive. We had to move out of the way.

Atop the pier, I spied the small freighter steaming at full speed towards our little harbor. While I tugged from shore and Sim worked lines aboard, *Siboney* slipped into a corner of the man-made harbor. The rusty freighter, belching blasts of diesel smoke and madly churning its propeller in reverse, edged its way to the space we had occupied only moments before.

The freighter's rusty decks contained a mountain of goods, all loosely arranged. A dozen passengers crowded the equally rusty upper deck. A cow and two goats, secured to the bow, complained bitterly about conditions aboard. Everyone in town was on the dock to greet the boat. Taxi drivers drove passengers to town. Local merchants claimed their cargo. Dozens of youngsters gawked at the only live spectacle in town. Many of the visitors dropped by *Siboney* for a chat and a cold drink.

The Mail Boat Master Loading Plan wasn't. Most of the goods destined for Great Inagua were on the bottom of the heap. All the bedding, chairs, concrete mixers, and planking first off-loaded were thrown back on board before departure. Left on the dock were piles of concrete blocks, cement, an odd variety of doors, cases of food, and dozens of sacks of fertilizer. The animals, still complaining, returned to sea. Sim and I, pushed into our little corner of the basin, watched as the originally clear sea water received a heavy dose of oil and litter.

Sim took advantage of an idle taxi and ran into town. She returned with ice, a few sad looking vegetables, and two packages labeled frozen chicken that looked more like sea gull. The fuel truck driver unloaded his full load of diesel into the Mail Boat and promised to be right back.

We talked for a long time with an old-timer who told us that an old friend, Woosh, drowned after falling overboard at night while on a fishing trip off the coast. Woosh had come to save *Siboney* late one night after I ran her aground on a rocky beach off Great Inagua in 1977. Sim and I had looked forward to seeing him again to thank him one more time for his help. Simonne that night prayed for Woosh.

While I slept, Simonne had continued to read. At eleven, on a trip to the head, she stepped down and was alarmed to find ten inches of water over the cabin sole. She shook me awake and switched on the bilge pump. The bilge emptied in minutes. Heavy with stores, the boat floated below the bilge outlet. Sea water had siphoned back into the boat through a valve which normally needed not to be closed unless underway.

Had Sim been asleep, the water may have reached us at bunk level and soaked many of my electronic spares. We hastened to empty the storage under the bunks and dried each can, though we left the soggy labels in place. We worked through the night tidying the mess.

This was a warning from Woosh, Sim had said. Later, in a dream, she had heard him call out..."Be careful. Be careful, my friends. There are dangers on this trip. Take good care of yourself." Poor Woosh. Such a great guy. His time had come much too soon.

Sunday dawn found us still tired and shaken from the near sinking. Calls to the owner of the fuel truck always ended with a promise that he would arrive in less than an hour. At three in the afternoon, we gave up and sailed for Panama with fuel tanks short twenty gallons.

The Windward Passage was windless. Seas calmed as we approached Haiti. We motored, but wishing to conserve fuel for use later in the trip, we did a lot of drifting. The current pushed us south and west, much too close to Jamaica and the perilous reefs that surround it. A wind shift got *Siboney* back on track, and at eleven in the morning on May 11, a tall white lighthouse stood off our port bow.

Morant Cays, an inviting set of tiny Islands fifty miles east of Jamaica, tempted us to pay a call. Several fishing boats worked nets to sea, and, when one of them turned our way, I brought our 9mm handgun on deck just in case. Two fishermen motored up, waved, and asked for cigarettes. We had none and tossed them a couple of cold drinks. They offered fresh fish and then sped away.

The rest of the Caribbean was equally windless. How we wished we'd been patient and loaded the extra fuel in Great Inagua. Even so, we would have saved less than a day. At last, on May 17, a month out of Miami, we approached the entrance to the Panama Canal.

Our SATNAV fixes helped steer us right to the main Canal outer breakwater slightly after midnight. Sim, at the helm, followed a string of green high-intensity lights into Cristobal where I dropped the anchor in an area set aside for small boats. In seconds, we were asleep.

In the morning, we began to feel our way around the formalities of transiting the Canal and quickly found that a yacht must follow the same paper trail as does a large ship. The Canal operates 24 hours a day and 365 days a year, but small boats are allowed to transit only on Tuesdays and Thursdays.

Visits to Immigration and a half dozen other public offices yielded a variety of multilayered forms and ultimately a scheduled departure for the following Tuesday. This worked out fine as Sim needed time on shore to prepare both mentally and physically for the long trip to Hawaii. Actually, we'd both been on the go for months and were much in need of quiet time.

Our six days on shore were, what should I call it, different. The country was on the verge of a revolution. The economy had slowed down for months. The people had revolt in their hearts but dared not show it. Both Sim and I speak fluent Spanish which helped us make new friends quickly. Taxi drivers, Club employees, and other Panamanians privately plied us with their frustrations. Most were ready to give up their peaceful existence and leave their wives and loved ones to do battle with their corrupt and despotic leadership. We listened to their plight but were heartened by the very visible show of U.S. forces in the air, on land, and around the waters surrounding the Canal.

We were warned never to leave the Club on foot because assaults were all too frequent. We taxied everywhere, usually with Arsenio. After completing our chores, he would take us on tours of the Canal where the US military had closed off the traditional vantage points. He ran us by his home in town where we waved at his wife and baby son, who looked down from a first floor window as we drove by.

An extremely peaceful man, Arsenio seethed. He told us, "Give me a gun. I am ready. The time has come to free Panama." In the public markets, Arsenio turned into an expert body guard. Along the way, he enlisted friends as additional help. Pickpockets wouldn't hesitate to run a long sharp pin through us to get our wallets. We always had one person at our side and another behind.

The market teemed. Each stall had a specialty. At one, we picked up three pineapples. At another, we bought two large calabashes. Sim picked through piles of potatoes and onions to select the freshest. I took Sim to an old fashioned chicken stall, complete with boiling vats of water and cages full of cackling poultry. Where would we find fresher poultry, I teased. Never, she said, could she enjoy a chicken whose neck she had seen wrung.

We looked all over for fuel containers in which to carry extra diesel for the jaunt across the doldrums. We finally settled on four large pails that at one time had been full of pig tails imported from the USA. Arsenio then drove us to a street where two young boys washed the pails while we waited in the car. These twenty gallons of diesel fuel would get an extra day and a half run out of the engine.

The Panama Canal Yacht Club is the main gathering place for all yachts sailing either to or from the Pacific. Our days tied to shore turned out to be old-home-town week for Simonne. Every other boat had a French crew. One couple had taken delivery in Panama of a large Taiwan built sloop. They were in the process, erector set fashion, of trying to put all the pieces together without the benefit of an instruction book. Another group of French men were delivering a fifty plus Benneteau to a charter business in Tahiti.

Next to us was a young New Zealand couple in a boat half the size of *Siboney*. They worked as line handlers and at anything else that came their way. When their coffers filled, they hoped to sail to Opua in the Bay of Islands, New Zealand.

Weemoon, out of England, was on its way to Australia with three enjoyable people aboard. Tied alongside *Weemoon* was a thirty two foot boat whose last port was in Brazil and its goal the South Sea Islands. Aboard was a young couple, him, Australian with a French grandmother, and her, the prettiest of Swedish girls. Sim met the girl on several occasions at the laundry room at dawn, both anxious to beat the heat of the day.

Out in the anchorage were two identical forty foot steel boats with the Australian flag and kangaroos painted on the windvane of their self steering gear. Also, to our surprise, was a sister or, if not, a first cousin to *Siboney*. Designed by Robert Clark, the cutter was built to slightly different lines. The couple aboard joined us on *Siboney* for an evening snack.

On the same night, Dan Jelsema, a young boy of sixteen sailing alone around the world, joined us aboard with his father, who had flown in for a visit. Dan had left Florida three weeks earlier, and when running through the Windward Passage on a rainy night, he had unknowingly closed in on the Jamaican coast. In the pitch of night, his boat ran up on rocks. Alone he struggled for hours. Free at last, he found the rudder destroyed but, nevertheless, managed to limp into Kingston for repairs.

Dan and his father were back in Cristobal to search for Dan's black cat. When time had come to transit the Canal, the boy's cat was nowhere to be found. Once moored in Balboa, they hopped the Panama Canal train back to Cristobal. Meanwhile Sim had found the cat near the Club's kitchen where it had joined a dozen other meowers in search of leftovers. Dan, overjoyed, lost no time dragging it away to the South Pacific.

Canal regulations stipulate that a small boat must have four line handlers in addition to the Captain and the Pilot-advisor. *Siboney* was under way by nine in the morning on our appointed Tuesday with two paid line handlers and the pilot-advisor provided by the Canal. A French lady doctor and Sim rounded out the line handling requirements. Sim steered while I tended lines. Emerton McDonald, one of our hired crew, was a good looking, engaging young man from Jamaica, who turned out to be interesting company on our two day trip from the Atlantic to the Pacific Ocean. Emerton works at the Panama Canal Yacht Club in Cristobal on a boat owned by a man who rarely spends time aboard. This allows Emerton time to earn a little extra money helping boats through the Canal. The other line handler was the son of a maintenance man at the Club. His father had asked us, as a favor, to take his son on his first trip through. The contract price was forty dollars each.

We motored to Gatun along with six other sailboats and rafted inside the first lock with a forty foot sailboat, *Rose of Devon*. As we prepared to rise more than fifty feet, McDonald took the bow line when thrown from shore while I backed Ricardo up in the stern. With the other five boats similarly secured, the control valves opened. Tons of water rushed into the lock. Powerful eddies pushed us towards the concrete walls. The two line handlers on *Siboney* and both on *Rose* heaved mightily to keep all four lines taught as water flooded in. Our pilot was the better of the lot. He had positioned *Siboney* in front of a mid-lock door where the force of the eddies was least.

Once full, the giant doors opened, allowing us to enter the second set of locks. Sim handled the controls and synchronized our speed perfectly with the lady on *Rose*, also at the helm, as they chatted away non-stop. Minutes later, we rose another fifty feet. There, as we exited the lock, the cruise ship, *Regent Star*, waited to enter. Passengers waved and took snaps of *Siboney* and the other sailboats. We then motored across Gatun Lake, past many large merchant ships awaiting their turn to transit, and up Gaillard Cut through lush jungle that led us to the overnight anchorage at Gamboa.

Our pilot was a young man, not yet thirty and married with three children, the oldest now ten. He hoped to have his full license as a Pilot before long. He was sick with the regime although always careful never to directly divulge his feelings. Once anchored, the pilot launch picked up the advisors while the rest of us spent the night in a tropical wonderland. Ricardo and McDonald joined the other line handlers for a fresh water swim as Simonne prepared a scrumptious rice and chicken dinner for the crew. The two ladies slept below. McDonald, Ricardo, and I squeezed into the cockpit, with Ricardo, the shortest, sleeping on the cockpit floor.

A light drizzle provided the morning shower. With the pilots back on board, we proceeded to the down locks of Pedro Miguel and Miraflores, and at noon, on the 24th of May, *Siboney* re-entered the Pacific Ocean. Fuel and water tanks were topped-off at the Balboa Yacht Club and the coolers fully iced. We added picturesque Club T-shirts to our collection. With a sole farewell wave from the fuel attendant, we set out on the next leg of our voyage around the world.

Hilo, in the Hawaiian Islands, lay 4500 miles ahead. There we would stop briefly to buy fresh food before continuing to Honolulu, the first major stop in our four year globe circling sail. From Honolulu, we'd sail to Hiroshima, Japan, with 25 other boats. The cruising rally was to start June 18. Not only would it be safer, but our arrival in Japan would be more fun. Japanese books and tapes aboard would help Sim, the ship's linguist, pick up basic Japanese.

Sailing the Inland waters of Japan in the late summer months of 1989 was to be the true highlight of our four year trip. October would see *Siboney* cruising through the Ryukyus, past Taiwan, and on to the Philippines. I dreamed of following *Siboney's* wake in waters I often sailed when living in Manila. We would enter Manila Bay between Corregidor and Bataan and then on to the Manila Yacht Club where I had been Commodore from 1967 to 1969. With all of our flags flying, I longed to salute my old friends.

I had a list of projects planned for my carpenter and friend in Manila, Pacifico Cadion. Simonne and I would fly home to visit family and to take care of taxes and other inescapable landborne chores. In February, 1990 or earlier, we planned to sail south to Brunei, over to Singapore, to Sri Lanka, and the Maldives. We couldn't linger as we had to keep sailing to stay ahead of the changing monsoons. From Djibouti, we would push up the Red Sea before head winds set in. A marina in Turkey would be our home for the winter of `90.

We planned to cruise the Greek Islands, Yugoslavia, and parts of Italy in 1991 to end up in a wintering spot near Menton in the south of France. There we'd lie in a marina less than a mile from Sim's childhood home on the beach which she had left at age twenty to discover the world.

In early June, 1992, we would anchor in Cadiz, Spain to join the America's 500 regatta. The start would take place in Palos and would finish in Miami, with stops in the Canary Islands and San Salvador in the Bahamas. This rally, to follow Columbus' "small boat cruise" of 1492, was to be a perfect finale for our world cruise.

A bright rainbow to the south drew us away from the Balboa Yacht Club early in the afternoon of May 24, 1989. My heart raced with excitement; I was on my way to join the ranks of the circumnavigators...Slocum, Morgan, Magellan. I aimed the bow of our sturdy boat away from land without so much as a backwards glance. I was anxious to swing into the open ocean where peace reigns, where man tests his skills against the earth's essential elements.

I held Simonne's hand as we motored away in silence. Again and again, she looked past our stern. Her eyes reached out to the land which she knew soon would not be there. She later told me she had prayed for a miracle, even secretly hoping she would break a bone, so as not to make this leg of the trip. She sailed only because she loves me.

Simonne dislikes long ocean passages. Her longest so far, aboard *Siboney*, had been twenty one days. On this leg, she had argued for a course that would take us coast hopping along Central America, up as far as Puerto Vallarta in Mexico. She could handle the three or four week sail from there to Hawaii. Unfortunately, May 25 was too late in the year for a direct shot towards Hawaii via the Great Circle route that skirts the coast. The hurricane season in the eastern north Pacific had started in April; I couldn't risk it. We had to play it safe and take the southern route to Hawaii. This called for a 0two hundred mile leg south from Panama, away from Hawaii, to reach the westerly flowing current. At four degrees North latitude, we would head west and sail 2400 miles before turning north towards Hilo on the island of Hawaii.

Under cloudy skies and light variable winds, *Siboney* clawed its way south. We burned half of our fuel supply to get out of the Bay of Panama and down to four degrees north of the equator, to where the current flows west. An island called Malpelo would be our turning point. What a strange, ominous name for an island. In Spanish, Malpelo means bad luck. A dark, cloudy, foggy night found us closing in on this spooky island. At midnight, the radar range to Malpelo was twelve miles due west. The breeze was gentle and steady out of the southwest. Sim napped below and I cat-napped on deck. At one in the morning, when Sim joined me on deck, the range was seven miles, still west.

The black night and heavy mist dropped visibility to less than a half mile. Simonne shuddered in my arms. I held her tightly as we strained into the blackness for a sign of Malpelo. The name connotes so much evil that we grew uneasy every time I made a new plot of our position. Light rain began to fall.

At two in the morning, the radar showed Malpelo at five miles. At three, the radar range was seven miles...we were going backwards. At three thirty, Malpelo suddenly disappeared from the radar scope. As I adjusted knobs on the radar and still received no echo, I kept wondering: Who discovered it? What happened there over the years? Why is it considered bad luck? What disaster overtook mariners on Malpelo? Some unseen force draws us closer. Was it no more than curiosity? Or was it danger? When I told Simonne what was going on, she shivered and said she didn't like it at all as she pushed closer as if looking for protection.

SIMONNE:

I closed my eyes and felt a force that clawed at me and pulled me towards this evil island. Then something strange came over me. I heard people cry. I saw people from an ancient shipwreck in the water. Their arms flayed wildly. It was dark, foggy ,and rainy, the same weather we had now. The cries were for us. These people were in trouble. They needed our help. Come in closer, closer, they called. Save us.

The stench of fermenting seaweed became stronger. We were much closer than we thought. Why did the island disappear from the radar? What powerful force. I turn towards Bill and whisper: "Let's get out of here. I'm scared."

BILL:

I didn't need much coaxing. I tacked the boat right off to the south and put ourselves on a course parallel to the spooky rock. At dawn, when we had again tacked, the Island loomed large on the horizon to the north. It stayed with us throughout the day. When the wind died, we ran the engine and used precious fuel; we had to be far away from the clutches of that evil place by nightfall.

On the following night, two fishing trawlers passed close by headed out to sea. Soon after, the weather turned nasty and stayed that way for the next two weeks. The wind changed every five hours. No sooner were the sails set to handle a blow than the wind died. Or when calm, with full sails flying, the wind would start to whistle. Unless I kept the sails properly set, the boat wouldn't move at her best speed, and we would reach Honolulu days later than planned.

Towards morning, on the eleventh of June, when we were 500 miles north of the Galapagos Islands, the wind shifted around from southeast to south. Dawn revealed an overcast sky with low, dirty clouds scudding fast towards the north. Sunrise was red and ominous. The wind steadily increased and, within an hour, reached twenty five knots. Soon we had gusts of thirty. I rushed to deeply reef all sails as Sim secured all hatches and the skylight. The boat was ready for heavy going. Seas continued to build as thirty five foot swells from the south roared and foamed and broke on *Siboney*. Each wave sent sheets of wind-driven spray over the boat and strained the self-steering gear to maintain course.

We hurtled over waves and rode atop swells larger than railroad cars. Our sailboat remained buried under mountains of frothy water. When the self steering gear lost control of the 12 ton boat, I would grab the helm and coax her back on course. There was no turning back.

Then a second storm broke.

Late on the second day of the southerly, I noticed Simonne had become quieter than normal. She didn't read nor listen to her Walkman radio. When I stroked her head, she exploded and lashed out at me for bringing her on this trip where she didn't want to go, for taking her away from her family and the life she loved, for putting her in danger. I tried to calm her, but my every try upset her all the more.

Her fury lasted hours. Trapped in the cabin during the storm, she had become claustrophobic which added stress to a premonition of danger. I tried to soothe her without success. Finally, I dug into the cooler for one of my last cold Heinekens and escaped to the equally stormy deck.

Eventually, she calmed, then slept. Later, as we talked, I confessed that I too had a feeling of foreboding. She said she knew. She had watched me sneak quietly on deck during the storm. She saw me flash the lantern on the rigging as I checked and re-checked new creaking sounds. We hugged each other, made love, and slept.

Through two days and three nights, seas streaked with foam and flying spray lashed *Siboney*. White water cascaded over the cabin and down the deck and finally gushed over the lee side. Hour after hour, the wind howled, and the ocean screamed at us as if questioning our right to exist. The self steering gear battled the monster seas that insisted on pushing *Siboney's* bow north. Unable to control the boat, I gave up. I let her run where she wanted. Unbridled, she took off like a runaway mare. In the next two days, we logged three hundred miles on a course closer to 300 degrees than the 270 we needed.

While the storm blew, we spent most of the time in our bunks sandwiched between pillows reading or napping. When we awoke around mid-morning on June 13, the wind and seas had calmed. The sun again warmed the decks. We opened the boat and hung our bedding out to dry. Brunch in the cockpit and a sea water bath revived us.

A dozen Satellite fixes over the past two days confirmed that the storm had pushed us ninety miles north, off our intended track and right into the strong North Pacific Equatorial Countercurrent. The easterly stream cut our speed by close to a knot or more than 25 miles a day. The start for the race to Hiroshima, Japan is but a few days away. When we committed to enter this regatta three months ago, I told the committee we'd be late for the start. We must find a way to make the boat move faster.

I had practically memorized our sector of the pilot chart for the North Pacific Ocean in search of a way out of our plight. The westerly current is about 100 miles to the south. If we tightened up, we could get there in a couple of days unless, of course, another storm blows in...and another is soon due, for they appear to hit on cycles of one week. Or we could head north with the next big blow, across the doldrums in search of the easterlies and the westerly current. That three hundred mile trek might take us a week even if we burned up most of our fuel. What to do? It was now the fourteenth of June, nearly midnight. I will go on deck and take a look around. The fresh air might clear my mind.

chapter one

MIDNIGHT WEDNESDAY JUNE 14, 1989
ABOARD *SIBONEY* IN THE PACIFIC OCEAN

The ship's clock struck. Midnight. An oppressive overcast smothers the stars. The southeasterly has been blowing steadily throughout the long Pacific night generating a deep swell which our 38 foot cutter, *Siboney*, slices through on its westward course. Its wake coils briefly behind us, then vanishes, devoured by the hungry night. The sole glow in the immense blackness of this vast ocean is the feeble gleam of our masthead light.

The Pacific Ocean, 1200 miles west of Panama, is more intimidating tonight as neither moon nor starlight penetrate the dense, low lying clouds that stretch to the horizon. With every roll, *Siboney* speaks softly with her many voices; the creak of the dinghy pulling against its lashings; the rattle of the leeward backstay banging against a stanchion; the knock-knock inside one of the storage lockers. Like a faithful workhorse, *Siboney* plows on, jousting easily with both wind and waves, its heavy frames yielding to the pressure of the sea.

The warm breeze fills our three sails which push our speed over the water to four and a half knots, the best we've been able to maintain as we're deeply loaded with fuel, water, and stores for the long sixty day passage from Panama to Hawaii. The strong easterly current continues to slow our progress. Hawaii lies 3000 miles ahead; not only are we hopelessly late for the start of the race to Hiroshima, but it's now obvious that just catching the stragglers will be an impossible feat for *Siboney*.

Simonne has at last drifted off to sleep, and her soft steady breathing comforts me. Our last satellite fix was at six this afternoon, June 14. It put us at 5 and a half degrees north latitude and at 98 degrees, 1 minute west longitude. My anxious finger punches the keypad on the Satellite Navigator in search of an updated position. There is none. I question the little black box for future satellite passes, and within seconds, it displays the answer: the next acceptable satellite will dawn at three thirty this morning.

I climb the short steps that lead to the cockpit. A splash and a gentle blowing sound surprise me. Streamlined shapes plow through the water alongside. *Siboney* is surrounded by what appear to be dozens of black dolphins. They pace the boat, surfacing to blow out old air and suck in new, and then, with a strong twist of the tail, they dive and vanish deep in the inky sea. Wherever I look, black, quarter-moon shaped dorsal fins cut the surface.

When Simonne stirs, I whistle lightly. Within moments, she joins me on deck. I knew she would enjoy their antics. "They're wonderful!" she says. "You know, Bill, we haven't seen dolphins in nearly three weeks, not since we left the Panama Canal."

"Well, I'll tell you what, we're seeing them now! Look at them, Sim; there must be hundreds of them."

Simonne leans across the life lines to get a closer look at our visitors. Not satisfied, she reaches for the electrical panel and flips on the switch to the tower spotlight. Instantly, the boat is bathed in a spectral whitish-green aura, the black masses now brilliantly alive. She studies the shapes closely then slips her arm through mine and whispers: "They're not dolphins but whales. Pilot whales. I'm sure of it."

They move like an armada on a purposeful mission. With each plunge of *Siboney's* bow, larger whales appear. There is nothing concrete yet, just a slight tightening of the herd. Up to now, we have had only good, positive thoughts and an all encompassing bonding with the whales. But their mood is changing. And so is ours. A flash of tension passes through our clutched hands. Are we infringing on their space? The unthinkable begins to form in our minds, and we no longer enjoy the charm of their company.

Sim shivers and, without a word, she returns below. An hour passes, then another; each half hour dutifully announced by the ship's clock. Soon, I hope, the pod will pass, and we'll be alone once again in the vast emptiness of this unfriendly ocean. How I wish we were sailing the Caribbean where the water is deep blue, stars twinkle, and flying fish play; Sinatra's tune runs through my lips..."we're on the way to Mandalay...so very far away... "

I return below. The display on the Satellite Navigator tells me it's four in the morning, June 15, Miami time. I touch the Position pad and instantly get the new fix, and I enter it into my Navigation workbook as: 0342 THURSDAY JUNE 15 1989 5 DEGREES 30 MINUTES NORTH 99 DEGREES 3 MINUTES WEST. I do some quick math and find that our speed since the last fix at 6pm yesterday evening is but three knots. The damned current still has us. I have to make a move soon, but where? To work our way south in search of the westerly current will take days and draw us away from our destination. My best bet could be to wait for the next storm out of the south and ride it into the doldrums. It'll be a wild ride, thirty five knot winds and thirty foot waves, but, yes, that's what I'll do.

Back on deck, I find the whales are now bigger, some half as long as *Siboney*. They breathe louder and act irritated. They rush at each other in an apparent struggle of titans for position. The boat trembles, and a sandpaper-like scratching sound echoes all along the starboard side...a long winded rough caress that rights the boat and lets it go again.

"Did you feel that?" I heard Sim's dimmed voice ask from below.

"Yes," was my terse reply. I had so much to add, but I was speechless. What I wanted to say was that the whales now are bigger; they surface more often, and when they blow, it's more like a snort coupled with a sneeze. Water caught in their blow rises like geysers. They are clearly angry at each other...or are they irritated with us?

Once again, a nagging sense of uneasiness slips into my consciousness, an intrusion on my practical mind, and although I can't put a finger on it, I feel there is something terribly wrong. Their rhythm has definitely changed. Larger whales now pack both sides of the boat. They pace *Siboney* and rush at each other for room. When they blow, air and water fly over the boom. We are prisoners, surrounded, encircled, and held hostage by a pack of maddened whales. Whales turned terrorists. Our complacent admiration changes to deathly fear. I disengage the self steering gear as another whale scrapes the bottom of *Siboney* from stern to stem.

A whale bumps us to starboard. In rapid succession, two hard blows to port echo like the boom of a kettle drum. The boat heels far over to starboard, holds, then straightens up. More black shapes close in. These whales are no longer a mindless force, but a conscious one bent on a single purpose: our destruction. I move the tiller to bring the boat up into the wind, but a titanic jolt knocks me into the lifelines. *Siboney* reels. Sim is thrown from her bunk and cracks her head against the galley. The shout most dreaded by any sailor echoes in my ears: "Bill! We're taking on water! Oh, God, it's coming in fast!"

I leap below. An ominous noise much like a waterfall meets me. Water gushes through the floorboards. The ocean pours in with rip-tide determination. I start the bilge pump then search for the damage. The sound of water pouring in comes from behind the cooler and the galley range, deep below the water line. It can't be in a worse place. The cold box insulation has six inches of foam covered with fiberglass. The panel behind the stove is a heavy sheet of stainless steel for fire proofing. Water is coming in so fast I'll never have time to rip it all out.

Frantic, I start the engine, close the engine salt water intake, and remove the top of the filter. This turns the motor into a giant bilge pump, drawing its cooling water out of the bilge. Will it be enough to keep the boat from sinking? Is the leak behind the engine? I pull off the engine box and toss it on a bunk. My lantern reveals no rush of water from the stern. It's all happening too fast. Disbelief, confusion, and fear paralyze me, but as the water rises over my feet, one thought becomes clear: we must save the boat. That's all that counts. We'll have to bail.

Water rises over my feet.

SIMONNE:
My son Chris' words flash before me: **"Mom, be careful with whales. I just saw a movie...a boat was sunk by killer whales..."** The thought galvanizes me into action. I grab my toilet kit and scramble out of the cabin. Bill clamors for the bucket and I hand it to him. He dips it into the rising water and shoves it at me. Again and again, he plunges the bucket wildly into

the water and thrusts it at me to empty over the side. With mad determination, eyes glued to the water inching up his leg, he bails. The engine roars. He fights to save his boat.

Water rises faster than bailing and the pumps can manage. I call over the din of the engine: "Bill. We're sinking. Stop bailing. I'd better get the raft. Hand me the knife." I can see the knife in the sink. Bill, bucket in hand, stands there, stunned. I call for the knife again, this time louder. The engine noise is deafening. I cup my hands, take a deep breath, and scream as loud as I can.

"BILL. WE'RE SINKING! *SIBONEY* IS SINKING. PASS UP THE KNIFE."

Water has reached the engine. Drive belts spin salt spray throughout the cabin that blinds Bill. He starts to turn off the engine but hesitates. He needs this backup pump but he also needs to see. He reaches over and stops the diesel. An eerie silence follows, broken only by the splash of waves and whales and the rush of water in the cabin.

Without a word, he pushes the knife into my waiting hands. My legs are weak, like cottonwool. I creep along the port deck and inch my way towards the dinghy. The knife is so dull that I need to saw more than cut through the half inch ropes that hold our fiberglass tender to its cradle. I pull, and the bag suddenly breaks loose, almost sending me over the side. That's when I notice the decks are less than a foot from the ocean. Whales swim alongside, oblivious to our torment. Are you happy now? Are you placated? An enormous bull splashes next to the boat. Inches closer, and it would have struck us again. I try not to panic. There's no time for that.

I drag the heavy bag down the deck and roll it into the cockpit. My nervous fingers tug at a tightly tied trash bag. Inside I find a second bag. Bill always overdoes it. I'm shocked. My God, the raft isn't in this bag. It's a spare sail. Where's the raft?

Bill is on the radio, his calls desperate:

"MAYDAY MAYDAY MAYDAY THIS IS SAILING VESSEL *SIBONEY* WHISKEY XRAY UNIFORM 5908 MAYDAY MAYDAY STATION KILO CHARLIE FOUR JULIET CHARLEY VICTOR WE ARE SINKING POSITION NINETY NINE DEGREES TEN MINUTES WEST LONGITUDE FIVE DEGREES THIRTY MINUTES NORTH LATITUDE. HIT BY WHALES. WE ARE GOING TO THE RAFT MAYDAY MAYDAY MAYDAY"

Hundreds of thoughts race through my mind. I remember the plane that crashed in the Everglades many years ago. The Captain calling...MAYDAY. MAYDAY. I am one with all the pilots, captains, and sailors who have ever sent SOS messages. The distress they felt is now mine.

"Bill," I scream, "Where's the raft?" He looks up and points to the other side of the dinghy. "There, Sim, on the other side. I can see it from here. Keep your cool; you're doing fine", he calls up, phone in his hand. A sob creeps up my throat. Cool now, keep cool, don't panic. I can do it. Please, legs, don't shake. And please God, help me stay calm.

I edge back out on the deck now almost under water. The whales blow and splash at my elbow; one could easily slide onto the deck. A powerful sea breaks over the bow and washes over my feet. The ropes that hold the second bag are loose and harder to cut. I'm frantic as I use the knife as a saw. It's taking too much time. The boat is going down. With unexpected strength, I pull the bag loose. It's much heavier than the other. I drag it along the deck, now inches from the sea. I open the bag in the cockpit. It is the raft. Thank God. I call Bill, "I'VE GOT IT! IT'S HERE! COME UP NOW!"

The water in the cabin is so high that I gasp loudly. Bill pushes his way through the flooded cabin to the companionway. Our fingers tremble as we silently rush to untie the layers of protection surrounding the life raft valise. At last, the raft pops out, new, compact, and so very small. Oh, my God, let it be OK.

Bill begins to pull the handle to inflate the raft but stops. First, we must clear the cockpit. He loosens one of the bimini ties while I undo the other. The wind quickly catches the bright blue bimini top and carries it over our heads and out of the way. Bill then moves to the starboard deck and tears away at the stanchions that hold the life lines. With incredible force, he pulls three of the stanchions out of their brackets and drops them over the side. Two feet high, the raft would have had to go over them, and doing so, we'd probably tear it.

Seas roll down the deck. Bill takes one more look around and says: "Sim, stand back. I'm going to inflate the raft." The raft has a handle with large letters that reads: PULL HERE TO INFLATE. His hard tug catches us by surprise, for we are totally unprepared for the explosion of high pressure air that rushes into the raft. Air hisses into the neatly folded plastic, each crease popping out in succession. Within seconds, a sturdy yellow raft fills the cockpit. A sudden puff of wind lifts it off the deck and threatens to blow it away. I hold on to it as Bill ties the painter to the winch. "Let's load it", he says and, with no further word, returns below.

I load everything on deck into the raft: bucket, cushions, flashlight, compass, gloves, T-shirts, shorts. From a cockpit locker, I pull out all the bottles of water and soft drinks I find and drop them in the raft. Now, I need Bill to hand up food and everything else we might need, but he's back on the radio.

BILL:

I searched the twenty meter amateur band for radio traffic but came up empty. No contacts. The band was either dead or everyone's asleep. In Australia and the Far East, it's four in the afternoon, a bad hour for reception. Back in the States, it's four in the morning, and even the most hardy hams are in bed. I then tuned to 13113.2 kilohertz, the Coast Guard weather broadcast frequency, and transmitted in hopes my signal would get through to some ship awaiting the latest weather forecast. As a last shot, I tuned back into the Pacific Maritime Net, sent my last MAYDAY, then locked the radio into transmit in hopes that someone with a radio direction finder would pick up my dying signal.

Now to load the raft with stores. We keep our food under the port bunk which is now piled high with the computer, the weatherfax, the camcorder, and heaps of bedding and clothing. I throw everything on the starboard bunk, tear off the cushions, and plunge my head into the diesel laden water to grope for the cans stored below. I drop each can into a plastic bag and, when full, pass them up to Sim. Suddenly, I remember there is something important I must do.

SIMONNE:

In water deep above his waist, Bill struggles with the heavy motor cover and cushions that block his way towards the bow compartment. In an instant, he vanishes. I want to shout, to tell him, "Don't go, don't go. It's too dangerous." The boat could sink at any minute.

A prayer, followed by a sob, springs to my lips. Long minutes pass until he returns with the water maker and two life jackets. I place the water maker under the cushions, then slip into a jacket. The raft appears to be strong, and for a fleeting moment, I feel reassured.

Bill again disappears, water to his armpits. I gasp. Gone for the longest time, he emerges at last with one large can of crackers and a roll of paper towels. I exhale, blowing like one of the whales. Whales, I've forgotten about them. Where did they go? Bill hands me a large ziploc with our passports, credit cards, money, and travelers checks. I put the packet in the top left pocket of my life jacket and close the flap. He throws up a large plastic bag with unused bedding. Water covers the lower lockers as he empties the upper ones into supermarket bags. I find a place in the raft for each.

The comforters on the bunks are soaked. One of my pillows, the one with the duck pillowcase on it, floats away. I bought it years ago and have kept it like a pet. Over the past weeks, I curled up nightly with my ducky. Now it's full of diesel, soggy, ruined. I wish I had it.

A bottle of cognac, half full, floats next to a can of crackers. Bill passes both up. The raft overflows with stores. Bill has been moving like a whirlwind in the flooded cabin, but now he hesitates and looks around. He cannot accept that his beloved boat is sinking.

"Bill, that's it; there's no more room. Let's get the raft in the water." He's not listening. He fumbles in the tool compartment, finds a screwdriver, and pries off the ship's clock and the barometer from their traditional places above the navigation station. I wave and point to the LOG book and my yellow Walkman radio. Water reaches his chest. I motion for him to come up, but he fails to move.

"Bill, get the radio and LOG and COME UP. PLEASE. NOW."

BILL:

I can't pull myself away from the cabin I've grown to love. I've spent hours at anchor and at sea breathing in the coziness and warmth of the deeply varnished cabin. The boat lurches as I grab an overhead bracket and step over the now strangely quiet engine and out on deck.

The floodlight shines brightly on the mainsail as it flails like a bird about to take flight. C'mon, *Siboney*, get up, let's go. You and I were ready to conquer the world. Don't leave me now, I command. You are part of my life. You and I have done much in these twenty two years. Don't rob me of my dream. We have so much yet to do. But the pull of the sea is relentless. Sim interrupts my musing.

"Bill, quickly! The boat's going to sink," Simonne pleads.

I return to reality. We must go. What am I forgetting?

"Butler, what's wrong with you? COME ON, LET'S GO!" she screams.

"I'm not ready." I know how my boat settles; my sons sank it twice in Biscayne Bay, and I re-floated it both times. It's not yet ready to sink. She has been my faithful partner, and I will stay with her until she leaves me.

"Lord. Have mercy on us. This guy is crazy. Who do you think you are? Captain Ahab?"

I look at Simonne. "I repeat; I'm not ready. Besides I need to get something out of the cockpit lockers."

"Bill, put the raft in the water. The boat could go down and pull us with it. I want to get off. Now."

Siboney, full of water, has righted herself, and she rocks gently in the waves, as if held in a giant cradle. Sim's desperation finally gets through to me, and I turn to her and say: "Ok, let's launch the raft."

We inch the heavily loaded raft towards the gunwale and slide it into the water. I take the twenty foot inflation lanyard and cleat it. When Sim jumps on top of our load of supplies, I push the raft off. It floats away with its bow line tied to *Siboney*.

I spot the fishing rod and set it aside. I probe in the aft locker for a bag of hooks. Six packages sorted by size should be there, each in its own ziploc. I search blindly in the rising water and find but four coconuts which I place on the deck. I feel around for a face mask. No masks. No hooks either.

I call out: "Sim, where are the face masks?" She yells back that they are in the bow, now submerged.

"Bill. For God's sake. Get off." She hasn't stopped calling me since she jumped into the raft.

The deck wallows under me. Waves roll over my feet. Should I take the fiberglass dinghy or not? It's been on my mind since we started to sink. We would have 100 percent backup for the raft. On the other hand, in rough weather, the dinghy will surely sink; what will happen then? Puncture the raft? Or tear it? Many reasons for and many against. I decide to leave it.

The bow is heavy with water. Waves roll down the full length of the deck, to spill over the stern. I will stay with you *Siboney* to the last. Soon you will be alone, resting eternally on the muddy seabed, thousands of fathoms of black ocean pressing down upon you, trapped forever in a darkened tomb, never again to sail into a strange port or to bound carelessly over the oceans of the world. We rode out a typhoon together, winds of more than ninety knots. The masthead touched the waves twice, but you emerged stronger and sailed further than ever before. Much water has passed under your keel, but on this last two mile leg...you will sail alone.

Simonne is barely visible just beyond the circle of light. I hear her clearly: **"BILL, IF YOU DON'T PULL ME IN RIGHT NOW, I'LL CUT THE LINE. THE BOAT IS GOING DOWN!! GET OFF NOW!!"** The boat lurches drunkenly. It's time to get off.

MARLTON, NEW JERSEY
0430 THURSDAY JUNE 15. 1989

Jim Butler's 230 pounds lie sprawled across the king size water bed. He dreams of *Siboney*, his father, and Simonne, far off in the Pacific, sailing along in a gentle breeze. The night is dark. He sees an undefined object approach *Siboney*. The object strikes. The boat shudders and heels over. Water floods the cabin. Then, suddenly, the sea is empty. There is no trace of *Siboney* or her crew...they have disappeared...they're dead.

Jim sits up in a sweat. He stares around his darkened bedroom, his pajama shirt soaked. The dream was so vivid. **Something terrible has happened.**

chapter two

ABOARD *SIBONEY*
0450 THURSDAY JUNE 15, 1989

The glare from the spotlight underscores the grim finality of the scene. A great sea lifts *Siboney*. A wave atop this mighty swell breaks on the stern. White water cascades into the open lazerette to hasten *Siboney*'s now inevitable plunge to the bottom, two miles below. Sea water fills the cabin where Simonne and I have lived the last two months in cozy comfort. The brightly lit mainsail waves a painful good-by. I turn towards Sim, who has constantly called for me to join her. A wave breaks against the cabin and covers my ankles.

I pull the raft towards the dying boat. Bright yellow and rugged-looking, it rides high though heavily loaded. Simonne, hair blown and lips pursed, hangs over the near end of the raft ready to fend off from the self steering gear. The roar of a breaking wave startles us. It washes over the cockpit coaming, collides with the raft, and propels it into *Siboney*. The surge overpowers Simonne and the raft brushes the stern. A loud blast of air rushes from the raft. The end closest to the boat deflates and sinks under Sim's weight. The raft begins to go under with all the stores we've saved. I start to pull it aboard in hopes we have time to loosen and load the dinghy, but in a flash, the raft fills out and continues to float as before. Internal sleeves filled to act as a back-up air chamber. Sim, her left hand outstretched, terror in her eyes, looks to me for an answer. I nod. We're OK for now.

The three inch gash stares at me. What if water floods in. Will the raft then sink? Though the raft has lost half of its air, it floats high. Will it hold the two of us? I hesitate to jump in, afraid my added weight might cause the raft to fill with water. I move towards the dinghy, but another wave breaks over the cabin. White foamy water cascades down the deck and pummels the raft. I can stay aboard no longer. *Siboney* is going down.

I pull the raft closer to hand Sim the fishing rod, then untie the line from the winch. Sim steadies me while I slide in next to her. The four coconuts float by, out of reach. We drift away from *Siboney* without a word; neither of us able to break the eerie silence. Lights continue to burn aboard *Siboney* while the distance between us quickly widens.

Sim and I remain motionless as the sea swallows *Siboney* and so many of our terrestial possessions. She squeezes my hand; we kiss. I search for words to reassure her but come up empty. Moments later, the tower is under water. Lights flicker and the boat disappears. Left in total darkness and so utterly alone, we embrace, and with anguish deeper than we have ever before experienced, we cry uncontrollably.

I tighten my hold around Sim and search the horizon. But search for what? We haven't seen a living thing except for birds in nearly three weeks. Never has a night been this dark and dismal. Adrift, deep in the Pacific Ocean, in an overloaded and torn raft, we are castaways in the true sense. When I glance at Simonne, face somber and stiff, I remember all too quickly that she is in peril solely because of me. Her death will rest at my doorstep forever. Dark clouds press down upon and compress our universe into a tiny ball of terror and anguish.

Sim moves her wrist near a small greenish emergency light attached to the raft. It's 0520. At 0420, we sailed along without a care, pleased to have the whales as company. In sixty minutes, our lives and destiny have been irrevocably altered. And in less than an hour of use, our raft appears so less sturdy than when first inflated. Then it had felt solid and sturdy; now it's soft and lies low in the water. We must fill it with air before it sinks, but where's the pump? What does it look like? Sim rummages among our stores and locates the emergency kit. In it, she finds a flashlight, two patches, a packet of seasick pills, two plastic knobs, and a bellows type pump.

She turns the flashlight to the instructions printed on the side of the raft near the valve. Large black letters read, "Screw the pump on clockwise until it is tight, then open the valve two turns." I hold the flashlight while Sim screws the pump into the valve. She turns it clockwise and starts to pump. The sound of air filling the chamber is reassuring, and once the raft becomes more solid, our confidence in the integrity of our new craft increases. She turns the valve to close it and removes the pump.

I don't dare tell Sim we're in the wrong raft, a coastal raft designed for a week or ten days which I bought to save money, space, and weight. Why didn't I buy a top of the line offshore raft? Will this one last until we're spotted? I look into Sim's disbelieving eyes, and when they catch mine, we cry aloud. What will happen to us now? Will our family ever see us again? When will help come? Our lives dangle from the thinnest of threads.

The emergency sleeves saved our lives. When the canister of compressed gas first expanded the raft, both halves of the air chambers inflated equally. Air pressure pressed two internal sleeves into tight balls in the middle of each side of the raft. When the raft tore, air from the whole half chamber filled the sleeves which then expanded into the empty half chamber. The raft floated as before.

Tens of thousands of square miles of empty ocean surround us. If we had but a moon or a few stars, daylight, anything at all to reach out to, we would feel less alone. The gloomy blackness of night drags on. Our anxiety deepens. We're coming up on 0600, Miami time. Out here, where we drift, the day runs about two hours later. The sun will not make its appearance until after eight, first light before eight, and sun up no earlier than 0830, perhaps closer to nine. This night, a night that has brought us closer to death than either of us could have imagined, has a long way to run.

There is no human life in any direction for hundreds of miles. Land to the east is more than 1100 nautical miles. Acapulco is 700 miles to the north. The wind could push us there, but the current will take us to the east. The Galapagos Islands are 600 miles to the southeast, directly upwind. To the west lie 4000 miles of empty ocean. The westerly flowing current runs a hundred miles to the south and one hundred fifty or less to the north. If we're pushed into either, we will drift into emptiness. Distance and time are now our most mortal of enemies.

I need not close my eyes to see *Siboney* in her final moments, decks awash, sails full. Then the ruptured raft. Could we have launched the dinghy in time? Should we have brought it? What will happen if the other end of the raft tears and the raft goes down? A vision of the raft sinking with all of our stores throws new shivers through me. We could not have retrieved another item from the waterfilled cabin.

Yet we are alive. Someone will surely find us soon. We have some food and the water maker. The Emergency Position Indicator Radio Beacon, the EPIRB, will transmit signals on two frequencies monitored by aircraft and satellites. Upon receiving a signal from an EPIRB, the receiving station can trace the approximate location of the signal. For the system to work, our EPIRB must be in line of sight with an airplane or a satellite.

Are we near a commercial airline route? Chile-San Francisco...New Zealand-Los Angeles...what others are there? None come close to where we now float. A satellite needs a shore station, and there is no shore within a thousand miles. I debate. Should I activate the EPIRB now or wait until we're closer? If we wait, it may be too late for it to do any good. We could be dead. We need help now.

If the EPIRB or MAYDAY signals fail us, our family will certainly take the necessary steps for our rescue. Today is June 15. We talked to Cris and to Susy on June 11. Susan reported my son Joe's baby, a girl, had been born a day earlier. Joe awaits our congratulations. Cris expects an answer on whether to rent the house or not. I had almost called the children last night, but now I'm glad I didn't. This way, we picked up four days. In a week, on the 22nd, it'll be more than ten days since they've heard from us. After we left Panama, we called home every three to four days. Our silence has to be a strong signal that something has happened. In ten days, when the boys compare notes, the air-search will be on.

Perhaps we'll be sighted by a freighter. Ships from Panama to Hawaii and to the Far East all run further north. Shipping from South America to the West Coast will run to the east of us. It's obvious...we're out of all regular shipping routes as well.

On the positive side, however, we're in a strong easterly current that pushes us towards shore. Aboard *Siboney*, it was our enemy. Now it's our hope and, very possibly, our salvation. The North Pacific Equatorial Countercurrent flows as steadily as the Gulf

Stream. If we're lucky, we'll stay in it all the way to the coast. If not, we'll drift into the trackless wastes of the Pacific Ocean...or into an endless eddy, to drift in circles, forever.

We remain motionless atop all the stores gathered in those last few minutes before *Siboney* sank. Though freeboard is no more than eight or ten inches, we float easily over the passing swells. Above the black, unfriendly sky presses closer. A sense of utter loneliness sets in, stronger than we have ever felt before. For Sim's sake, I must keep a strong, positive attitude. Poor Sim, she's so quiet. I can only imagine what desperate thoughts run through her mind.

Neither of us can doze, much less sleep. My eyes refuse to close. Sim lies in my arms with her eyes shut, lips pursed. The green glow from the tiny, salt water activated emergency light helps fight our overwhelming feeling of loneliness. I look at the pain highlighted on Sim's face and think of how much more pain she must bear before we are delivered. My eyes reach up to the heavens. How do we get out of this one? I've sailed the oceans for more than forty years. I'll find a way.

The sky at last grows paler; the horizon more distinct. Touches of pink tint both the eastern and western horizon. At sea, on *Siboney*, I always stood the early watch to experience "first light," that splendid moment when night suddenly yields to the force of a new day. It is at this moment of first light, when both the star and the horizon are visible, that ocean navigators the world over shoot stars to find their position. Minutes later, even the brightest star is no longer visible as we're welcomed by the break between the long sweep of the swells and the multilayered sky .

Thursday, June 15, 1989, dawns. Black clouds turn grey, then slowly evolve into isolated shapes that glide in from the southern horizon, pass close overhead, only to quickly disappear far off to the north. The horizon lies before us, naked, except for the incessant waves that form a jagged, tooth shaped silhouette where ocean joins sky.

We bob easily atop the ceaseless swells as the seas continue to calm. The sun, hidden behind thick clouds, is surely up. I change position slightly and stretch slowly. Simonne looks up and hugs me. Tears run down her cheeks while prayers form on her lips. We hold each other tightly as time stands still.

The skies lighten. We have enough light to fix the tear in the raft. The emergency kit contains two mechanical patches. Each patch consists of three pieces: an aluminum oval disk with a rubber gasket that will slip inside the tear; a long threaded screw runs up from the middle of this disk. A similar disk, except without a gasket, fits outside of the hole; a wing nut will tighten both halves together. A wire soldered on to the end of the screw with a cord prevents losing any parts.

I disassemble the patch and hand it to Sim. Careful not to unbalance the raft, I turn slowly onto my knees and reach towards the tear. The damage consists of a hole more than three inches long and two inches wide. I'm not sure both patches will plug it entirely. Sim hands me the first patch with the wire lead tied to a cord. I slide half of the patch into the air chamber to cover one edge of the tear, push on the outer cover, then tighten the wing nut. The second patch fits alongside and covers the hole with a hair to spare.

Sim pumped constantly while I fixed the hole. I lean back and take over. With each push of the pump, the air chamber tightens. I count my strokes: fifty, one hundred. Sim tells me to stop. A slight hiss from the patch confirms that some air continues to escapes from the space between the two patches. But it works better than I expected.

Sim gets down to the business of housekeeping. She barks like my old sarge at Ft. Dix as she orders me to lie down and to put my feet up on the side of the raft, then piles mountains of stores on me. The floor of the raft is but a thin piece of rubberized fabric. If we were to lie on it, we'd be cold and susceptible to attack by fish. Or we could tear it. When the far end of the floor is bare, Sim covers it with one of the cushions salvaged from *Siboney*. Atop the cushion, she puts the camcorder, the bucket, and the bag with bedding. In the bucket go the gloves, the knife, the camera, and several food cans. She clears space for the next cushion; each of which is three feet long and a foot wide. The second cushion fits easily.

I move again and Sim repeats the process. Soon all four cushions line the bare floor. Each of the two small cushions go under our bottoms while the life jackets and foul weather gear help lift our heads. The canned food becomes part of our headrest. The camcorder case with the camcorder and 35 mm camera lie against the air chamber near our feet. On top of it, she has placed the large bucket. The watermaker, wrapped in a jacket, is under my feet. Water, flares, and all our other gear have been squeezed in alongside us.

When Sim spreads two comforters under us and I move to my side of the raft, I find it's downright comfortable...that is except for the two 2 1/2 gallon water jugs pushing against my liver. Sim has put all sharp objects, like two pairs of scissors and a nail file, into the gun case with the .38 Smith and Wesson. I can't believe I missed the bullets. We have yet to find a home for the six foot long fishing rod with its razor sharp hook. For the moment, I'll hold it between my legs with the tip out the window.

I've kept a log on *Siboney* since the day we sailed for Hong Kong out of Manila in 1968. This latest Log is the eighth and began in 1987. Its last entry is: 0342 JUNE 15, 1989 DAY 21 OUT OF BALBOA, POSITION 5 DEGREES 30 MINUTES NORTH LATITUDE 99 DEGREES 7 MINUTES WEST LONGITUDE-SURROUNDED BY WHALES

Sim hands me a ballpoint and I enter:
0430 HIT HARD BY WHALE-OPENED SEAM-WATER RISING
0445 ABANDONED SHIP
0500 *SIBONEY* SINKS

On a new line I continue....
15 JUNE 1989 THURSDAY-DAY 1 ON RAFT
0800....

Also aboard is my navigation workbook with all of the satellite fixes received since leaving Miami. On the page opposite the fixes are notations with my radio contacts. We have no charts, but I will construct one with the satellite position data.

It's time now to put our new home together. When I look around for instructions, big bold letters on the side of the raft tell us first to: "DEPLOY SEA ANCHOR BEFORE ERECTING CANOPY TO REDUCE DRIFT." Giving it no further thought, I unwrap the sea anchor and toss it over the side.

Next we inflate the two arches, one on each end of the raft with the small bellows type air pump. These arches are ten inches in diameter and run across and over the raft. When they stand erect, a rubberized fabric sewed into the arch covers both ends of the raft. Another flap, also fastened to one of the arches, zips into the opposite arch and forms a roof. Two flaps attached to the long sides of the oval raft zipper into the arch and become windows. With the canopy roof in place and the windows zipped part way up, we begin to feel more secure, safer. Our new home has quickly become dark and cozy. Sim, exhausted from her chores, lies next to me and closes her eyes.

Seconds later, she turns my way and asks: "Bill, will anyone search for us? Do you think they'll find us in this immensity? We are miles away from anywhere. Will the raft hold up?"

"I hope so," is the only reply I can conjure. The same thoughts have been twirling in my head, and I haven't found a single positive answer to any of them.

We turn toward one another, embrace, and hold each other for the longest time. We kiss and tears flow. Sim looks up at my tear streaked face and says in a low voice: "I heard a voice last night, soon after we drifted away from *Siboney*. The voice was low, much like a whisper, and over and over it repeated..."forty days, forty days"...I can't get that message out of my mind. What do you think it means?"

Forty days. We'll be dead in forty days. The design life on this raft is no more than two weeks. We don't have a prayer of a chance to squeak out of this one. Sim breaks in:

"Bill. Will we live? Will we be found?"

"Of course, we'll be found." What else could I say?

"When? In 40 days and nights?"

"It'll take a few days, maybe a week."

"I hope so. Bill, I love you."

"I love you too."

~•~chapter three~•~

1000 THURSDAY JUNE 15, 1989

"You bastard. And you are a real bastard. Your disgusting jealousy is what got us into this. You had to separate me from my children. You forced me on this trip. And here I am, in a miserable miniature raft where I'm certainly going to die."

I try to break in but her broadside continues.

"You ugly beast. You just lie there and smirk. You want me dead, but you went too far this time. You're not going to get out of this alive either. I'm going to die, but you will die too. What will my invalid mother do with me dead? You are a criminal of the worse kind, Butler. We must pray we die quickly and without pain, for there is no hope in praying for life."

I start to argue, but it's like throwing gasoline on a raging fire. She goes on for what seems an eternity...my madness, my children, her children, her poor mother, hopelessness, death. Exhausted, she slows for a second, and I try for a change of mood.

"Sim, find the EPIRB."

Momentarily distracted, she stops the cannonade and digs under the pile of stores under her feet and quickly finds our bright red emergency signaling radio. I extend the antenna, then read the instructions. "KEEP IN A VERTICAL POSITION" is the first thing I see. I turn the switch to TRANSMIT. A small green light flashes which indicates our signal is now beamed to satellites and airplanes.

I can't find a place for it to hang vertically, so I hold it outside the canopy for almost an hour. I find a strap on top of the canopy which holds it upright. The batteries are designed to power it for three or four days. I stretch out again and glance over at Sim.

She looks up at the EPIRB and says: "That will get a signal nowhere. It's all we have, so I'll shut up. I've said too much already. I wish I was dumb and unknowing. Perhaps I'd feel more secure."

"Sim, it's transmitting. It should work."

"Cruising World said that most of the EPIRB's don't work. They tested a bunch, and only one or two in ten did the job."

"I heard you before and I hear you now. You must believe this is the one in ten that works."

"And they also said that the system isn't working worldwide. There are many gaps. Considering the desolation out here, we have to be in one of the gaps."

"Damn it, Sim. Can't you think positive. It's working. Help will come."

"You're dense for an engineer. The system needs an earth station. There isn't a chunk of earth within a thousand miles of here. And as far as hoping for an airplane, anyone flying overhead is in worse trouble than we." Sim spoke the last words with a strange smile.

"Ok, baby, I know. It doesn't work. What's wrong with humoring ourselves? Besides, what do we have to lose? I still think we'll see results. Someone will pick up our signal. They have to. I feel there is a ship heading our way right now." Sim's grin broadens. She shakes her head. I throw up my arms. "Ok, so I'm more than a little punchy."

When we try to get comfortable, we quickly find there is hardly room for the two of us and the stores piled high around and under us. A large trash bag full of spare blankets and comforters for use in the higher latitudes has been in the way since we first cast off. Sim pulls it open and finds three comforters, a heavy cotton sheet, and a wool blanket. In a flash, she throws two of the comforters over the side.

While still in sight, we have second thoughts. "Perhaps we should have kept them," she says. "They were my babies' favorite comforters, and we may have had use for them." We agree to throw nothing overboard for another day or two. We move the remaining bedding around to soften up our head rest, and except for various lumps under the bedding, our raft turns out to be genuinely cozy. Under the canopy, it's dark and cool. We lie on our backs, which is fine for Sim as she can stretch out, but the raft is eight inches too short for me. I push my head up until it touches the end and put my feet on the air chamber at the other end.

When rain starts halfway through the afternoon and pelts the raft with giant drops, we and our stores stay dry. The dark blue coat of waterproofing cuts out much of the light. We've been on the raft twelve hours. Our last sleep was before one in the morning. I feel limp and tired. My eyes close. The regular patter of rain quickly puts us to sleep.

When I awaken, Sim rummages through one of her cosmetic bags. She pulls out a miniature set of dominoes, and I lose no time challenging her to a game of double sixes. We hold the pieces in the palm of our hand as the raft rocks too much to place them on the cushion that is our playing table. Sim wins the first game and also the second with the score entered in the Log. We call it quits half way through the third game when stomach and back muscles complain loudly. Besides hunger tears at me. We had our last meal aboard *Siboney* before sundown yesterday, more than twenty hours ago.

Sim takes over her traditional role as meal planner when she announces: "We'll ration food and maintain a three meal a day schedule. We'll eat the crackers first..one cracker in the morning. At lunch, let's eat two with peanut butter. At night, we can go back to a single cracker."

Her plan sounds acceptable, but it's missing an important ritual. "Before supper," I counter, "We'll have happy hour as usual."

Sim shakes her head: "OK, borracho. Tomorrow we'll have a can for lunch. We can't afford to let our bodies go down too fast." I nod in agreement.

Sim digs under the covers and comes up with a can of Keebler's Export Sodas which have been a 20 year staple aboard *Siboney*. They stay crispier longer than any other we have tried, even in humid surroundings such as on a boat. I gulp down half a cracker and gag. Desperately, I reach for a bottle of water, open it, and wash the cracker down.

Sim watched the entire scene and suggests: "You're taking too big a bite. Look, bite off a crumb at a time. Like this. Then let it melt on your tongue with your saliva and, when it's soft, swallow it."

I nibble on my second cracker. Breakfast stretches out to fifteen minutes. Several gulps of water give me the sensation I'm full. My eyes close...

Sim sits up with a jerk and brings me out of my snooze. She's rigid, like a hunting dog.

"What's that?"

"What's what, Sim?"

"That bump? Didn't you feel it?"

"I'm not sure. Wait."

I'm jabbed in the middle of my back. Then there's a bump to Sim's bun and two to her legs.

Sim leans on her elbow and whispers: "What can it be?"

I shrug my shoulders and shake my head. The bumps continue. It feels like we're hitting a log which could have nails that could puncture the raft. A scratching sound runs down the side of the raft. Sim jumps up, opens the window, and looks out.

She calls out: "Bill, it's a huge turtle."

"A what?"

"A turtle. It's more than three feet around. It's going to puncture the raft."

I zip my window down, grab the orange oar, and row the raft around. A huge sea turtle paddles leisurely towards the raft. It lifts its head out of the water to breathe and looks directly at me. Large black rings surround its eyes. Barnacles cling to the light brown armor plating of its carapace as it heads under the raft. I hit it with the end of the paddle. It kicks with all four flippers, splashes, and dives. Message received.

Small rain drops start to fall from a dark grey cloud overhead. We quickly zipper the two windows closed as the drops turn to a downpour. Under the waterproof canopy, we stay dry. We snuggle, embrace, and sleep. Sim prays...God save us...please God. I fail to recall a single prayer. Besides I can get us out of this.

My watch chirps. I find the flashlight next to my head and untie my reading glasses that hang from the inflated arch. It's midnight. We have been on the raft for nineteen hours. Heavy rain pours down, but not a drop has fallen on us. I pull our cotton comforter up, bunch the pillow, and begin anew the process of falling asleep.

I think back to yesterday at this time. What did I do wrong? What should have I done differently to save the boat from the attack? Why did the whales suddenly turn on us? They appeared friendly and never bothered us as they swam alongside for hours. Our hull, painted a dark red, may have looked like a large baleen whale in the black of the night. Did the pod of pilot whales consider *Siboney* a menace to their young? In this case, they would have attacked instinctively and not stop until we, their prey, lay mortally wounded, no longer a danger. That would explain why they didn't come after the raft.

Or, being carnivorous of nature, did they attack in the belief we were edible? I've read stories of pilot and killer whales attacking large solitary whales in mid-ocean. Several of the pod position themselves under the large whale to keep it from sounding. Three or four more attack the tail to cut its means of propulsion and balance as one or two jump over the air hole to prevent the whale from breathing. Another dozen become a collective battering ram and hammer away for the kill.

Once the whale is dead, the entire pod feeds. Preposterous, but true. After all, had *Siboney* been a whale, it would have made dinner for the entire pod. In either case, we should be safe aboard the raft. We haven't seen a whale since we cast off. Hopefully, they will find nothing of interest in our frail craft. A lunge by the smallest of the whales would be our end.

When I awaken, Simonne still prays out loud in French. The air chamber is tight. I turn and sleep anew. When I open my eyes next, it's to a rainy dawn. When I stir, Sim reaches over and kisses me. I peek out the window but rain sweeps in, and I quickly close it and lie back down. Sim turns towards me with a faraway look.

We embrace. This isn't at all that bad, I muse. Rain falls and the wind blows, but we're dry, safe, and cozy. I have a sexy, naked raft mate. The comforter makes it feel like a feather bed; I'll test it out later. I try to perk Sim up: "Hey, Sim, this is like the Hilton. We'll make it. You'll see. Help will come soon like in the James Bond movies. What time is it?"

Sim is the raft time keeper. Instead of wrestling with my glasses, I find it easier to ask Sim. We saved two watches, my digital Seiko and Sim's Raymond Weil, the one I gave her when we flew to Venezuela for Christmas of '88. My watch chimes or, better yet, chirps on the hour. Both show dates.

"It's nine, Miami time. And it's Friday, June 16." That makes it seven or so local time. On *Siboney*, I had planned to change ship's time to Hawaiian time in another thousand miles. This would have given our biological inner clock a chance to adapt to a new rhythm before arriving in Hilo.

The time has arrived to do a little formal navigation. My navigation workbook contains my calculations on course changes and daily distance traveled summaries since leaving Miami. My last entry aboard *Siboney* was the 0342 Satellite fix. Thirty hours ago, we were safe and secure...better not to dwell on that. That fix put *Siboney* 1200 miles west of Panama. The Galapagos Islands lie 600 miles to the southeast, upwind, unreachable. To the west, there are 4000 miles of empty ocean...the nearest land, the lonely island outposts of Christmas and Fanning Islands.

With the good position fix at the point where we sank, I can calculate where we are. To noon today, June 16, we have been adrift one day plus seven hours or a total of thirty one hours. At three fourths of a knot, our easterly drift is about 25 miles for these thirty one hours. I can't measure the effect that the current has on the raft, but I can feel its push. It's like riding one of those escalators that aren't set right and jerks along. An inexorable and invisible force holds the raft so firmly that neither wind nor waves alter our course.

The rain has stopped which allows us to open the windows and expand our horizon from the two to three feet we have in the tightly closed raft. The clear weather will allow me to measure the drift caused by wind and waves. I cut a two inch square piece of paper and drop it to windward where it quickly wets and floats under the surface. Sim has her watch ready as I call out.

"Mark."

I wait until the paper is ten feet away from the raft and again call: "Mark."

"Thirty seconds," Sim calls.

"Sim, check wind direction." She digs the compass out from under the bedding, holds it up to the wind, and calls out.

"South, 180 degrees."

A little mental arithmetic. Ten feet in thirty seconds. 20 feet in a minute. 1200 feet an hour. 6020 feet to a nautical mile. The drift caused by wind and waves is a bit over 1/4 mile per hour or knot. In the 31 hours on the raft, we have drifted north seven miles. Of course, my calculations are rough, but I'll keep them up until we're found.

Light rain begins and again forces us to close the windows. The wind increases. We play dominoes. I win, six games to Sim's five and enter the results in the Log. Larger waves break on the raft. Spray splashes over the window and onto us. We tighten the window ties and cover up.

Sim sops up the water that has collected in the bottom of the raft with a small sponge. She then squeezes the sponge into the pail. My job is to hold the pail and dump it when full. Sim reels, sea sick. We have pills in the raft emergency kit if she gets worse.

At one in the afternoon, we open a can of Diet VEG-ALL...Diet of all things. Just what we need. We have no eating tools and quickly master the use of the toothbrush and lose not a single tiny piece of our precious food. We save half of the can for supper.

The wind dies towards late afternoon and the rain stops. We open a window in hopes the fresh air will dry us out before night sets in.

"Bill, what's that?" Sim's in her hunting dog pose.

I don't hear a thing. "What do you hear?"

"A noise. Listen. Let me look."

Sim opens the window a little further.

"My God, Bill! There's a freighter coming straight for us! Oh, my God! They found us. We are saved! Oh, thank you, dear God! Thank You!"

"Let me see." I struggle up and look to where Sim is pointing.

A large freighter with a dark blue hull and white topsides steams straight for us at high speed, pushing before it a high bow wave that curls off the bow. Never have I seen a more magnificent sight. I rejoice and call out: "Oh, baby. We are saved. Quick, get dressed."

The heat has kept us naked from our first moments on the raft. Besides we're short of clothes. We saved the clothes we were wearing plus a small plastic bag with two pairs of shorts and two T-shirts. Last night, we had worn T-shirts to keep warm. We dress quickly, then open the windows, and zip back the canopy.

The ship, less than three hundred feet from our raft, heads directly for us. We embrace, laugh, and cry, unable to believe our incredible luck. I raise my hands in thanks and shout. Simonne wraps one hand around me and cries with uncontrolled joy.

The huge propellers bite into the churning sea with what appears to be increased power. "Sim," I cry out, "Look, he's slowing down."

We scream with glee. Castaway in the depths of the Pacific...one moment we're alone, and suddenly...there's life heading for us. We're going to live after all. I cry out with unrestrained joy.

"Wow, something really worked. The Mayday got through. No, they're homing in on the EPIRB. We're saved!"

Sim doesn't take her eyes off the ship. She nods and says: "They're coming for us. There is no question they've seen us.

Otherwise, what would they be doing out here? What phenomenal luck."

The bow of the ship is two hundred feet away. The air chambers throb from the thundering boom of the huge diesel engines. The sides of the ship rise high off the water, neatly painted. When they do stop and come alongside, can we make it up to the deck? What will they throw down for us to grab on to?

The ship's bow pushes tons of water before it and is now abreast. We ride the breaking crest of the bow wave. Our eyes are on the door to the pilot house. Someone will emerge any second now and wave to us.

The bridge approaches. We see no one on the bridge, but then it's hard to see through the glass windows. Have they not seen us? We scream for help. Sim waves a white shirt. With the bridge abeam, we yell even louder and wave frantically. Something is very wrong. The sides of the ship are barely fifty feet away. The bastard almost ran us down. I look towards the fast approaching stern. Are the engines in reverse? Or are they? They MUST be.

Sim breaks the spell: "Bill, it's not stopping."

The confused propeller wash is indicative of reverse. I try to explain, "Sim, it takes miles to stop a big ship," but then cry out, "Where is everybody?"

The deck of the ship remains empty. The bridge passes. Nervous and desperate, I command unnecessarily: "YELL, Sim, YELL!" She is already screaming louder than I. I call out desperately: "Where are the flares? Get them quick!"

Sim digs under the covers, finds a flare, and hands it to me. I look up. The bridge has passed; It's too late. No one looks out the stern. With only three flares, we can't waste one on a long shot. I shake with nervous desperation and plead, "Sim, yell!"

She needs no prodding. She has screamed since the bow passed and has waved her shirt all the time. The stern comes into view. Large white letters proclaim it's the "TER ERIKSEN" out of OSLO.

"Norwegians. Wake up, damn you. HELP!"

"Sim, they're turning, aren't they?. They must be."

"Why don't we fire off a flare? They're still so near."

The ship turns to starboard. Darker now, I'll signal. Sim hands me the lantern. I flash SOS...SOS...SOS.

Sim signals with her shirt and continues to yell as I blink SOS'S. A mile past us, the "Ter Eriksen" shows its starboard side in what appears to be a wide turn. Minutes later, the ship is but a blur on the Eastern horizon. The turn was an illusion. They did not see us. When I look again, the sea is empty, and once again, we're alone.

We refuse to accept the obvious and continue to scan the horizon for signs of the returning freighter. Jagged waves create constantly changing patterns against the lighter sky. I wrap my arm around Sim to pull her closer as more minutes pass. With night closing in on us, it is obvious that rescue will not arrive, and we must prepare for our second long night.

We continue to kneel and to stare at the darkening horizon and hope the ship will return for us. Long minutes pass and we remain embraced. Heavy tears pour from all eyes. Darkness swallows both the ship and our little world. We cannot speak or, for that matter, comprehend this new event. Slowly night shuts out day and we're again alone. More so than before. We struggle to fathom all that has occurred to us in so few hours. Our latest narrow escape has shattered what little hope remained. How could the "Ter Eriksen" fail to post a lookout? Any lookout could not have failed to see our bright orange raft drifting less than 100 feet from their deck. As we give up all hope of rescue, we turn to lie on our backs. Simonne is the first to search aloud for an answer: "Why didn't they see us? We were so close. My God, they almost ran us down. If a ship that close fails to see us, what hope do we have of ever being rescued?"

I too despair and say: "I really screwed up. I should have fired a flare when we first saw him."

Sim puts her right arm around me and pulls me closer. "We were so sure they were going to stop. It wasn't dark enough for the flare, and besides there was no one looking. Anyone on the bridge looking out would have seen us. Particularly with all the fuss we were making."

We hadn't seen a soul on board. They probably had a radar similar to the one on *Siboney*. They set a ten or twenty mile guard zone around the ship and need not worry about collision. A ship or land will make the radar beep. That's why, whenever we sailed, one of us or the radar was on watch. Even then, we had been convinced that large freighters do not maintain lookouts.

Sim's eyes drop as she edges into my arms. The cool night air makes her tremble. "It's hopeless. The MAYDAY messages didn't get through. The EPIRB is trash. We're 1200 miles from help. When help does arrive, we're invisible. God help us. Let us live. I don't want to die, please God!"

I zip the canopy closed and lie back down. I put my arms around Sim and pull her closer. We hug and cry. Sim calls out to God as tears stream down her cheeks: "Oh, Lord, help us, send us another ship. Give us another chance. Please...send help." We feel more alone now than yesterday after *Siboney* sank. Humans, safety, so close, beyond reach....

Her cries of anguish pour out: "Cris, Alex, my babies! Do something! Sally, call the Coast Guard. Do something! Anything! God save us; let me see my sons again. I am not ready to die. Bill isn't either. We have so much yet to do." She looks up and cries out: "Why, oh, why did this have to happen to us? What have we done, dear Lord, to merit this punishment? We are not evil. Forgive us our sins! Help us!"

"Calm down, sweetie," I say, trying to be reassuring. "We'll make it."

With that, she turns. Her eyes flash, her voice thunders: "You. You are the one who got me into this predicament. You pushed me into this. I didn't want to leave Miami. I was happy in my house. You were obstinate, mad, blind. We should have sailed the Caribbean for a year. This long trip could have waited until we arranged everything on shore. No, we had to leave now. We had to hurry, and for what? Butler, answer me. For what? To have whales almost kill us and now, in this junk raft, lost in a desolated ocean, surely to die?"

"Desolated? May I remind you a ship full of people almost ran us down just minutes ago."

Sim shoots me another seething look. "Those bastards. But you are the evil one. You insisted on separating me from my children before I was ready. My mother is sick and I left her alone. Suppose something happens to her? She knew we were going to have an accident. She told me over and over to be careful, not to go. When we don't report on the radio, she will be the first to worry. She knows the boat sank and she knows we're barely alive. The worry could kill her. And it will be all your fault."

This argument is going nowhere. What can I say? We're going to make it or, better yet, we've got to make it. I try to reason with her: "We've patched the raft and it's holding air. We have water and we can fish. We sent messages..."

She cuts me short: "None of that is worth a damn if some big shark comes along and starts chewing on the raft. Then we will be dead...Butler, do you know what dead is, or are you a zombie. Through. Finished. No one will ever know what happened to us. I'm praying; why don't you try? It may do you some good. Or don't you remember how to pray? You certainly don't. The Lord sent this tragedy to you as a warning. You'd better start soon or it may be too late."

"I receive the message, but he really didn't have to go this far." I search for a way to calm her and say: "Let's examine our mistakes. Haven't we led good lives?"

"I'm not that sure. When we divorced, I hurt my husband, and your wife was heart broken by the whole affair. We hurt them and we hurt our children."

Sim continues while staring out her window: "It was such a difficult situation. As much as we tried not to hurt our loved ones, we ended up hurting everybody, including ourselves, because we couldn't be together. Then, when we got together, we couldn't be happy because we knew our exes weren't. It was traumatic for the children. They all suffered, mine, yours. Had we been closer to the church or had we received counseling, we could have resolved this situation in a smarter way. It was a Catch 22 situation. It was either them or us. We chose us. We had glorious moments, but we paid dearly for it.xxx It's hard to rebuild on ashes and ashes we left behind. The worst part for me, but I think it was the same for you, was leaving people behind: my husband, your wife, who we still love in a certain way, and it hurt to see them hurt."

Sim remains inspired and I let her rattle on. "Yes, but for both of us, life as it was couldn't go on. I couldn't function. I felt caged. Something had to give."

She's right. What a strong feeling had swept over us. It was like a tidal wave, a monster tsunami. Nothing could stop it, and God knows we tried, both of us. We had met at the Tamanaco Hotel pool late on a sunny afternoon. Sim had sent her children home. I awaited, with two associates from GE, for the arrival from Brazil of a turbine specialist. The attraction was instantaneous. As we were both married, we fought the intense captivation. How often after that did we try to stop seeing each other? Always, always, this indescribable obsession drew us back together. "Love is crazy," I mutter.

"Love is crazy and a two edged sword. It's hell and heaven at the same time. Every little piece of heaven is paid in hell. But I don't regret being with you. What I do regret is what it cost to get here. If I had the choice again, I'm not sure I would have the guts to go through with it all. For us, it was everything, passion, desire, an all-consuming obsession that swept me away. Too bad, I didn't meet you when you were young, free, and single."

"Yes, except, when I married at twenty one, you were only twelve years old. A little young to marry, wouldn't you say?"

"Yes, but you could have waited for me," Sim sighs wistfully, not without a tear.

The sun drops under the horizon. While light remains, I ask Sim to read the prayers. Yesterday, she found a half dozen cards with printed prayers, parables, and psalms in her toilet case. She read them for the first time last night. For a brief moment, while she reads, I escape into a world of hope and light and beauty. As she concludes reading, the shadows of night deepen and close out our second raft-born day. Sim takes a last look around, and I do the same out of my window. Low, dirty clouds cling close to the sea. Deep in thought, we hug, and so embraced, we are lulled into a deep sleep.

When I next look at my watch, it's just before midnight. In the near total blackness, I find Simonne, rosary held tightly between her hands, eyes closed, lips synchronized to her prayers. When I push the air chamber, I find the raft had needed air earlier, but Sim let me sleep. I screw in the bellows type pump, fill the chamber until it's tight, close the valve, and remove the pump.

As I lie on my back in the complete blackness of this quiet Pacific night, my mind begins again to try to make some sense out of our misfortune. I see little hope of rescue, either from an organized search or a random find by a freighter. Someone must first miss us bad enough to stir up a search. And when they search, where will they look? We will be impossible to locate unless the EPIRB works. I must give some thought to turning it off and saving it for later. I dare not betray any of these thoughts to Sim. I must keep her hopes up. It'll be better that way. Simonne hasn't slept at all, so far as I can tell. Too many worries. I watch her pray and feel better for it.

Waves jostle the raft as the southwest wind picks up. When I look out, clouds hug the sea and have turned blacker. We pump air. I obviously nap, for when I next open my eyes, the air chamber is again limp. We're losing air much too fast. I must locate the leak and try to stop it or at least slow it down. When I finish pumping, a faint grey glow overhead tells us that Saturday, June 17, will soon dawn. Heavy rain greets us on our third day adrift. Wind speed increases to fifteen then to twenty knots. Wave speed increases proportionally with the wind until mountains of water whisk under us at not less than twenty five miles an hour.

In the ocean, far from land, swell height is of no real significance to a small craft. Much like *Siboney*, the raft floats easily from the top of one 30 foot swell down to the next trough and up again to the next crest. Swells the size of small hills emerge from the sea, careening tons of power; they roll towards us, ever steeper and larger. Most waves approach from the south, but a few approach from the east, and yet others from the west. The distance from crest to crest is far over one hundred and fifty feet. On each, four to six foot waves add power and confusion.

Waves that ride the top move faster than the swells. When a wave crests at the top of a swell and then breaks, it submerges the raft in up to a ton of water. The roar of an approaching wave prompts us to grab hold of the internal life lines. The wave breaks and collides with the raft with a sonorous boom. I lie poised to jump to windward in case we start to roll. Will our tiny vessel take the beating? Will the ballast bags do their job? We have so much to learn about heavy weather performance of our new vessel. Other waves, flush with unspent energy, glide beneath us and speed away on their journey towards land.

Each minute turns into an hour as we hang on to the safety straps. The roar of the sea drowns out all words. The wind screams in our ears. Simonne, on her back, eyes closed, hair soaked and matted, rosary held tightly in hands joined on her chest, prays incessantly. The driving rain stings my eyes whenever I blink them open. I lie on the windward side and receive the full force of the breaking waves. My mind races. What can I do to get out of this predicament? How could I have created this disaster? To be lost at sea in a small plastic raft is tough enough but to be lost more than a thousand miles from shore stacks the odds against us. Damn it. I've got to come up with a solution. Meanwhile I'd better prepare for a roll-over.

Hundreds of miles to the south, tempests we will never

experience generate the seas that pound our fragile raft. These towering multi-story mountains of water arrive confused; their journey interrupted by the Galapagos Islands now more than five hundred miles to the southeast. Waves out of the west, not as large or powerful as their southern brothers, have a fetch of more than four thousand miles. Some have been heading our way for more than a week.

When the two wave systems meet at the point where our miniscule vessel floats, the mighty collision creates a ten foot high breaker that slaps the raft with the force of a car crash. We're thrown, soaked, and quite often, the raft spins 180 degrees. When turned around, the leeward window, kept open for ventilation, faces the fury of the ocean. I quickly zip down my window and row the raft back, not without an eye on a new breaking wave. One moment, we're at the top of the swell and we can see over the horizon. The next moment, we are surrounded by walls of water. Minutes later, another wave smothers us and we spin again.

Every eighth or tenth wave is twice as large as the others. Tons of water dumped on the canopy collapses it and sends a shower of salt water through both windows. Bathed and sopped, we are at odds to find a way to escape the soaking. As the wave breaks, we slide down the swell with the inertia of a roller coaster. We jump to windward when the raft heels perilously, threatening a roll. A wayward wave could lift the windward edge of the raft allowing the wind to catch the bottom-side of the raft. We remain tensed awaiting that split second when our world will turn upside down. The deafening noise keeps us braced. Three out of four waves that roar in break and pass ahead or behind us. Each blow on the raft resounds inside the air chambers with a cavernous boom. Every breaking wave sends us surfing.

Yet the waves are our allies. They push us home. We need high winds, strong waves, and heavy currents to reach shore. Time is against us. The longer we are at sea, the higher the chance of meeting with some unknown hazard. Or we could become ill or weak from lack of food. I feel like crying out: Let the wild wind blow...let the waves break...take us quickly towards land.

The ballast bags that hang under the raft have kept the waves from overturning the raft. There are four bags in all. Two small ones, two feet long and black, are at the ends. On each side, a bag four feet long and light blue provides most of the stability. All four bags are a foot and half wide and deep and have three inch holes punched along their sides near to their point of attachment to the raft. Eight inches of chain are sewn into the bottom corners of each bag.

When we launched the raft from *Siboney*, the chain pulled the bags down. They quickly filled with sea water. Whenever a breaking wave hits and threatens to roll us over, it must overcome the weight of the water in the bags. When the full force of a breaking wave smashes against the raft, the holes in the bags let some of the water out reducing stress, but most of the water ballast remains and provides the vital stability.

Each wave smashes the raft with sledgehammer force. We cringe as we hear it approach with what sounds like the roar of a freight train. When the wave hits, the raft, caught in its swirling waters, skids ten feet, pops back out, straightens itself out in the current, and quickly resumes its previous course. We've secured the watermaker and water bottles to the raft just in case we do flip.

It was before dawn when Sim threw her bolt out of the blue. "Bill, how could that freighter not see us? He came so close."

I banter back. "They had a satellite antenna. They were relaxing, eating, or drinking beer or schnapps. God knows."

"Not schnapps, Aquavit."

"Whatever."

"Norwegians. I thought they were good seamen. No one was looking. How can a ship travel at that speed and have no one looking out? What's going to happen to us? Will anyone find us in this watery desert?"

"We'll be OK. The raft will make it. We have water. It's just a matter of time. They'll be looking for us soon."

"Who will be looking? Where will they look? Bill, only we know where we are. Nobody else does."

"Help will come," I declare as forcefully as I can. "We can survive for many days, even a week or two. The EPIRB is still sending. I checked it first thing today. There is a chance the MAYDAY'S got through. Besides someone will soon miss us. When a week passes without a call, that will be a strong signal."

"I sure hope so." Sim remains quiet for a moment. Then her face breaks into a smile. "Guess what. I heard Alma Llanera on the radio. It was beautiful." Alma Llanera is the Venezuelan equivalent of "America the Beautiful," a song we learned to love in our nine years in Venezuela.

Sim has tuned her little yellow radio, tucked near her head, sparingly every night to conserve our only set of batteries, the ones Sim had put into the Walkman a day or two before our shipwreck. This is our only contact with the outside world, and how lucky we are to have it. We have tacitly agreed, without really discussing the matter, that only Sim will listen to the radio. I hope it helps her get through the long nights. Happy for the distraction, I ask: "When did all this happen?"

"You were asleep. It was three or four in the morning. I picked up a lot of stations. I heard the news from the Voice of America. Eight Chinese have been sentenced to death because of the riots. Your old buddy, Mr. Marcos, just had emergency surgery. Storms knocked out power in Washington, D.C. And tomorrow is Father's Day. Congratulations."

"Every day is Father's Day, don't you know? And though I lived nine years in the Philippines, Marcos is not my pal." It was an old joke of Sim's. In fact, the general economic downturn brought about by Marcos' policies was the main reason I left the Philippines. "Anything else on page 1?"

"I heard mostly Mexican music, which means Mexico is closest. I get nothing as soon as the sun comes up which means we're far from land. My best reception is between one and three in the morning. I picked up a station in Oklahoma, but it faded out right away."

While I wonder how long the batteries will last, I notice the raft needs air again. I ask Sim for the pump which she pulls out from under my head. The pump, four inches in diameter and of the bellows type, is our only means of putting air into the raft, for I have not yet discovered a way to blow air in by mouth. The raft has two valves, one at each end, plus a valve in each of the arches.

I screw the pump into the valve closest to my head and turn it to the right to open it. My fingers hold the bottom of the pump. I move the bellows in and out and count strokes by tens. At one hundred and twenty, the air chambers are tight. When I try to remove the pump, the valve won't close, and I must work the pump continuously or the raft will quickly deflate.

I need pliers, but I know we have no tools on board. Oh, to have taken a few before we sank. *Siboney* had every tool imaginable for any type of repair. I was ready to tackle any job: mechanical, electrical, refrigeration, engine, rigging, or carpentry. I had spares for everything. Here we have nothing except for a knife, two scissors, one tweezer, and the can opener. With a sudden twist, I force the pump loose, but the valve remains open which I plug quickly with my finger and call out to Sim:

"Sim, look for the can opener." She plucks it from the pail and hands it to me. Using the two legs as a pair of pliers, I am able to loosen the valve and close it though I can still hear some air leaking. We need to plug it. Sim digs through the parts bag supplied with the raft and comes up with a yellow plastic knob with threads on the bottom. It looks a lot like a yellow mushroom. I try it, but the threads are too small in diameter.

"Wait a second", says Sim. She pulls a pair of scissors out of the dark green suede gun case and proceeds to cut a strip from her T-shirt. I wrap it around the threads and screw the assembly into the valve. Sim returns the scissors to the case and zips it closed. The valve holds air. For now.

The raft, when fully inflated, is an oval five and a half feet long by less than four feet wide on the inside. The total floor area is under sixteen square feet. I am six feet long by almost two feet wide at the shoulders, and when I lie down, I need at least eleven square feet. Sim takes up eight or nine square feet, so without counting stores, we are missing four square feet. We've tried lying on our side; then knees and bottoms don't fit. We've tried head-to-foot and head-to-head, and honestly I can't tell which is best or worse. We just do not fit.

The damned bucket is always in the way of my feet as are the two containers of water. The camcorder case, also under my feet, is full of all the large sharp objects like the fishing reel, can opener, and camera. The two life preservers and the two large cracker cans are part of our headrest.

A printed nameplate on the side of the raft glares at us boldly: "SWITLIK-FOUR MAN COASTAL RAFT." How are the two other people going to squeeze in when they arrive? A couple of gorgeous blondes, well that would be something else. Four people could fit...for about an hour, or two if they're real cute...we've been aboard almost 50 hours.

A southerly wind pushes the seas to twenty feet. The roar of breaking waves is the only sound we've heard since we sank. Except, of course, for the "Ter Eriksen." In another three days, they should be entering the Panama Canal...

Sim prays aloud in French. I try but can't get started. I haven't prayed for dozens of years. I can't even recall the Lord's Prayer or even remember when I prayed last. It was possibly thirty, maybe forty years ago. Now, lost in the vastness of the Pacific Ocean, I feel terribly alone. Sim, rosary in hand, has found company, someone to communicate to, someone to lean on, support.

A tear runs down Sim's cheek as she says: "Bill, this rosary is a miracle. My mother gave it to me last October when we visited. I didn't know I had it with me. I was looking through my toilet kit, and there it was."

She continues: "This is my rosary from my childhood, from my first communion. I can still remember how pretty we were...dozens of little girls, all dressed in white. My mother and I spent days shopping for my dress. It was so pretty...all white. When we filed into St. Michel church in Menton, we looked like a bunch of angels."

Misty eyed and choked, she continues to reminisce: "Until I was twenty, I went to church all the time. I was very close to God. As soon as I left home, I began to drift away. I have missed church so much over the past thirty years. Why, oh why, did I wander away? Things would have been so much easier. And different."

A massive wave breaks over the raft and interrupts Sim's musings. A bucketful of water pours through the closed window and soaks us once again with Sim getting the worst of it. As she spits out salt water and wipes herself dry, she says: "We've got to make it. I want to change. I want to go back to Church. I now understand what has been missing in my life."

"We'll make it, Sim. And we will go to church."

Her thin smile tells me she well knows the nearest church is more than a thousand watery miles away...miles which we must inch across propelled by nothing but wind, waves, and current. If we but had a sail or some way to increase our speed. To really speed up, we would have to remove the ballast bags or at least press them flat against the bottom of the raft. We'd reduce drag, but then the first breaking wave would turn the raft upside down. On the other hand, the ballast bags keep us moving at the same speed as the current. As our raft continues its slow-moving journey, I reach for Sim's hand and squeeze it tightly in mine. It will take a mountain of miracles to see us through this one.

The raft is just too heavy. Its freeboard is under ten inches, less when it's rougher and when the air chambers need air. The lighter the raft, the safer we will be if we hit a storm or if the raft suddenly loses air. I suggest that we should inventory what we have on board. Simonne readily agrees.

Sim starts at the far end of the raft under my legs and calls out each item as I make entries in the Log: two 2 1/2 gallon plastic water jugs, seven bottles of Evian and two big bottles of Perrier (a good French girl never leaves a sinking boat without them), water maker, one and a half cans saltines, eight cans with veggies, five beers, 1/2 jug cognac, compass, barometer, ship's clock, two watches, camera, camcorder, two life preservers, the full set of six cockpit cushions, can opener, knife, gun, two sponges, two sets of foul weather gear, one big trash bag with bedding, a large blue sail bag, Walkman radio, EPIRB, three flashlights, log book, writing material, three flares, five small cartons of juice, two pairs of shorts (both Sim's), four T-shirts, fishing rod and reel, one hook, three of Simmone's toilet kits with odds and ends, and a large white bucket.

We also compile a list in the Log of the important items we missed...things we should have on board the raft to help us survive. When I last saw it, thirty flares in a sealed plastic container were on top of the trash bag with the bedding. The bag made it to the raft but the flares did not. The flares should have floated but I don't recall seeing them.

I kept a full case of charts next to the Log Book. I missed the air horn. With it, we could have signalled the "Ter Eriksen" and, at this moment, be on our way to Panama. We have virtually no clothing. I have no pants. We had a full inventory of medicine on board *Siboney*. None of it, not even a bottle of merthiolate, made the raft. We have no shoes, but then who needs them now?

The empty Veg-All can has been transformed into what we've come to call a "pee-pee-pot." It's so much easier to use than the large pail. The pail is always stuffed with the knife, gloves, and the gun, all of which we must put in a safe place while using the bucket. Besides Sim creates quite a scene when she climbs onto the bouncing bucket. When nature calls, Sim struggles to her knees, which, at 3 in the morning in twenty foot seas, is a real undertaking. A real trooper, she sticks her head out the window and takes a look around for the one ship that will come to save us.

It's time for formalities. Every vessel I've sailed has had a name. I announce:

"Sim, let's christen the raft. What shall we call it?"

"It should be significant. Do you like SECOND CHANCE?"

"How about LAST CHANCE?"

"Good name. THAT'S IT. I'll get the cognac."

Two drops of cognac for the raft and two drops each for the crew, and we are in a properly christened vessel.

I propose a toast: "May the stout raft "LAST CHANCE" see wild west winds and rough seas."

Sim glares at me. "What are you saying? Are you crazy?"

"Do you want to make it to the coast or not? A strong wind will blow us to safety. Wind, current, and waves are our allies. Time is our enemy."

I love the passage in Mitchner's Hawaii where the Polynesians, in their catamarans, were set to sail for legendary lands to the north. Many people were aboard. Food and water were limited. They had to speed to their destination or die. The high priest invoked the Gods to send them the "wild west wind." We now need the wild west wind. To push us to shore before...I shiver with the thought.

I embrace Simonne which brings on another flood of tears. The utter hopelessness of our situation is so real we dare not talk about it. There's nothing to say. There is no point in fooling each other. We face so many variables and countless unknowns. Our enjoyable pleasure sail, our retirement cruise has become a deadly nightmare.

Simonne, who has been pensive, suggests we lighten ship, and I jump to agree as the lack of room has me in a constant cramp. Without a second thought, the camcorder goes over first. As we watch it float away, I think back to how proud and happy we were when we bought it in Miami and of our plans to film an around the world video. So far, we've shot but twenty minutes while passing through the Panama Canal.

Next goes Sim's 38 revolver. I can't explain how I missed the bullets. They were right next to the gun. I cleaned everything out of her locker, or so I thought. The gun would have made a terrific signaling device. A couple of shots to the topsides of the "Ter Eriksen" would have brought everyone aboard on deck. Or if that hadn't worked, a shot to the pilot house would have brought the troops out. Then maybe they'd have run us down or shot back.

The ship's clock and barometer are the next to go. I find it ridiculous when I think how, in water chest high, I had pried them off their place on the bulkhead near the galley aboard *Siboney*. The ship's clock, when we are not at sea, hangs on a wall in our bedroom where it chimes away the hours and half hours. On sleepless nights, I keep track of exactly how sleepless the night really is. Otherwise, we never hear it.

The barometer would be handy to have on board except that the glass cracked last night, and the needle fell off and has disappeared. We collected all the glass and threw it over the side. Sim has looked all day for the sharp pointer with no luck but will continue tomorrow, for we need no new holes in the raft. Besides, why worry about future storms? We'll find out soon enough anyway, and there's no safe harbor in which to hide and no way to get there if there was.

Sim breaks into my musings: "Bill, quick, we're filling with water. Look."

"I don't see any water. The raft isn't leaking. Take it easy, baby."

Still excited, she points: "See, here, look. There it is." Sim runs the sponge under one of the cushions and squeezes not more than ten drops into the can. "Where's it coming from? We must have a leak. The raft is falling apart."

Exasperated, I suggest: "Taste it, Sim."

She looks at me quizzically, makes a face, then dips her finger into the bilge, and confirms: "It's not salty."

"That eliminates the leaking, sinking, falling apart raft."

Sim searches under the bedding and finds we've lost water from one of the large water jugs. "You squashed it," she says without looking up.

After Sim rests for an hour, I propose: "Madame, do you not think it is time for a repast? Yesterday we lunched at one and dined at seven. Breakfast today was at nine. Let's keep those hours. I feel like I digested all the meals quite well. You are a first class raft cooky. Stir something up real quick." She glances at me and quickly adopts my mood.

"Whatever you say, mon capitaine. Let me look into the cupboard to see what we have on the menu. Perhaps a cracker with peanut butter with a raisin on top."

"Dish it up, cookie dear. Let's eat two crackers for lunch. What a shame, we missed all those jams and other jars of peanut butter and the sardines and the tuna."

I take four crackers out of the can under my head while Sim digs into the peanut butter with the handle of the toothbrush. As I chew small bits of cracker, my thoughts go to shore...this is Saturday afternoon...what are our children doing?..**Sally, Joe, Cris, Alex...do something...call the Coast Guard...call our friends...we're in trouble...we're going to die.**

Sim's right on her analysis of the EPIRB. The Mini-B is trash as far as doing us any good out here. My Mayday signals did go out on a live band, but there was no one tuned in. During the daytime, the bands are dead, made so by the presence of the sun. A dead band gives just that impression. There is nothing, not even static unless there is a thunder storm around.

Though the band I tuned to was live, I found not one station on the air. I ran from one end of the twenty meter band to the other. The time of the day was against us. It was four in the morning Eastern time. The Americas were asleep. Even the most sleepless amateur radio operator had gone to bed. The sun could have killed our signal to operators in Australia and the Far East. No contact means just that. No one heard my signal. I hope someone was tuned to the Coast Guard weather frequency and heard my plea for help.

Our single best hope lies with family and friends. When will they miss us? I know my boys. They consider *Siboney* unsinkable. The single side-band radio is new to the boat, and they have no idea how powerful it is. Besides *Siboney*, in most of its 35,000 miles, was known for its lack of communication. We never engaged in VHF chit-chat. We turned the radio on only for short periods when approaching a marina. The boys probably think the radio died and that I'm happy; they know I like a quiet boat.

Between Miami and until ten days after leaving Panama, I was too busy with boat chores to spend much time working the ham bands. Single side-band radio contacts are often tedious and tiring unless atmospheric conditions are just right. It takes time to scan the band to find the kind of contact I'm looking for; then I must wait for a break to place my call. Many initial calls go unanswered. When sailing in close contact with shipping and land, I'm too occupied with navigation, course changes, traffic, sail changes, and boat chores to have the energy to chase around on the short wave bands.

At six in the afternoon, on June 2, with *Siboney* settled into a two thousand mile leg to the west, I tuned the radio to the ten meter band and listened for traffic. I heard a CQ, which in amateur radio talk is a request for a contact. I made my call and, to my surprise, back came my call sign from a ham radio operator in Georgia.

When I looked over to Sim, she was misty-eyed from joy; we were in live contact with the outside world. I gave my new friend a rundown of our 'round-the world trip and then asked him to put through a call to my son Joe in Miami to find out if his wife had made me a grandfather for the seventh time. In seconds, Joe was on the telephone listening to my voice booming off the speaker. The Georgia ham relayed his messages to us. The baby was not yet born but time was short. Everyone else was fine. We sent our hellos to all, gave our position, and promised to call back in a couple of days.

After that first contact, I tuned to the ten meter band at six every evening and each night talked to an amateur radio operator in a different part of the USA. The radio signal on ten meters skips off the ionosphere and where it lands depends on sky conditions on that particular day. I was never able to renew my contact with Georgia for my signal dropped the next night into the Oklahoma-Texas border. On the following nights, I made contact with radio operators in Washington D.C., Indiana, Connecticut, and with a man on a sailboat anchored off Puerto Rico.

On June eleven, anxious to talk directly with our children, I switched to the commercial marine frequencies. I tried to reach the AT&T high seas operator in San Francisco on a dozen different channels with no luck. WOM, in Ft. Lauderdale, was constantly occupied with calls from passengers on the dozens of cruise ships plying the Atlantic. When I was given a chance to break in, my signal did not get through. Out of desperation, I tried one of the higher commercial frequencies. A surprised shore operator, unaccustomed to receiving a call on such an unusual channel, answered right back though rather perplexed. Our first call went to Susan in Texas and the second to Simonne's boys in Miami. We gave both our position, our projected course to Honolulu with our expected ETA. Susan told us that Joe's baby, a girl, had been born the previous day, the 10th. I told Sue that I would call Joe in two or three days to congratulate mother and dad.

Cris said our house had yet not sold, but he had someone to rent it. Were we interested? We told him to hold off for a couple of days while we thought about it. I told him we'd call back with an answer later in the week. Cris was to call Sim's mother in France and tell her we were fine.

My nightly contacts on ten meters continued. Sim beamed whenever I chatted with hams in far away places. On June fourteen, the night we sank, my signals landed in southern California. My last contact was with Jesse, N6SBV, in Hemet, a town near Los Angeles. He was anxious to maintain contact with us as our sail progressed, and we set up a schedule for future nights. I thought about asking him to call home but decided to wait another day.

Today is June 17th. Our last contact with the children was a week ago today. How will they react when they receive no further calls? Perhaps it's too early for them to worry. In another week, when fourteen days go by, they will know something happened. A search should follow soon after. We will have to wait another week. Unless, of course, the EPIRB or MAYDAY do their job...

Sim announces the start of her period and quickly begins to search for protection. With a jerk, she pulls the heavy cotton sheet out from under my head, for it's the driest item on the raft. I hold one end while she cuts long strips about four inches wide then cuts these into pieces about a foot long. What do we do with the soils?

Increase air loss forces us to pump every half hour. Sim sniffs around for their source and soon finds not one but two leaks. The patch that covers the tear leaks between the two patches, and air leaks out of the valve. Sim hands me a piece of white tape she salvaged, and I wrap it around the valve then tighten it with a length of cord. An hour later, the air chamber is still tight. Something positive for a change. I'll work on the patches if the leak gets worse.

One question keeps running through my mind: how long before someone starts looking for us? Another week? Two? By the time we're off the scope for two weeks, our children and friends should conclude that something has happened. I voice my thoughts, and Sim nods, hopefully: "Exactly what I was thinking. Nothing will be done this week though you told Joe and Cris that we would call. They'll surely think we are having trouble making a contact." Her face falls, lips drop. "I really miss my babies. I should never have left them. Why did I ever let you talk me into going on this mad adventure? I was crazy to leave my beautiful home. You always get your way. Nothing I could have said or done would have changed your plans. You're crazy and a self-centered egoist of the worst kind."

"Wait a minute. We talked about it for two years. You never said you didn't want to go. You really amaze me. Last October in France, you were as excited as I when we shopped for dried food to take on the trip. Why didn't you at some point say, 'Bill, I cannot go'...something that simple?"

Sim nods: "We didn't talk enough about this trip. We were always so busy. We never had a quiet moment. Every time I broached the subject, you became uptight. You did not want to listen to me. You had your plans and projects all set. You had all the details worked out, and anything I said met your disapproval."

She continues, "I don't know when you changed all the plans. If you remember, we had talked about going to the Caribbean for a year. We would hop from Island to Island. You know them all, but I don't know any except Barbados and Martinique." She pouts for a moment. "We were going to socialize at exotic anchorages, make new friends, relax, have fun. No. It couldn't be. You wanted it your way although you know how much I hate long passages. Panama to Honolulu has to be the longest ocean passage in the world."

Sim barely takes a breath before continuing. "You are a monster of egoism. As long as you are satisfied and your needs met, everything is fine. Who cares if you trample everybody's feelings? Mine, my family's, your family's. I gave up my beautiful dog, Seda Linda, my house, my furniture, and my children to follow you on this miserable trip. I must be out of my mind."

She keeps hammering away: "Look where we are now. It's time you get a hold on your life. If we ever make it, you will have to make some drastic changes. You got away with too much until now, Butler, but your luck is running out. If God lets us live, I swear I am not going to listen to you blindly in the future. No, sir. That is over. I refuse to be your slave, your toy, your tag along."

Sim again begins to boil over: "Don't you realize that you went too far? That we are going to die some horrible death? A stupid and useless death. You, the big hero. Superman. Show me how you are going to get us out of this one...squirm out of this one, Butler."

"Come here, baby, let's squirm."

"Don't touch me, you monster...keep your hands off me. Use your energy figuring out how to get us saved. How could I be so dumb to fall for your crazy "Round-the-World" cruise in your old boat? Oh, Lord, have mercy on me." Tears roll and I squirm. She's right up to a point, but then she could have always stayed home. The great silence that follows is a relief.

Heavy, low ashen clouds sweep overhead. To the west, a low black cloud line rings the horizon. Night envelops us. I close the window, then rearrange a corner of the bedding around the cracker can as a pillow and settle down. Poor Sim. She is so right. We should have talked more to better synchronize our hearts, our dreams, and our feelings. Adventure it was, and the dangers were there. We both knew that. She, being more of a realist than I, surely saw the negative side more clearly. For me, this was to be the realization of my life's dream. I was on a high, blinded with excitement and joy at having accomplished so much work on my boat.

Never had *Siboney* looked so beautiful, so prepared, so ready to roam the seas. Was I an egoist? I think so, but how could I not be? Soon old age will cut my wanderings down to near shore day sailing. This was my last chance.

I take Sim in my arms and hold her while she cries out her frustrations, her fear, her homesickness. I cry with many of the same feelings. When Sim regains her composure, she reads, then we pray quietly. Simonne's mind wanders to her home in France....**What can my mother be thinking? Is she worried? She has to be. My poor mother, old and sick and alone. What will she do when I don't return?**

0200 SUNDAY FRENCH TIME, JUNE 18, 1990
ROQUEBRUNE-CAP MARTIN, FRANCE

Madame Marie Saissi knows something is wrong. Three candles burn in her bedroom. Unable to sleep, she strolls out to her balcony. Monte Carlo, engulfed in its usual haze, is off to her right. The Mediterranean stretches below. Evenly spaced swells roll into the shoreline to break on the sandy beach. Her thoughts go to Simonne. **My baby is out there. She's in trouble. I know it. In my dreams, I have seen danger. I have known this trip would end badly for at least six months.**

Whenever she called, I warned her not to go on the trip. Simonne, I would plead, get Bill to postpone the departure. 1990 would be better.

No, they had to go. They wouldn't listen. And now, something terrible has happened to them. Tonight, I'll light another candle. I will pray constantly for their safety. There is nothing else I can do....

chapter four

ABOARD THE RAFT "LAST CHANCE"
0000 SUNDAY JUNE 18, 1989, DAY 4

My watch chirps, and I shine the small white flashlight on the dial. It's midnight. Or should I say, it's only midnight. Nights seem so much longer than their eleven hours. If I'm lucky, I'll sleep through half of it. The other five or six hours turn into endless attempts to sleep interspersed with long, silent sessions of speculation as to what tomorrow will bring. If we do live through tomorrow, will we see the next? Will the raft hold up? That is our key unknown. Should the raft lose its buoyancy, how deep will it sink? Will the inflated arches keep it from sinking from under us? How long can we survive chin deep in water? I try to think of all that can go wrong before it happens.

The endless night creates within me a deep loneliness made more penetrating when I glance at Simonne lying by my elbow, forlorn, so vulnerable. Past her, through the open window, there is no moon, not one star. I play games with my eyes. Open or closed, there is no difference; the darkness is so absolute. The ocean appears as a sinister black monster waiting to claim two new victims. Specs of light from minute phosphorescent plankton dance below the surface; their light sources triggered by the splash of the waves. Life surely abounds around us, but so far we've seen neither fish nor bird. What monsters lurk below us? We dare not speculate.

I think back to the "Ter Eriksen"...oh, that was close. A hair's difference in its compass course, and the raft, LAST CHANCE, complete with crew, would be no more. Had the hand that put the course into the automatic pilot turned the setting knob to starboard the width of a sheet of writing paper, the large freighter would have run us down. I shudder again when I picture the ship's bow aimed directly at us as it plowed a giant path through the seas. The displaced water, as it climbed up the cold steel knife edge of the bow, formed a comber that rose high towards the deck, then curled and broke furiously ahead of the ship. Had the ship been heading for us, we could not have rowed clear. I can't erase the evil picture of huge, clinging barnacles first ripping the raft then tearing into Simonne and me. As the stern approached, the powerful pull of the propellers could suck us in and mince us. In all of our misfortune, we've had a huge dose of good luck...someone is looking after us....

Scattered drops that turn into incessant heavy rain break my incubus and lull me closer to sleep. Sim prays incessantly, rosary in hand. Again I try to pray but cannot. I remember the first part of the Our Father...Who art in Heaven...Hallowed be Your name...but no more. Sim mumbles on in French audible over the pounding deluge.

The wind picks up and the weather worsens. Waves build quickly under a light gray overcast. Clouds, low and ugly, scud ever faster to the northward, indicative of worse weather to come. Large seas roll us around inside the raft like cement in a mixer. It is fortunate to be in a small raft and packed in tightly, else we'd tumble around like a loose barrel in the back of a truck. The roar slam of a wave jostles me awake. It washes the entire raft as it passes and spends itself in a sea of foam. Soon it will build in strength and break again and again on its journey to land. How I wish we could lasso its crest and charge with it towards shore; in two days, we would be on land and safe.

Wind whistles through the canopy as heavy, continuous rain pummels the raft. The raft loses air faster. As Sim never sleeps for long, I wait until she stirs to pump air. I pump while Simonne prepares the paper for the plug. I've tried doing it alone several times, but I always lose most of the air and must start again. When the chamber is tight, I remove the pump; Sim plugs the hole with her finger, then screws in the plug. She never misses. She's terrific and a good crew if she wouldn't rag me so much. Every day, so far I've had a two hour scolding...same themes....

In the last hour, I've become increasingly dizzy, and now I can't turn or get up without losing my balance. I've probably lost salt as a result of the sinking and the strain of the first day. I wash out the can, fill it with sea water, and take a sip. The first few sips go down OK, but I gag on the rest. If a ship were to find us now, I couldn't save myself. Once or twice in the past hour when I moved my head, I felt the entire raft roll upside down. I look at Sim and cannot see her although she's inches away. I search for her hand. It darts into mine. Her squeeze tells me she is happy to have me close by.

Seas strain to destroy the raft. The roar of an approaching wave cues us to tighten our grip on the support straps. One, two, three waves miss the raft. When we relax, a ton of water slams into us. Breakers roll our way in an endless parade. The ballast bags, with hundreds of pounds of sea water, hold us steady. But for how long?

Should the raft capsize, the arches might help us through a complete roll. How will it happen and how do we react? Capsize would be sudden and catch us unwary. A wave crashing against the windward air chamber would lift it until a gust of wind slips under the flat bottom of the raft and blows it over. By then, we will be falling off the crest upside down. A new wave will crash into us as it and the wind pushes the raft through a full roll. Inside our weight would be on the canopy and arches with our gear piled on and around us. Will I have to leave the raft to bring it around, or will the wind and waves do it alone? In any event, we've tied the water maker and bellows pump to the raft. If we keep the windows closed, most of our water and stores should stay with us. Yet we're bound to lose something. We could even damage the raft or hurt ourselves. I rehearse this dreadful scene until I sleep.

At long last, our fourth day on the raft dawns--dark, cloudy, and rainy. Where has the sun gone? We haven't seen it since we've been adrift. Salt water has soaked everything aboard. The strain of the day's-long vicious storm has left us sore and worn out. Sim is seasick and I remain terribly dizzy. Whenever I turn, I sense the raft spin and topple over. Simonne supports my every move. In an emergency, I would be useless. I drink two more cups of sea water followed by two gulps of fresh water. The repugnant salt taste stays with me. Many experts claim that drinking sea water can be deadly, but I can think of no other solution to my dizziness.

A caravan of hissing mountains of water pummels the raft all morning. Waves break constantly around us. One in four scores a direct hit. We keep the raft pumped up tight and rigid and hang on. Sim sponges the floor of the raft every half hour in an attempt to keep our stores dry. In the early afternoon, wind and waves ease allowing us to release our grip on the life lines.

Sim notices I have my eyes open and says: "Bill, today is Sunday. Let's do something special Sundays. We'll eat a can only on Sunday. We have four cans left. Rescue will come by the time we get down to the last can."

"I like the idea, except let's skip today since we had a can yesterday."

Sim shakes her head. "No. We're both weak and you're dizzy. We need to help our bodies adjust gradually to less food. We'll open a can today. Besides it's Father's Day. The children must be thinking of you. Cheers."

"Thank you. Thank you. We'll have a can of chick peas. Can you figure out which one it is?" I move my head as Sim digs under my head rest. She pulls out a can with the right shape. "I'll open it," Sim volunteers.

The can opener was one of the first items Sim loaded onto the raft. She opens the can and it does have chick peas. We first sip the salty broth before it spills.

"Bill, let us give thanks," she says as she recites the Lord's Prayer in French.

By balancing one pea at a time on the end of our toothbrush, we finish half of the chick peas. Since the weather is relatively cool, the other half will stay fresh until this evening. Rain has not stopped, and monster waves continue to punish us as we drift along. Bored and tired of just hanging on, I dig out the Log and my navigation workbook.

I have always maintained a detailed Log of our activities at sea. Whenever *Siboney* left the dock, even on a one or two hour sail in Biscayne Bay, I entered a one line summary of the weather, distance travelled, and time away from the dock. Each of the 35,000 miles sailed by *Siboney* under my command are recorded in eight Log Books, all but the last safely stored in Miami. In all Logs, I have summarized at year end nautical miles sailed, hours under way, and days at sea.

With time on my hands, I leaf back through the Log to my last totals which were for year end 1988. I add the jaunts around Miami, then add on totals for the leg from Miami to Panama and Panama to where we sank. Since March 1968, when we sailed to Hong Kong to race in the China Sea Race to the moment of sinking this produces totals of:

NAUTICAL MILES SAILED: 34,794
HOURS UNDER WAY: 8,020
DAYS AT SEA: 582

Over time, I developed my own system for the Log. If I sailed six hours to an anchorage 30 miles distant, stayed three days, then sailed back in six hours, I logged 60 NM, 12 hours under way, and 3 days at sea. I will now follow the same procedure as on *Siboney* with a day running from midnight to midnight, except for Day 1, June 15. With the boat sinking at 5 in the morning put us on the raft but 19 hours on that fateful day.

Today is Sunday, June 18, day four on the raft. So far, Sim and I have taken turns making entries in the Log twice a day. On *Siboney*, I made my first entry whenever I first awakened after midnight, usually between two and three. Now given our snail's pace and to conserve the life of the batteries in the flashlights, we enter the new day as soon as the sun is up and we're both awake. We update the Log at four or five in the afternoon before night sets in.

In my navigation workbook, which we saved together with the logbook, I set up a table with columns for the Day number, the day of the month, the speed and direction of the set created by the power of the wind and waves, and the speed and set caused by the current. The last two columns are Latitude and Longitude and begin with day one at 5 degrees 30 minutes N Latitude and 99 degrees 10 minutes W Longitude.

Whenever I can look out without getting soaked, I try to get a fresh feel of how fast wind and waves push us north. I hold the compass up into the wind and waves and find both are due south. The wind was light on our first day; it picked up on the second and has blown hard for the last two. With a scrap of paper, I've just timed our speed to the north at a bit under 20 seconds to cover ten feet. That comes out to more than 1800 feet per hour, about a third knot. I enter a set of 8 miles to the north for the last two days, with 4 miles for the first day and 6 for the second. The average direction of the total set of 18 miles is north.

The current is impossible to quantify, but it must be strong to hold us on an easterly course though wind and waves pound us from east and west of south. I enter an easterly set of 20 miles per day for all four days. With this dead reckoning data, I come up with a position at midnight tonight of 6 degrees north and 98 degrees west. We've drifted more than 100 miles to the north northeast since we sank. With shore now 1100 miles to the east, we'll be there in 44 days if wind, waves, and current hold up. That'll never happen. Besides the raft will be hard put after 44 days of the same ferocious pounding.

Sim returns the Log and workbook to its dry place in the white plastic compactor bag. The pen goes into a small yellow plastic case with a dozen others she bought in Panama. Sim watched me prepare the dead reckoning table and then read the Log entry. Looking out of the window at a far away cloud, she talks as if to herself: "Lost. We are lost. Even if anybody in our family or our friends worry, even if the Coast Guard is willing to search for us, where will they start? We are so far away, so far away."

"You need faith," I say, hoping to instill some of my positive thinking and make her feel better.

Sim looks at me with fire in her eye: "Look, who's talking about faith. You? Butler, you are the most faithless person I've met. You don't even know how to pray."

I fight back. "Knowing how to pray helps, but it isn't the key to faith. You have to believe we will be saved."

Sim looks out into space. "Look who is preaching. My God. The devil himself. I have never seen you even kneel in church or, for that matter, anywhere, much less pray. Give me a break."

I look her straight in the eye. "We'll be saved, Sim. Get that through your dense head. We aren't the first to be adrift in a raft. Many others, like us, have had their boats sink from under them and have been saved after many days at sea. So cheer up."

Sim eyes brighten. "Cruising World had a story of a man who drifted seventy one days alone in a raft in the Atlantic. I think his name was Callahan. I wish I had read his book. He was alone."

"And you're not alone. You have this gallant, handsome raft mate for company who'll whisk you to safety."

"I can swallow the gallant part, but handsome? Have you seen yourself in the mirror? Your hair is matted; you're unshaven; your T-shirt looks like you found it in the bilge of *Siboney*; you're dirty; you smell..."

"Ok, skip the handsome portion. How about witty?"

"Butler, get serious. We're in deep trouble. And we can't do anything."

A cramp has me search for a new position that will yield a semblance of comfort. Most of the time and that means up to eighty percent of the day, we lie on our back because it is the most efficient, space wise, and most comfortable position. Sim has done a great job storing and fixing our "bunks." My bottom lies on one of the four boat cushions placed laterally on the floor of the raft. One of the smaller cushions is under my back. Under it, Sim placed a life preserver to raise it higher so that my head, resting on the air chamber, is in line with my back. Under my neck, she has piled the binoculars in its case, a large can of crackers, and the spare parts bag. Her bed's made up about the same. On top of the cushions, she has spread the large striped comforter, and under my head, I have the wool blanket we bought in the Andes. She detests the feel of wool so uses the cotton spread. My feet are also raised by the multitude of stores she's stuffed under the comforter...things like the water maker, foul weather gear, and other life preserver. My feet rest easily on the opposite air chamber.

We have drifted two days without sighting human life. Next time we do we must be instantly ready to signal. Sim must keep a sharp lookout, particularly at night when flares are most effective. She keeps wondering when will someone look for us...realistically. Will it be two weeks? Three weeks? I try to imbibe her with my optimism and insist that our stay in the raft will be short and say: "Every day that goes by increases our chances of someone finding us. Today is the eighth day since our last radio contact. One of the children will react soon. They must be worried now and soon they will do something."

"I pray every minute for that...."

Sim bleeds heavily. The soils go into the empty cracker can. Slowly, the stormy weather relaxes. Seas lessen. A breaking wave hasn't struck us for almost an hour. Clouds lift and the rain stops. We turn back to back, close our eyes and sleep, for when we again look out, the sun is an hour from setting.

I can't stretch out fully and complain to Sim. "My knees hurt. Could it be arthritis?"

Sim, naked and lying on her side, shoots back. "If you've got arthritis, it's in your brain. What you have is simple. Your muscles get rigid from lack of movement. I have the same problem. We have to lie on our back and exercise our legs. Bicycle in the air."

"What we need is to relax. You've been too uptight since the first night on the raft."

Sim turns towards me, a wild look in her eyes: "The great Captain says relax. Relax? How in hell can anybody relax? I'm afloat in a sinking raft, a thousand miles from anywhere, packed in like a sardine, and punched all night as if in a bout with Mohammed Ali. Read my lips, you dummy. **W E A R E G O I N G T O D I E.** Do you understand? Nothing is going to save us. The expensive radio that didn't get your MAYDAY'S through. The EPIRB that never sent a signal. When I think we paid $500 for that worthless piece of junk. We should sue those guys who sold it to us. The crazy skipper who doesn't know where he is or where he is going. And the big macho says "relax." You are hilarious, Butler. Relax. You're going to die and you don't even realize it. You've got the great habit of always saying relax whenever you have no answer to a problem."

I shrug. "What can I say? I am a failure. How about a game of dominos?"

"Dominos. Throw them overboard. Stick the dominoes up your big ears."

"Pass them over; I'll check the fit."

"Bruto." Sim smiles and says: "Ok. Let's play. What else is there to do? I get tired of listening to your bull." With a groan, we inch to a semi-sitting position. I take my place on the starboard side as I move my legs across the raft. It feels good to sit up. My initial dizziness goes away gradually.

We refer to the end of the raft with the patch as "the stern." It has been facing west for the past three days and away from the full force of the breaking waves. Facing east or towards the bow, I am on the right side of the raft, and Sim lies on the left. My side faces south, the direction from where the waves approach. Though the ballast bags have worked perfectly, my weight on the high side offers an added margin of safety. Besides Simonne can't stand the full force of the waves that break with vicious blows against the air chamber to then catapult over the canopy. On the other hand, the person on the low side, away from the waves, often gets soaked. When a roller breaks and hits the raft, water squirts between the canopy and the window with such force that it shoots over me and onto Sim. How do the French say it...c'est la guerre? When she receives a bucketful of water, I turn my head to hide my snicker.

In today's domino game, we play points. We both hate to loose. Sim plays a determined game and easily takes me to the cleaners. I hope it improves her disposition.

"You've won first prize, baby, here I am."

"I won YOU? Take a look in my mirror and come back to the real world."

"Perhaps a little kiss instead. It's still Father's Day."

"I don't trust your kisses."

I banter back, figuring it's time the rafts sees a little action. "Me? Just because you're naked and lovely and scrumptious doesn't mean I'll take advantage of you. My intentions are purely platonic...uh, therapeutic."

"Butler, you've taken me on your platonic voyages before. I know how little platonic they end up, and I know all about your cure-all therapy. Stay away. Besides I've made promises."

"What sort of promises."

"It's a secret. Hold on to me. I'm going to take a look around." Sim turns over on her knees, opens the top part of her window, and sticks her head out. The swells are still well over thirty feet but long, and the crests aren't breaking. Sim comes up with a weather report. "We have better weather ahead. Seas are down. Wind is between ten and fifteen knots from the south. I'm coming back in, hold me."

"Hold you, where?", as I run my hand up her thigh.

"Ayyy, not there. Bruto. Be serious, Butler."

"Just trying to help a damsel in need. It beats falling over the side. What, no thanks?"

Sim settles back in and says, "Let's read before it gets dark." Sim takes the set of cards with psalms and prayers from a small ziploc that has snapshots of her children and family. Tears roll down her cheeks as she stares at the faces of her mother, her sister, and her boys. Slowly she regains control and reads.

When darkness engulfs our little world, Sim's personal problem gets worse. We don't dare throw anything over the side to avoid attracting sharks. The flashlight helps us settle down in this darkest of nights. We pump as much air into the raft as we dare and doze off.

Sunday night turns out to be rather peaceful for a night deep in the Pacific Ocean on a thin plastic raft. Our bunk remained warm and comfortable; Sim and I synchronized our turns at the same time, and no arguments over space erupted. We pumped three or four times and slept well between pumping. The night passed quickly. If they all pass at this speed, we'll be out of this one in no time.

Waves today are higher than 15 feet. I make my daily estimate of drift: twenty miles east, eight miles north. We feel the push of the strong current as it grips the ballast bags. It nudges the raft with a gentle jerking motion, much like a car with an ignition problem.

Meanwhile Sim is bleeding heavily and is now dizzy as well. Eyes closed, she prays for help in getting our message through to God that we are in desperate need of His hand. Sim has tied several medals to the canopy with images of Mary the Miraculous, St. Michael, and our Lady of Lourdes. She touches them all the time. Poor Sim, hair matted, dirty, her drooping lips giving away her feeling of deep despair and hopelessness.

A thump announces the arrival of another turtle. It first bumps Sim in the middle of the back, then hits me. It's Sim's bottom next, later my legs...and on and on for over twenty minutes. Sim, her head and shoulders outside the raft, awaits for it to surface. The small paddle in her right hand, she's ready to strike. When the green sea turtle emerges for air, Sim swings for its neck and hits. The turtle kicks and dives.

It quickly returns but Sim is ready. "Take this, this, this, and this...you monster...," she calls out in fury.

"Sim, cool down," I insist, for I fail to see the need to get so worked up.

"I'm going to kill it."

"Sim, baby, the turtle isn't doing all that much harm."

"That's because you are blind. That turtle is going to sink us."

"How can it sink us? The top of his shell is round and smooth. It's just hitting the ballast bags. It can't do any damage. Relax."

At that moment, the turtle surfaces, and Sim swings madly as she yells: "Take that, and that, dumb bitch. Go away! Leave us alone!"

She hits the shell with a dull thud. The turtle swims ten feet away from the raft and turns again towards us. It lifts its ancient head out of the water. Its two large black eyes stare at Sim with a curious, quizzical look, obviously the first time it's encountered our species and promptly swims back towards Sim.

"Ay. I'll fix you this time," she screams.

Sim hits the turtle. Again it swims six feet away and returns. The scene repeats itself until Sim, exhausted, excitedly passes me the paddle. "Here, Bill, quick. It's on your side. I can hear him scratch the raft. It's full of barnacles. It's going to puncture the raft."

The turtle has its shell half under the air chamber and paddles wildly taking us with it. I hit the turtle which tries to swim away but cannot. I hit it again then see that it has a flipper tangled in the boarding ladder. I lean over the side of the raft and turn the moss and barnacle laden shell until I can reach the tangled flipper. The turtle strikes back with its beak narrowly missing my fingers. I unwrap two turns of the webbed nylon boarding ladder from around its front flipper. Once released, it dives gratefully into the deep.

"Hold the paddle, Sim, I'm going to tie the boarding ladder so this doesn't happen again." I roll the red straps of the ladder into a ball and use two ties to hold it closely to the raft.

Minutes later, the turtle is back under the raft. Sim simmers. I lay back and try to relax. We're bumped ten times in a row. Sim boils over. She's ready to jump overboard and wrestle the beast to the end.

"What is that male monster doing with us? What does it

want? It's going to tear a hole in the raft. Why doesn't it go away? Butler, answer me! Why am I surrounded by dumb males?"

"Which question first? I really don't know what it wants with us. I would normally guess it's looking for shade from the sun. That doesn't explain today or last night when there was no sun. Why get all worked up over one turtle? Let's only worry about turtles with broken edges or barnacles. A turtle with an even round shell can't damage the raft."

"Butler, you live in wonderland. Can't you hear it scratching right now? How many scratches can this junk raft take? This turtle is going to work its way right into this raft!"

"A shame it's not a female. Maybe there'll be a little action on this raft."

"Is that some sort of complaint?"

"No, of course not. What would make you believe that? It couldn't be your conscience because you have none. Besides I'm considering taking up a monastic life when I get to shore. I'll lead the simple life."

"We had the simple life. Then you get restless and cook up this crazy around the world excursion. And here we are."

"This is the simple life. We relax, lie back, float, and make mad passionate love until we're found."

"Get that out of your head. The raft is too shaky for funny things, and I'm not in the mood. Besides I made promises."

"Let me try to get you into the mood, my little bonbon. Come to zee capitaine's exotic Pacific waterbed. Perhaps, a leetle keess? You still haven't told me what your promise is all about."

She quickly changes the subject: "It's one o'clock, time for lunch." Our usual cracker with peanut butter tastes like a filet mignon dinner today. A crumb at a time then two full gulps of fresh water satisfies our hunger. Five raisins for dessert round out an exceptional meal.

"Madame, I challenge you to a game of dominos." Today we play games not points. I win the first four rounds. Sim smiles when she wins her first. We're forced to stop when large seas again pound the raft. The wind began to build late in the morning and is now blowing more than fifteen knots. Waves are picking up speed too. We're surprised how quickly seas build and how long it takes for them to settle back down after the wind stops.

The crash of a violent wave jolts us awake just as water cascades over the window and drenches us. A quick look out to weather reveals mountainous grey seas rolling in from the south. Clouds race overhead, dense and grey. They speed towards the northern horizon, towards the doldrums, where they will collide with that perennial weather wall to create formidable climatic towers. We tighten the windward window as today's torment begins. Sim reads early.

Sim's reading before the onset of night again fills us with an aura of peace and tranquility that bolsters our will to survive the fearful eleven hour night. Again I try to contact Sally. I close my eyes, concentrate on her apartment, and transmit my pleas...Sally help us...we are in danger...we are going to die...the boat sank...we're in a raft in the middle of the Pacific...we need help...NOW....

With my eyes still closed, I strive to reach my twenty eight year old daughter in Mt. Vernon, New York. Of all the children, Sally is the most likely to receive my messages. She and I have made contact before. So many times, back home in Miami, I would call her, and she'd pick up the phone on the first ring and say, "Hi, dad, I knew it was you. I knew you were thinking about me."

Besides she is the one least burdened with outside activities. She spends most of her day at home taking care of her year old baby, Cody. Her husband works hard to hit the big time as a drummer. If I can get through to anyone, it will be to Sally.

I continue...Sally, listen...concentrate...your daddy is in deep trouble...call the Coast Guard...call friends...we need someone to start searching... HELP...HELP...Sally... I distinctly feel contact. It's nine p.m. in New York. I picture Sally in her large stuffed chair watching TV. Cody is on her lap. I try again and again to reach her. I feel I am getting through. **Sally, you're my big hope. Do something. Send help...now...**

MOUNT VERNON, NEW YORK
2130 MONDAY JUNE 19, 1989

Sally Smith is in her favorite recliner. Baby Cody suckles busily while mother watches TV. Sally finds her mind drifting away towards the deep Pacific Ocean. **Dad and Simonne last called Susan and Cris more than a week ago. Joe had a baby on the 10th of June. It's now a week later. Why hasn't Dad called Joe?**

There's no need to worry just yet. I do wonder how it's going for them. They left Panama three weeks ago. Dad said he expected a sixty day trip from Panama to Hawaii. He should be calling this next week.

Sally's eyes begin to close, senses dulled by the drone of the TV. A new picture forms in her mind. She sees an immense black void. Faraway, she hears her father call:

SALLY, HELP! HELP! YOUR DADDY IS IN TROUBLE! WE ARE GOING TO DIE! HELP! GET HELP!

Her eyes pop open. **What was that? It was so vivid. Has something happened to dad? What's going on?**

chapter five

ABOARD THE RAFT "LAST CHANCE"
0900 THURSDAY JUNE 22, 1989, DAY 8

The storm lasted two days. Mountainous seas hammered our miniscule floating home, each wave threatening to engulf and capsize us. Our senses remained constantly alert. With each roar of a thunderous wave, we'd jump to windward seconds before an avalanche of boiling water buried the raft. The raft would slide into the trough and, just when it appeared we would no longer emerge from our watery grave, out we'd pop, soaked but safe. Two or three breaking waves would miss us until another mid-ocean collision between opposing weather systems buried us anew. Soon one wave more powerful than all others will roll us over and down to the deeps, to release us only after expending its awesome power. We could not survive long.

The ride over smooth rolling waves after the seas flattened out late yesterday provided a surprisingly quiet night's sleep. We slept right through our one week anniversary. When we had to pump air but every three hours last night, I felt I was in castaway heaven. The comforter was dry and the air temperature perfect. Sim slept bare which gave me a chance to give her plump torso a full examination. Another couple of weeks on our three saltine a day diet, and she'll have a knockout figure. I kept an edge of the comforter over me to keep my cold blood warm. Neither of us sleep longer than an hour and a half at a stretch. When I awaken, it's only long enough to pinch the air chamber, take a quick look around, sense all is as I left it, and doze back out.

But that's all behind us. The raft's performance was first rate. Not once did it become unstable and threaten to flip. I hope it stays that way. The morning has dawned clear and bright. Of course, what we now call clear is considered quite cloudy back in Miami. Clouds no longer press us into the ocean but are higher, light grey, and not so dense. Sim points to a sliver of blue sky, the first we've seen while adrift. We greet the sun as a long lost friend. It's not a perfect day for an air search, but it's the best we've had yet. We scan the skies and genuinely expect to hear a far away hum which would signal help has arrived. Soon after, a glistening Coast Guard falcon jet will make a low pass overhead. It'll dip its wings in recognition ...and it'll all be over...we'll be safe and on our way home....

Sim's voice cuts into my fantasy: "Don't tell me sleeping beauty's awake. You've missed half the day, Butler. I've been pumping, cleaning, beating off turtles, and you've slept through it all."

"Good morning, sweety. I've been busy dreaming. Did you see the Coast Guard jet that flew over this morning?"

"You may be joking, but I did dream about a plane waving its wings at us. It made several passes before it flew off. Let it be true, oh God, let it be true."

I am sure they will launch at least one search flight today. But will they look in another part of the ocean? Susan and Cris had our position on the eleventh of June. What's going on?

I gave the ham operator in California our coordinates as of eleven hours before we sank. He will send a QSL acknowledgment card to my address. Will the children sense its significance and call him?

Perhaps Karl can. Karl installed the single sideband ham set aboard *Siboney*. He would have to transmit an emergency CQ on the ten meter band. That is, if he can, for his Collins radio may not have crystals for that band. Even so, it would take days for a net to form to trace the station in California with whom we had our last contact. Too many "ifs."

I turn towards Sim and ask: "Were you able to pick up any news on the radio?"

"Lots. A Russian cruise ship, the *Maxim Gorki*, with nine hundred and fifty people aboard hit an iceberg in the north Sea and is sinking. I hope the children make a connection...they sink and we sank. I shouldn't say this, but it's luck for us. Now they should get worried. They are bound to put two and two together and conclude they have no news from us because the boat went down."

I voice my agreement: "They should definitely make the association. Come on, gang. Think! Think! Get your brains in motion. Call our friends. Act! Now!"

Simonne continues to escape the confinement of the raft to touch the land borne world so far away with the little yellow Walkman radio. Careful not to drain the batteries, she listens but minutes at a time beginning after midnight when reception is best. As the signal skips off the ever changing ionosphere, she must continuously re-tune to new stations or let a minute or more pass until her original station reappears. Mexican stations come in strongest for Acapulco lies some 700 miles to the north. If we're out here another week, I'll have her track the strength and source of the many stations she picks up to help me verify our drift towards shore. Though every sign convinces me we're drifting to the northeast, I'm hard pressed how to prove it to Sim when she casts doubts on my navigation plots.

I add our last day's run in my dead reckoning log and total our way made good in the week since *Siboney* sank. I find we've drifted to the east with the current a total of 135 miles, and we have been pushed 45 miles to the north by the wind and waves. I jot down our new latitude and longitude in my workbook. But what I really need is a chart to better visualize our progress. I'll make one. I draw a half inch grid on a page of my navigation workbook and label the coordinates for latitude and longitude at intervals of one degree for each square. Longitude will run from eighty to one hundred degrees west and Latitude from zero to twenty degrees north. We're in there, somewhere.

In the navigation notebook, I find the exact position for Balboa and for Punta Mala, both in Panama. Balboa is the Pacific Ocean terminus of the Panama Canal, and Punta Mala is a Cape south of the Canal that all ships going north must round. I enter both positions on the chart. I remember that Acapulco is right on 100 degrees west and close to 17 degrees north. I enter a dot on the chart and label it. As I remember it, the coast between Punta Mala and Acapulco is almost a straight line, so I draw a line between the two points. The Gulf of Panama goes north from Punta Mala to Balboa and drops in a semi-circle to the southeast.

With Sim's help, I locate the borders of the Central American countries. Costa Rica is north of Panama, of that we're both sure. Then it's Nicaragua. We know Guatemala is next to Mexico. We can't remember if Honduras or Salvador is next to Costa Rica, so we leave the entire area blank for now.

I put an X on the chart where we sank which is twenty squares from the coast. Each square is a degree, sixty miles, so that means we're 1200 miles from Panama. 1100 miles from the nearest Central American coastline to the east. Seven or eight hundred miles north to Acapulco. Sim watches my every move.

"How far away are we from the coast?"

"Oh, about nine hundred miles." I always knock a few miles off my estimates.

Sim knows this and adds twenty percent to everything I say. She asks: "Where are we headed?"

"This current will take us right into shore. We're at seven degrees north now. The current will push us east until we approach the coast. The wind and waves will push us north."

I can't remember what happens to the current near shore. Does it swing north, or does it go south? But why worry about reaching the coast? Help should be on the way soon. We need several clear days and we'll be out of here.

Sim runs her fingers along the crease between the floor and the air tube in search of anything sharp. She has repeated this precaution every day, afraid that abrasion might open a hole in the air chambers. We still haven't found the barometer needle. She also watches me all the time to insure I don't leave scissors, a file, or the hook near the plastic tubes. She knows how careless I can be. She keeps the scissors, the nail file, the hook, and the knife in the leather gun holder. When I use the scissors, she keeps her eyes on me until they're away safe.

We emptied both two and a half gallon water containers and tossed them over the side. Now I have only the large plastic bucket to contend with. We've almost drained two of the seven bottles of Evian which means I had better check out the water maker and see how it works. Sim retrieves the machine from under my feet and removes the foul weather wrap which protects it and keeps it from damaging the raft. The device has three plastic tubes. One of the two larger ones is the salt water intake and has a mesh filter fitted to the end. Waste salts wash out of the other large tube. I drop both large tubes over the side. Sim hangs on the third tube from which the fresh water will hopefully emerge.

The body of the pump is almost two feet long and has a two foot handle attached to one end. As I stroke the handle and salt water is sucked in from the sea, the pressure needed to move the handle increases. After a dozen strokes, bubbles and finally water drips from the small tube which Sim holds over the side until the water is clear.

I put the tube in my mouth while I continue to pump. The water is salty at first, but ten strokes later, the water becomes sweet and pure. Sim puts the tube into an empty plastic bottle and holds both until the bottle is about a quarter full. Sim then takes over. She's a sight pumping, naked as a centerfold. I ogle, whistle, and get a dirty look. Sim and I trade the water maker back and forth after six or seven minutes when our muscles start to ache.

Each liter takes twenty minutes to fill. We do thirty strokes in thirty seconds or one stroke per second. Twenty minutes has 1200 seconds so a liter needs 1200 strokes. We'll keep trim and our muscles in shape, at least from the waist up.

Sim has the first sip and announces the taste as first class. "As good as Evian," she declares which, from a Frenchwoman, is an exceptional stamp of approval. If the machine continues to work, water will not be a problem. We fill a liter in less than twenty minutes; our day's supply in forty.

We make a second inventory as Sim again reorganizes the raft in hopes of gaining a few extra inches of floor area to spread our bodies. The food and liquid inventory yields: one can vegetables, four cans with unknown contents, one can with juice, 2 beers, 1 can clams, 1 large bottle apple juice, 2 Perrier, one half bottle cognac, one half liter coke, 1 small Sprite, 2 bottles of Evian, 1 can crackers, 7 liters of water, and three boxes of raisins. Sim makes it all disappear under us in what we now call the bilge.

The day continues sunny, and the breeze is light from the south. Seas are six to eight feet but calm enough for me to open my window. Sim opens hers and part of the canopy, and we hang a corner of our bedding out to dry. What joy we find in again being part of the world after seven days locked up inside our tiny raft. I tighten my hold on Sim's hand as we gaze out of the open window at passing clouds and birds that circle the raft in search of a meal.

No land-locked aquarium approaches what we have below our raft. We can see more than a hundred feet down. Dorados are everywhere and they jump and splash in glee. Schools of brightly colored school fish similar to parrot fish dash around followed by what look like yellow tails. Among them swim small sharks. Four orange triple tails swim within an arm's length. They barely move and stay inches under the surface, not up and down as other fish but swim sideways. One eye looks straight up at us. I could snag one if I had a harpoon. Perhaps I can make one.

I untie the fishing rod from the air chamber where we secured it that first day right after *Siboney* sank and, with the large knife, cut the rod in half. With four feet of monofilament fishing line unspooled from the reel, I tie the hook to the end of the thin half of the rod.

I watch my prey as they circle closely. With one eye up, they appear to watch me. Before the gaff was ready, they swam right up to the raft. Now they come no closer than ten feet. I wait. Minutes go by. At last three triple tails slowly coast in. I jab the hook under the closest fish, pull, and miss. All the fish vanish into the depths. I wait but I know fish...they're gone...these will not be back. I'd love to catch a dorado, but how do we land it without damaging the raft? One small hole in the air chamber, and we'll sink. We've used up all the patches and we now rely on the emergency tube.

If I had a net when the triple tails first arrived, I would've caught one. How to make a net? What knot do net-makers use? I'll give it a try. I know that the first item all net makers and menders need is a spool. I pull more line out of the fishing reel and wind ten feet onto one of Sim's ball point pens. I hang the small half of the fishing rod between the arches and wrap a dozen loops of the nylon around it stretching from one end to the other. Then I practice making knots. When young, I had watched Cuban fishermen mend their nets. Sim, back in Menton, had sat with the fishermen on the old breakwater as they worked on their nets. We take turns practicing, but the right knot continues to elude us. An hour later, with nothing but a tangle to show for my efforts, we give up and throw the odd pieces of nylon over the side. What a shame, I'm sure I could catch something with a net.

When I look out again, the yellow fish are no where to be seen. In their place, dozens, possibly hundreds of dorados swim playfully under the raft. These are the Atlantic sea dolphin; the Hawaiians call them mahi-mahi. They dart in schools of six or more below the surface. Their bright blue and yellow colors liven our underwater world. Some dorados, with bright phosphor blue pectoral fins and yellow tail fins, skirt inches from the raft and tempt us to catch them. Suddenly, one will shoot out of the water to land flat with a slap and a splash. Unquestionably, it's done out of sheer happiness. They celebrate life with exuberance and joy, so pleased to be in their element. Our element is so many miles away...among green fields and fat cows and trees with long leafy branches...will we live to see land again?

A flying fish takes off in a frenzy, just in time to escape some large pursuer. There is blaze of gold and blue in the sea. The flying fish remains aloft while a swift shadow beneath it shows where a dorado keeps pace with its flight. Flight energy expended, it falls into waiting jaws and vanishes in a flurry of foam.

I inch around onto my knees and lift my head over the canopy. Twenty foot swells, graceful now and far apart, roll under us on their way to some distant shore. Skies are clear to the north and west. Clouds ring the horizon to the south. A few hours of sunshine is all we ask.

Birds fly and feed all around us. Boobies sweep the crests of waves in search of an airborne flying fish. Their large wings help them soar effortlessly in their quest for food. I count thirty two boobies, mostly young with light and fluffy feathers and fuzzy markings. At any one time, half are in the air. The others perch nearby on the water either squabbling or preening.

Simonne calls out: "Here, Pretty Boy. Bill, look at this beautiful booby. He's my friend. He came yesterday and the day before that. He spends the night with us along with another dozen or so birds. The others aren't as pretty as this one. Look at its black body, its white chest so rounded, so soft. Have you seen his eyes?

They look straight at me. Agate eyes. It's a male, and the brown and beige ones are females. Why is it that in the animal kingdom the males of the species are always the most striking?"

"Pretty Boy" swims closer. "Is he good to eat?" I tease.

"Don't you dare joke about it. Isn't he gorgeous?"

"It looks more delicious than gorgeous. He has me salivating. Here, pretty bird, here. I bet he tastes great, and he'd make super bait."

"Bill Butler, stop your eternal dumb talk. You're not going to touch one of my birds. Here, sweetie, come to me. Look, he isn't afraid. He loves me."

I'm glad to see Sim relax who continues: "He's really pretty. And look below; look at all of those dorados and other fish. We're in wonderland, above and below the surface. But what are they doing this far from shore? There's nothing out here but water. The nearest land must be the Galapagos, and that's more than five hundred miles away."

Sim remains excited: "Look, next to "Pretty Boy", there's a beauty of a young female. Her eyes are black, and she looks like she has makeup. Her beak is blue, and her face mauve and violet. She looks like Elizabeth Taylor in Cleopatra. I'm going to call her Cleopatra. And there's another but not as pretty as Cleo. Won't the sharks eat them?"

"I'll bet!" When we first saw the birds, we wondered whether they would be shark bait as a shark, when hungry, will eat anything. As days passed, it became obvious that cohabitation on the high seas is a natural phenomenon sorted out millenniums ago. The birds watch everything that's going on and, although alert, do not act overly preoccupied. Sharks swim among them just feet away. The boobies watch them unflustered and soon continue to preen and cackle.

Meanwhile our sea family grows. More than forty sea birds swim with us. They sleep and scuffle nearby and drink salt water. The boobies discharge excess salt through special nasal glands. They shake their heads vigorously and the salt flies. A dozen birds swim lazily near the raft. At first when they dipped their beaks in the water, I thought they were drinking salt water, but they'd pop if they took a sip with every dip. Now I'm convinced they're but checking out what's going on below. Pretty Boy and Cleo approach within several feet of Sim, who entertains them with running chatter.

The boobies are forever busy preening. When perched on the sea as they ride the waves, they work on waterproofing their feathers. We watch as they bend their heads around and push their beak into a spot near their tail feathers. There, with their bill, they squeeze droplets of fatty oil from their preen gland and convey the oil to their feathers in nibbling and wiping actions.

Twenty birds float alongside, all busy with their feathers, not one interested in Sim or I. That is, except for Pretty Boy, who's fallen in love with Sim. He watches her every move and cocks his head when she talks. Sim says Pretty Boy is her guardian angel in disguise. I hope so. We need all the protection we can get.

On the way out from Panama, we saw very few birds. Every day or two, one would fly with us for an hour, and once in a while, a booby would rest on a spreader, but I'd shoo them off before they messed up my sails. Three or four days before we sank, I woke up in the morning to find the mainsail stained with a heavy dose of droppings. I scrubbed it for an hour and threw several dozen bucketfuls of water on it before it was white again.

High overhead, head into the wind, soar the keen-eyed, always watchful frigate birds, their great wings spread to their full six foot span. Their flight is at times motionless, stability provided by distinctive twin tails that act as rudders. I haven't seen one yet come near the surface. Do they stay up there all night? If not, where do they go?

SIMONNE:

I so love these birds. The males have such striking markings-white and black or white and brown. The color of brown is the most beautiful I have ever seen. I reminds me of a monk I had seen once in Assisi in Italy, who prayed alone in a church where I had wandered in search of shade and silence.

It was summer outside. As I knelt, a ray of sunshine shone through a high stained glass window. It gave the monk's robe a glow that appeared to come from inside. The color of the booby reminds me of that moment.

Whenever I see birds, I always think of St. Francis...his boundless love for all life on this earth. Birds flocked to him. They sat on his shoulders, ate from his hands. Animals obeyed him. I respect people who love animals because God gave these to us and we have a responsibility towards them.

I learned from the old fishermen in the south of France to preserve and respect the environment. They gave their prey a chance. My brother Serge, a good underwater hunter, caught most of his meals..octopus, sea urchins, and squid with his bare hands. He never used gloves or a knife. If they were what he wanted, he kept them. Otherwise, he threw them back.

BILL:

With Sim's steadying help, I turn from my back to my knees then stretch up to take a look around. I'd love to stand, to test my legs, but that's impossible. The full majesty of the deep blue ocean spreads in every direction. Swells big as hills roll in formation from the south to lift us gently until we stand on top of our watery world. White caps dot the oceanic swells that raise us to their crests until I can see over all other waves. Each time we rise, I focus on a small part of the horizon, hoping to spot help on its way. The sea remains empty.

When the crest passes, we drop slowly. Ten, twenty, thirty, forty feet down into the sea. I look up to towering peaks of water as they surge towards us and get the sensation we may not emerge from the trough. But we do rise to soon stand again on the pinnacle of our watery world. I breathe in the vast vista...constantly changing, ever on the move, powerful, punishing, yet sustaining...both friend and foe...a soothing balm and a dedicated killer.

I stay on my knees long after they begin to pain, for I can't get over the feeling that a ship is nearby and will come to our rescue. The small lamp on the EPIRB continues to blink and could bring help to us. We have been at sea seven full days without sighting human life. Today makes eleven days since our last radio contact. Our family must soon miss us and activate a rescue mission. I repeat my mental signals to Sally. She's our big hope. Do something, baby. Call everyone you know. Involve our friends. You won't find us easily, but the pieces to the puzzle are in place. Simonne concentrates on Cris. She has a special bond with him, her eldest. When Sim hears a whistle in her ear, she's sure it's her mother thinking of her. Her mother knows we're in trouble, but she's so far away and sick...what can she do?

As daylight wanes, boobies come in to roost. Our raft becomes a birdport. To leeward, a dozen birds, lined up in formation, much like planes approaching an aircraft carrier, close in on the raft with wings slightly curled, webbed feet extended. Their approach is perfect until they collapse their wings and put their weight on the canopy. It probably looks solid from the air, but it's only thin cloth suspended between the inflatable arches. The canopy folds, and the booby slides right off and lands in the water with a belly flop and a surprised look...their hope to spend a quiet, dry night perched atop our canopy dashed. Sim and I explode with laughter as each booby touches down on the canopy only to slip off and land in the sea with a splash. Seconds later, another bird touches down and belly flops into the ocean. Their antics keep us entertained until at last we tire and I wave them off with the pole. Undaunted, some go around for a second try. Others quietly swim away twenty feet to windward. They stay close, providing companionship and reassurance for the long night ahead.

We eat a cracker each for supper followed with a long drink of water out of the bottle. Sim reads the prayers. This has been a great day, and we can take many days like this one. Perhaps we will survive after all. A bright red-orange sunset tops off our best day so far. I prop my head up with a life preserver to see the bright scarlet western horizon. Sim gazes out the window, pensive, dreamy until darkness is complete. Our flock of boobies are all bunched together. They quack at each other as they float easily on the breaking waves. I check my watch. Total darkness is at eight forty five.

The seas have flattened further; the raft loses less air, and the turtles have gone elsewhere to scratch their backs. The gentle breeze lulls us to sleep. I'm ready for another dose of raft heaven.

"Bill, look, there's the Virgin Mary."

"That's Venus."

"I know it's Venus. We call it Stella Matutina, Star of the Morning. It's my favorite star. It's always been there when I need Her. She is the first star in the sky and the last to disappear. A guardian of souls. Our guardian."

"It's not a star. It's a planet."

"Whatever. Look, there are some more stars. And the moon. Oh, it's so beautiful. We won't be alone tonight. And the seas are much calmer. This should be a pleasant night without those awful waves."

The raft surges violently. My heart leaps out of my chest. What in the hell was that? Something hit the raft with a sledgehammer blow. My mind races as my hand finds Sim's. Our sole movement is an imperceptible tightening of our hands. Another violent blow sends the raft spinning. I lean into Sim and put my index finger up to my mouth. Sim is wide-eyed and whispers, "Shark." I knew that was the answer. All four sides of the raft receive hard blows in rapid succession. It feels like Babe Ruth is out there slugging homers.

We remain immobile and clutch each other more tightly. Adrenalin rushes through my body. Whatever it was, did it leave? I hear Sim's heart pound. Mine feels like a kettle drum. Waves lap against the side of the raft as if counting time. We wait in silence, powerless. Death has knocked. Is this the end? The shark must be huge. What does it want with the raft? If it's a mako or a tiger shark or a hammerhead it'll soon be over. If it's a great white, we have only seconds left. In three passes, it will swallow the two of us and half of the raft. I have never felt panic like this. My life will soon be over. How stupid. I sail away for pleasure and now I will die. Damn.

A powerful blow freezes my blood. Sim squeezes my hand until it pains. Poor Sim. She didn't want to sail away on this trip. I talked her into it. Her children and mother need her desperately, and here she is where she will die with me. My mind has been running through every experience I have ever had with sharks. There must be something I can do. I inch up to a sitting position, zip the window down part way, and lean over the side. Twenty feet away, shooting at high speed towards the raft is a torpedo shaped trail of phosphorescence. It slides by my side and, when abreast, kicks the raft with its tail. The plastic of the raft is no deterrent. It's paper thin. I lie back down and whisper to Sim:

"It's just a small shark playing with the raft." I lie.

"Small shark," Sim exclaims much too loud. "It feels like an express train. What do you mean by small? Twenty feet?"

"Shhh. No, baby, four or five feet." I chop a couple feet off our predator. Why scare her any worse than she is?

The raft of a sudden receives another ferocious blow on Sim's side. It's another shark, or is it the same one? We hold still as Sim prays with a new intensity. What is it they want with the raft? Minutes turns into hours as I lie in cold sweat, unable to devise a defence or escape. We are again held hostage. First by whales that destroyed *Siboney*. Now....sharks...an invisble menace, a force fully capabable of instant destruction. Lord have mercy on us....

I can't describe the panic that grips me, for I have lived most of my life in close proximity with sharks. One of my fishermen friends in Cuba lost half his face to a shark he had boated and thought dead, his deformed face a testimonial to the wanton, destructive nature of these most primitive of animals. We have absolutely no protection. We're at their mercy. I know their habits...first they'll play with us, and when they tire of that game...they'll get down to serious business.

The shark attacks stop when a light drizzle turns into a downpour. Perhaps the decrease in salinity caused by the rain or the noise made them leave. For more than an hour, I try to catch rainwater. I pull the canopy down into the shape of a funnel and hold an empty bottle outside under the bunched up cloth. Water pours everywhere except inside the bottle. The bottle slips out of my hand. The canopy flops in the wind. Sim complains when water drips off my elbow and onto her cover. After an hour, I have filled but a quarter of a bottle. I offer Sim the first taste. She gags and exclaims: "Pure rubber."

I take the bottle from her and take a full gulp. She's right. The rubberized canopy must be washing off, and who knows what chemicals it releases. Now we have a choice...die poisoned or die eaten...which is best? I give up catching water as the rain continues.

The shark or sharks do not return. Perhaps it was but a curious, lone shark.

Simonne prays. I listen to her murmur, then doze. Morning finds us rested which is a miracle considering how it started. The shark didn't return. The wind shifted to the west. The raft heads north and south which means we're out of the current. At least the monster waves are behind.

Living to see and breathe this new day is no less than a miracle. Never have either of us lived such cold fear...fear and overwhelming conviction that our next breath would be our last...fear of a lingering death...fear of mutilation and a painfully slow death by drowning. When my eyes find Sim's, I sense she is as filled with gratitude as I. When she suggests we read the psalms and prayers, I readily agree. We must heal and strengthen our hearts for what lies ahead.

Simonne reads first a psalm written by the Ship Ministry that so aptly fits our situation; men who go to the sea in ships and who see His wonders in the deep. Tears stream down my cheeks. How weak are we. How could we ever make this trip alone? We need help...and only God can help us. Simonne next reads my favorite parable, the parable of the lost sheep. I am a poor lost sheep. In so many ways. Is it too late to be saved?

chapter six

0130 TUESDAY, JUNE 27, 1989, DAY 13

The hammering seas and the howling wind bore like augers into our pith. Cold, lonely, scared, and miserable from the incessant beating of wind, wave, rain, and shark, we cling to each other and search our inner senses for an answer to what yet awaits us. Many hours ago, when the last rays of light yielded to murky darkness, the wind started to rise. Soon it screamed as if questioning our right to exist. The seas quickly responded. Ferocious waves raised up to punish us and showed us no mercy. Great seas lifted the raft as they roared and foamed past us. The resounding boom of the waves against the air chamber reached into the very marrow of our bones. We embraced, searching for mutual reassurance. With respite from no quarter, we gasped for breath and awaited the one wave that would ultimately destroy us.

Now, an hour into this new day, one wave after another attempts to overwhelm us, to do away with an unwanted intruder, an orange and yellow blemish on its blue white frothy mantle. Hundreds of tons of water propelled by the wind at more than twenty miles an hour hurtle past us. Fresh sheets of spray bury our fragile vessel. The canopy fills with spray. Gallons of cold water spill inside and on us. We remain naked as the wind-driven rain flies under the canopy. Under the salt water soaked comforter, we fold into each other to search for and draw out the other's warmth. Will this now be the end?

Simonne's cries reach out to heaven. She pleads with God to listen to her...to please open His heart and forgive her. Her sobs are only broken by the thunder of a breaking wave. Tears pour down my cheeks when I dwell on the hopelessness of our plight and the thought that we may both soon die, never to see our children and their babies again. I damn myself for insanely barging ahead on this trip and for my hardheadedness which took us so far out to sea, outside of shipping lanes and probably out of range for the EPIRB.

Minutes turn into long hours. With the roar of each avalanching wave, we tighten our hold and squeeze to windward. The inside of the raft is so totally black I see nothing. No sooner does a minute pass without a breaking wave and we start to relax our grip when a wave larger than most buries us once again. When will this punishment end? When will we earn a moment's peace?

Simonne's prayers are at last answered. I look at my watch. It's 2:30. Rain slows and then finally stops. The wail of the wind and the rumble of the waves no longer drown out all other sound. We force ourselves to relax to begin the lengthy process of putting our mind to sleep. I hold Simonne's hand tightly as the raft rocks along. Only God knows where we are. The wind dies, but the waves still sweep over us. When the wind dies, the waves take a day to reflect the change. When the wind starts to blow, wave action picks up in an hour. That's not right. But the whales sinking our boat wasn't right either. My eyes close and stay closed as my mind fills with savory sleep, Simonne's prayers my last conscious mental impression.

A violent jolt as though a fifty foot high breaker had collided with the raft jars the raft violently and instantly shocks us out our musings. Sim leans closer and whispers, "He's back." We embrace tightly. Less our visitor detect the presence of a meal, I shish, unnecessarily, and hand signal Sim, "Not a word, not a move." The next strike spins the raft around 180 degrees, my side now to leeward. Five more blows in a row brings panic. Neither of us moves. Not a word is spoken. I hold Simonne tightly; my mind wildly trying to sort out this new situation.

Whack. Whack. Whack again. Sim whispers, "Pray." I search in vain for a prayer. Dear God, help us. The shark leaves. I wait, immobile except to feel for Sim's outstretched hand. She squeezes mine. Four successive blows rock the raft. These are followed at machine gun speed with more than a dozen raft spinning slaps. Time stops as we are punched, shoved, and knocked around until we have no doubt our existence will soon be over. Unable to defend ourselves or escape, we brace ourselves for the worse. In the dark, I visualize hundreds of razor sharp teeth set in jaws wired to the brain of a wanton killer...the jaws open, row upon row of teeth pushed ahead of a powerful body travelling at high speed. The shark first bumps its prey to better sense what it is. Then it attacks. I look up to the heavens and plead for help. Help us, dear Lord.

Between attacks, minutes turn into eons. On our backs, eyes fixed wide, heart pumping wildly, we gasp for air and wait. I play many different scenes, all to myself. How big of an animal is it? The bash to the raft felt like Mohammed Ali swinging a two-by-four. The shark must be Ali's size. What type of shark is it? I dare not guess. They're all deadly. Mako, tiger, or hammerhead sharks are wanton killers. Why do they beat on our raft? Is it curiousity? Are they testing this strange floating object to later plan their final attack? With my free hand, I feel for the air chamber in search of reassurance but find but a thin layer of rubberized plastic. We are definitely going to die. Only divine intervention will save us now.

Two hours pass without a visit by a shark. We have an hour to go before we can expect relief from this infernal darkness. When day comes, I will see what's swimming under the raft. When at long last the first vestiges of dawn creep across the sullen sky, we are utterly exhausted yet exuberant. We have been born again. I never expected to make it through this fearful night. I kept a brave outer front for Sim's sake, but I know sharks. I have fished and fought sharks all my life. I have more than a dozen true shark stories and a wall full of shark jaws. Is this their revenge?

Sharks are skillful killers; their senses sharpened since the earth's earliest days. Sharks, as we know them now, have been around for a long time, much over 25 million years. Their roots go back even further. More than twenty five species of sharks attack man and boats while most sharks are scavengers and carnivorous. Tiger sharks eat everything from a wide variety of fish including other sharks to turtles, birds, seals, squid, garbage (including plastic), and carrion. The shark that attacked wasn't a Tiger; we would now be dead and devoured if it was. All sharks love warm water except the Great White which will go anywhere for a meal. The water temperature here is about 25 degrees C, 80 F, a perfect habitat for sharks. Our problems are but beginning.

I can hardly wait for full daylight to see what we're up against, but I do know that there will be more than one shark since they grow up in packs. Mature sharks segregate by sex and come together only during the mating season. When parturition is imminent, the female moves to a nursery area, gives birth, and abandons her offspring with other newborn. Sharks have a slow rate of growth, one to three inches per year. Males of the same age stick together because, if they mix with larger sharks, they will become part of the day's menu. If we see many sharks, this will signify immatures. A single shark will signify a mature member capable of a predatory attack.

Dawn greets us with rain falling on all horizons. I sit up, stiff from the dampness and our tense night and look out over the window into a deep blue ocean wild with motion. I love the early morning blend of the pure and unknown. Above clouds scud heavy with rain. Sheets of water in changing patterns tumble from black squalls that dot the horizon. Up wind, a dense black fringe covers ninety degrees of horizon. I iron out lumps in my bedding, bunch a part as a pillow, and lie back down.

"Weather forecast," I call over to Sim. "Storm fast approaching from the west. More rain. Residents on raft to get soaked."

As Simonne serves up our breakfast saltine, a loud crack of thunder is followed by a long roll. A second bolt lights up the inside of the raft. Much louder thunder follows. I count seconds between the flash and the crash. The next one is forty seconds. Sound travels at seven hundred feet a second. At forty seconds, the storm is thirty thousand feet away or under six miles. Soon Sim calls out twenty seconds. The squall moves in.

We close both windows and tighten the canopy to the top of the window. A flash brighter than the midday sun followed by a thundering boom brings Sim into my quivering arms. "Ten seconds," she whispers. I know Sim ponders as I do. Will lightning strike a raft?

The storm breaks with a blast of cold, moist air. Thirty knot winds push the raft at over a knot. Stronger gusts threaten to topple the canopy as it strains to become airborne. Sim throws her weight to windward. Rain beats onto the raft and mixes with the wind driven salty spray flowing over the window. The last shards of dry bedding soak up drips too many to count.

Sim lashes the water making machine and water bottles to the inside of the raft and tightens the window tie downs. A gust heels the raft to leeward as waves grow steeper. Sim edges further up on the high side to add her weight to mine. We brace for capsize, and I mentally play out how to recover. Is this what hell is like? We remain immobile, exhausted and bewildered by the continual punishment. Long minutes pass until the worst of the storm passes. Seas no longer threaten to bury us. The wind no longer whistles. Sim lowers the window in hopes that the moisture laden breeze will somehow dry our sodden bedding.

When will help arrive? Seventeen days have passed since our last radio link with our family. Cris awaits our decision whether to rent the house or not. We haven't called to congratulate Joe on the birth of our new granddaughter. Failure to make contact should generate a strong signal. They must be marshalling forces and developing strategy for an air search at this very moment. Today we should keep a sharp lookout for an airplane.

Our radio silence will bring action. If we don't call, there could only be one reason: the radio isn't working. The radio could only be inoperable if it broke or if the boat sank. If the radio failed, we would sooner or later contact a passing vessel via VHF radio and ask them to relay a message home. Perhaps it'll take them another week for the family to be fully convinced we're in danger and to get a rescue mission in motion.

Waves are so high that we experience the characteristic lull in each trough, the gusts on each crest. If anyone is out looking for us today, the monster breaking seas will make our raft invisible from the air as we're in the trough most of the time. We wouldn't be seen in a direct flyover. Even the orange coating on the outside of the raft is turning white. Soon we'll appear as just another breaker.

Where in the hell are the planes? We've been off the scope for seventeen days. What better signal do they need? Where do the children think we are? What do they think we're doing? Isn't anyone thinking about us? I yell out the window: "C'mon gang, we need help...now...."

If we had a hand held VHF radio, we could've signalled the "Ter Eriksen." I left ours behind on *Siboney*. In the storm that pushed us off course three days before we sank, a huge wave had soaked it. I then rinsed it off with fresh water and put it aside to dry before charging. When we sank, the radio was still wet; the batteries uncharged.

Waves ever so slowly abate. The bedding dries, and I turn in hopes of finding a softer spot. "My captain," says Sim when she notices I am awake, "Would you like the morning news with your breakfast?" I grunt and nod, and she continues: "Everyone got off the Russian ship before it sank after it hit that iceberg. The leaders in China shot seven more men. Someone found the battleship *Bismark* that went down in the second World War. And in Cuba, there is a big flap over a bunch of officers involved in drug trafficking. The ringleader is a friend of Castro called Ochoa." I still find it incredible that we can stay abreast of world events even while lost to the world. Somehow I feel less lost and less alone.

The story of the Russian ship sinking should get one of our children or a friend to think about *Siboney* and the possibility that it may have sunk. Or will it? In several days, we'll be off the scope for three weeks. An air search will be launched in a matter of days. Soon we'll be found and on our way home.

A scraping sound that runs from one end of the raft to the other brings Sim's hands shooting into mine. When I sit up, I see a large shark racing for the raft. Inches away, it dives to surface on Sim's side. A quick spin and back it darts to pass alongside, its white belly up inches below the surface. The shark skims along my side of the raft and, when abreast, whips its tail against the air chamber, the violent blows we felt last night. The shark then sweeps along the other two sides of the raft and gives each a mighty whack. I hold the pole outside the raft pointed end down. If the shark follows the same pattern, it should approach from my right. A light grey shape shoots my way. I plunge the pole at the fast moving shadow and miss. The shark pummels Sim's side, then the bow. I wait. It shoots under me before I can react. On its next pass, I jab it in the middle of its stomach. Its tail flips high and sends water all over me.

Two more sharks circle below. One approaches a foot below the surface and within reach. I poke its head. It jerks and swims away. An hour passes quietly. To my dismay, a shark twice as long as the raft swims by the window, not ten feet away. I glance at Sim to be sure she isn't looking.

The monster circles but maintains its distance. I close the window and hide behind it. If that shark were to attack, it would be all over in seconds. The large black mass swims, its huge dorsal fin slicing through the water. The top edge of the fin has a white spot...a white tipped shark...a deadly man eater.

Sim asks, "Did you see anything?"

"Nope. Rain is letting up."

I lie. The four to six foot sharks that are our constant visitors worry the devil out of Sim. If I were to tell her we had a twelve foot shark ten feet away, she would sleep even less. I zip both windows up all the way, so there's no chance Sim can see out. We both lie quietly. I fall asleep. Sim prays most of the night. After midnight, the smaller silky and lemon sharks return.

I am up with the first whack. I lower the window and ready the pole. There's nothing. I lie down. We're whacked. I'm up again and wait. We're struck on Sim's side. Mine should be next. I see it move in, strike, and connect.

"Did you hit him?" Sim asks.

"One hit. Zero misses. I can't understand what they're after. It's as if they're playing with us."

Sharks batter the raft all night. When they stop, a turtle arrives. It bumps us from head to foot, gets caught in a strap; I release it and it swims away casually. Between all the action, we nap when we can. Whenever we doze off, the sharks return. I bounce up, pole ready. They are invisible. I score not one hit. I lean back, take a deep breath, and close my eyes.

Sim shakes me violently. "Bill, quick, pump! There's no air in the raft! We're sinking!" I awaken from a deep dream. We were back on *Siboney*. Whales were furiously pounding the hull.

"What time is it, Sim?"

"Two." Rain pours down as I push vital air back into the air chambers. I had hoped it was closer to dawn. I'm so stiff I can barely move. On the positive side, the canopy keeps us dry. I pump air into the raft until Sim gives me the usual "OK." If I stop before she checks the air chamber, she will invariably find it limp and I'll have to start again.

"Bill, where's the flashlight? Quick, I lost my rosary." This is the third or fourth time Sim has fallen asleep holding her rosary.

When she tosses in her sleep, the little metal loops that hold the beads pull apart. She tears at the cushions until she finds all the little pieces.

Fear and apprehension keeps me awake for hours. Is the white tipped shark still around and will it attack? Sharks are timid individuals; they'll circle an object until their sensitive sensory glands confirm it's safe to attack. Vibrations, minute electrical charges, smell, taste, appearance will be fed into a central computer data bank compiled through the past 300 million years that will define whether it's safe to attack. If it receives a GO signal, our death will follow within minutes...perhaps less. There is nothing we can do; I dare not splash with the pole or make any movement...that may be the one signal that triggers its attack.

Motionless and cramped, I wonder if we will live to see dawn arrive. The night drags on into what seems like an eternity. The sodden bedding lumps, and the hard edges of the life preserver push into my back. I must remain immobile for any movement upsets Sim. My salt water soaked shirt needs to be aired, but I can't turn on my side, or I'll kick Sim. Anyway, it's better to wait until the sun is up to dry the sores that have formed on my back. I'm between two sharks...I feel like a piece of salami...Sim'll chew me out if I move, and the shark will chew me up if I move; this is surely the end.

In the east, pale clouds slowly turning crimson announce a new day will soon be born. Gingerly, red skies extend further north and south until our little world comes to life. How wonderful to be alive and to again witness the vanquishing of darkness by the might of day...thirteen new hours of hope and possibly of salvation. If the day turns out to be clear, search planes should be flying. Realistically, it may take them a day or two to locate us. Perhaps they've been searching. We've been off the scope for near on three weeks. On the other hand, there's a lot of ocean out here. If they could focus one of those super spy satellites this way or one with an infrared scanner to pick up the higher temperature of the raft over the surrounding sea....

As the first warm rays of the newly risen sun strike the raft, we burst out of the cage that has held us prisoners for so long. When we drape the sodden bedding over the arches to dry today, we'll be more careful. Several days ago, we played dominoes while drying and didn't notice an end had fallen in the water. To make it worse, it was Sim's end, her pillow part. It never did dry after that, and Sim had to turn the comforter to place the wet part near our feet. That was one hell of a drill as was the recrimination that followed. On the positive side, time does fly by as we argue over trivialities...but the constant nagging is working into my marrow.

Sim sounds the alarm: "Whale, a big whale. My God, he's coming our way!"

The massive black whale heads for the raft, dorsal fin purposefully cutting the water. Thirty feet away it blows, sounds, and we never see it again. Sim used to send twenty dollars to the "Save the Whale" fund. I could strangle her. The whale she saved is probably the one that sank *Siboney* This whale could have cut the raft in half in one pass. I should have brought the fiberglass sailing dinghy...what great back-up. As *Siboney* filled with water, I debated the pros and cons of cutting it loose and bringing it with us. We could now be sailing on the course of our choice and at two or three times our present speed. On the other hand, the savage seas that engulfed us over the past two weeks would have sunk it. Full of water, it would create a dangerous pull on the raft and easily tear out a piece...that's why I left it, so stop re-hashing your decisions, Butler.

I can see my Dyer dink still tied to the cabin of *Siboney*, suspended upside down in two miles of water. *Siboney*, sails set, flags flying, embedded in the mud in an unnamed Pacific canyon. If she could jettison her lead keel, she would pop back to the surface. There's no chance of that; the eight new one inch brass keel bolts will yield long after the hull has dropped away.

The lead keel that holds *Siboney* to the bottom kept it upright through the worst of storms. In 1967, caught out in a typhoon off Manila in the Philippines, a giant wave broke on *Siboney* and threw her down wind, mast down. The top of the mast, forty-five feet off the deck, touched the water. A second wave followed suit. *Siboney* bounced back each time, the lead keel doing its job.

Sim breaks into my musings. "Bill, why do the sharks come at night? They petrify me. The fabric on this raft is so thin. I've been looking at it during the day when the raft is low on air, and really it's nothing. A dull shark tooth could cut through it. What happens if the main air chamber goes? How can we swim with all those sharks around? Oh, Lord, help us."

"We'll survive, Sim. The boat cushions will float. The two arches are full of air, and they will keep us up. We float too. The only heavy item on board is the water pump. We'll be sitting in water, but we won't go down."

"Not go down? May the Lord protect me from your naivete. If we lose the raft, it's over. We're dead. There's no other way."

"You can give up if you want, but I'll struggle until I draw my last breath. And I know you'll battle all the way." I turn my back to Sim to get away from another endless argument and look out the window.

Triple tails swim up to the raft. They are so close that I put on my gloves and try to snag one. I touch one, but that's as close as I come. Perhaps if I make a spear...the hook, straightened and tied to the end of the pole, might work. I put the barb into the end of the fishing rod and slowly take the bend out of the hook, careful not to snap it. Luckily, it's a tough hook made by Mustad in Denmark. I lash it to the pole with nylon line.

The fish must have watched me. There isn't one in sight now. I wait. I nap, then look out again. Still no fish. Towards evening, three triple tails approach. I let them close, raise the harpoon, plunge, and miss.

"Bill, a turtle. This is a big bad one."

That's it. The triple tails follow turtles. The turtle scratches the bottom of the raft as Sim cries out: "Barnacles." I get the heavy pole ready, and when it comes up for air, I swing, miss the neck, but hit the shell. The turtle turns and dives.

Sim was right. This turtle has a heavy load of barnacles and a torn shell to boot; either of which can damage the raft. It emerges ten feet from the raft, takes a breath, then paddles lazily alongside until it lifts its curious head out of the water, looks me straight in the eye, and heads my way. I hit it again, this time on the neck.

I can't help but chuckle. These antediluvian creatures are on the "endangered species" list. I have never seen so many turtles in my life. There must be hundreds out here. We see four or five every day. What in the devil do they want with the raft? Make love to it? Seek shelter?

The turtle's repulsive eyes remind me of Dracula. Expressionless, dead, round, and black, surrounded by a black circle three inches in diameter, they appear to have a perpetual hang over. The eyes make the turtle look dumb, and dumb they must be. No matter how hard we hit them, they come back for more. We have to devise a better method of battling them.

Tonight I close the windows before dark. I can't let Sim see the size of two sharks that circle the raft. They're easily twice as long as the raft. Unexpectedly, she opens the window and looks out. I pray the monster is not around. "Bill, look at that sunset. We haven't seen one for several days. It's pretty. See, there's a cloud that looks like Mara. Do you see it?" I sit up and look down, not up.

"Yes. It even has her eyes." Mara was our schnauzer. She died two years ago while trying to deliver pups. At that moment, a 12 foot hammerhead shark circles, its dorsal fin fully out of the water.

"Sim, come on, lie down. Read the psalms."

"In a minute. I want to enjoy the sunset and watch my birds. We've never had this many spend the night with us. I can count over fifty boobies. "

I sit back up. There before us swims our monster. I can no longer divert her attention and wait for Sim to react.

"Bill, my God, there he is! What kind of shark is that? A hammerhead?"

"I, I think so." My game is up.

"It's been with us for a week. It comes every night at this time. It swims around the raft a dozen times and leaves. They probably wait for one of us to fall overboard."

"Do you mean you've seen it and haven't told me?"

"I didn't want to scare you. You have enough problems."

"Sim, baby, I've also seen it for the past week, and I didn't tell you because I didn't want to scare you. That's a laug. If they haven't touched us for a week, they probably won't. Let's forget them. Why don't you read?"

Sim reads before night sets in. We have two flashlights and a lantern on the raft. One flashlight came with the raft and is fully waterproof and heavy duty. The other flashlight is a cheap one I carried as a spare. The lantern is heavy duty and waterproof. All three work fine, but we use them little as we have no spare batteries. My entire stock of batteries, neatly packed in ziplocs, now lies in two miles of water.

At five this morning, we passed our two week mark on the raft. We missed the big event as we slept in after the all night battle with turtles and sharks. I have a new theory. A turtle under the raft keeps the sharks away. Who knows, perhaps we should be gentler to them. Anyway, the night was a drill. At three in the morning, all predators left, and we fell asleep...for an hour...that's as long as the air leak will allow us.

Thursday, June 29, dawns clear and bright. Waves are down. The raft travelled little all night and headed in no particular direction. Let's see how the navigation department handles that.

The birds are nowhere in sight. Every other morning when we awaken, we have enjoyed watching the boobies skim the waves in search of their meal. Two lone boobies fly in the distance. Perhaps the others are out fishing far off and will return tonight. Last night, they had formed a tight group fifty feet to windward and preened and pecked at each other as they bobbed on the waves, gently paddling with their big blue feet to stay headed into the wind. They had not met in such a large group before; normally, they form small groups of five or ten. If they are gone for good, where did they go?

The always present frigate birds remain. Aloft a young bird follows its mother. Both soar with their giant wings outstretched and head into the breeze without perceptive motion. The larger frigate of a sudden collapses its wings and drops. The young remains motionless above. The frigate plummets a hundred feet in seconds. A dozen feet off the ocean, it opens its wings, slows, and turns, still at high speed, in pursuit of a booby. The booby spots the frigate and, squawking loudly, tries to escape.

An aerial pursuit, Sim sees it as a ballet, ensues. We have not witnessed before such speed and mastery of flight. The booby bird uses its high speed and maneuverability to escape. The frigate, wings now fully extended, stays on the booby's tail. The frigate's attack is merciless. The booby's desperate squawks drown out all other sounds, but it's what the frigate bird waits to hear, for the pitch of the squawk tells the frigate if the booby has a fish in its crop. This booby has a muffled squawk which confirms the crop is full. The frigate gives the booby no respite and lives up to its other name: the "Man-O-War" bird.

We've watched frigate birds catch fish honestly. From way up high, they drop to the surface and run at high speed over the waves to scoop up flying fish and small school fish that venture too close to the surface. But they do appear to get special delight out of harassing boobies. This frigate chases the booby until its crop empties then catches the regurgitated fish in mid air. After a casual climb to its waiting young, mother feeds baby, much like in-flight-refueling. The baby, big enough to feed itself, soars at mom's wingtip, happy with the handouts.

While we enjoyed the morning acrobatic show, the skies cloud. The Western horizon is black, the portents of another heavy storm. The current is moderate and the raft barely swings. I try to fish without success. I should've grabbed a bird while they were still around except Sim would've out-squawked any booby. We make water, eat our cracker, then nap.

Minutes later, a flash of lightning is followed by long growling thunder. "Ten seconds," Sim calls. Again we button the window up against the canopy. Isolated rain drops turn quickly into a major downpour. This squall doesn't have the wind of the last one. Heavy rain falls until mid-morning. Sharks stay away throughout the shower. Rain, don't go away.

Sim spots it first: "Bill, the raft has turned around."

We remain motionless. The horizon spins in a full circle. I open one side of my window, and water drips in as I poke my head into the rain. A huge green sea turtle flaps lazily, one flipper caught in the boarding ladder. The pounding by the sharks loosened the nylon mesh boarding ladder from where I'd tied it days past. I stay clear of the gaping jaws, grab the tangled flipper, and unwrap the webbing. The ladder has caused more problems than it's worth, yet should either of us land in the water after a roll over, we might need it to get back into the raft in a hurry. On the other hand, we've been in several major storms and the raft has always proven stable; it's really more trouble than it's worth, so I take the knife out of the pail and cut it away. That's the end of that problem unless, of course, we end up going for a swim. If I were to reduce our situation mathematically, how many unknowns would we have...many too many...the answer is not in mathematics but with God. His is the true power. He will save us...if we seek and find His way.

Rain drops filter in through the canopy, but wrapped inside our comforter, we are dry and snug. And sharks don't attack while it pours, so let it rain. Bump. Sim lowers the window, sticks her head out, gets soaked, and sees nothing. The turtle is under the raft. We're bumped a dozen times, gently, never in the same place. Sim fumes as she shakes her head like a dog coming in from the rain, then explodes:

"I can't take it any longer. I'm fed up with turtles, with sharks, with the situation, and most of all, with you, Butler. It's all your fault. I hate you. I could strangle you. And don't laugh, you wretch. You look awful with your beard. I hate beards, I hate turtles, I hate sharks, and I hate you. DO YOU HEAR ME! HELP! HELP! SOMEBODY HELP!"

I cringe as she screams out the window. Every mako and hammerhead shark within miles will soon home in on us. She continues: "I hate this cretinous raft; it's too small, too slow. It's unbearable torture; it's insane. Why, oh why, did you have to be such a scrooge and buy the cheapest raft? You cheapskate, you. Always going for the bargains. What are you keeping your money for, tell me? You must want to take it with you..."

She runs out of breath and I grab at the chance. "You forget you couldn't lift a bigger raft when we were sinking. You had a hard time moving this one, and it's only fifty five pounds. Besides, I did spring for the water-maker."

"You could have helped mewith the raft, you nitwit. We would have such a better chance to live." She continues, and I try to tune her out. Some of her points I can buy, and others are best left lost in the Pacific. The word Pacific is such a misnomer...and doesn't rhyme with sinking, whales, sharks, turtles, or pissed-off wife.

Sim and the rain ease up in the late afternoon. The turtle swims on. Sharks return. I bonk a couple and get sprinkled in the process. Several booby birds are back. One perches on the canopy.

It's such a terrible night; we decide to let it sleep with us. We huddle together, angry words forgotten. We only have each other.

There's a new leak in the overhead canopy. Sim puts a can under it and catches many of the drops. When I change positions, I turn it over and it spills. Sim grumbles and sponges what she can out of the bilge. Nothing is dry any longer...except for me that is...a good shot of Scotch would work wonders right now.

As night falls, we pray. Sim reads early as the heavy overcast will hasten night. The reading soothes our mind and body and helps ease the transition from daylight into darkness and its many deadly fears....a spiritual balm on two souls adrift in a watery hell.

Through reading, Sim muses: "What a shame, Bill, that we didn't get the missal Dick Lloyd gave us at our going away dock party. It would be a blessing to have it now. I'm ashamed we never opened it on the trip out from Miami. We were always so busy toiling at something. His gift meant so much to me. I wish we had saved it. I never want to be so busy ever again that I have no time for God."

"Yes, I know. I didn't see the missal in your locker, nor did I see the bullets."

"That's a great association, Butler, missal and bullets. Oh, Lord, give me patience with this man. Besides sixteen days are enough punishment. Sharks, turtles, thunder, lightning, high waves, rain, and you, Butler. All at the same time. Enough is enough, Lord. Save me; do something. Do you hear me! NOW!"

"I can't believe what I'm hearing. You presume to tell God how to run His shop? He will decide when He will save us."

"I hope it's soon. I can't take any more of this. Lord, help me."

I tighten my hold on Sim's hand, and she begins to cry. I fall asleep to the murmur of her prayers.

Sim jolts me awake and calls out: "Two turtles this time. And they are doing it. The male is chasing the female. Oh, Bill. They're back under the raft."

"Relax, Sim. They're only doing what comes naturally. Besides they're endangered. They need all the babies they can make."

"Endangered? We're endangered! At least they are in their element. Get out of here, you perverts..."

Sim jolts each of the turtles and off they go. The female tries desperately to escape from the faster swimming male. There is no question what's on the male's mind. But what's on hers? A headache?

Heavy rains, pushed by a strong wind out of the west, force us to lock ourselves in once again. The current must be light as the raft swings wildly. Rain seeps in through the canopy. We use the pole to push the canopy up, like a tent. The rain water rolls off and less leaks in. I don't know why, but the canopy is disintegrating. The blue waterproofing on the inside has cracked and begins to peel and fall off.

Even the birds aren't airborne. One booby spent the entire night perched on the canopy. It defended its space with loud squawks from other birds who were also hoping for a dry perch. With all the rain, I don't understand the difference. Three boobies paddle nearby. But the large group has never returned. Where did they go? To Cocos Island? I have been looking for signs of Cocos to the north, but could it lie to the south? The best I can recall is that it lies around 90 degrees west. Whether it's five or seven or ten degrees north is beyond me. We sank at five and a half degrees north. In the two weeks plus adrift, we have been pushed perhaps 100 miles to the north which puts us near 7 degrees north. The current has pushed us steadily east at 15 to 20 miles a day or an average of 120 miles a week. That puts us near 95 degrees west, still a long way to Cocos. The birds most probably flew off to the Galapagos, now 300 plus miles to the south.

Between rain showers, we make three liters of water. Why didn't the people who made the raft think of putting a hole in the middle of the canopy with a small rubber funnel to catch rain water? When I try, most of the water either drips into the raft or misses the bottle, or the bottle slips out of my hand and spills. I get soaked; our bedding gets even wetter; Sim gets out of joint, and we end up, after an hour, with less than a half cup of water. And unless it really pours down, I catch nothing but drops. From now on, I'll rely on the water maker. Sim agrees. After all, it cost a bundle, and I risked my life to grab it from the sinking *Siboney*.

The lovers are back at it under the raft. She hides between the ballast bags. He chases after her, probably whispering sweet nothings. She strains to escape. I tell Sim that I can hear her repeat over and over...not now, later; I'm not in the mood, or did she also make a promise? I get walloped by Sim.

A full morning of turtle foreplay wears us down. First they are under the raft, then out fifty feet, and back under, then around, then out, later back. When they near, Sim defends us. When the orgy moves on to other waters, the sharks return to slap the raft without mercy. I beat some off, but more come. More than twenty sharks circle ten feet under the raft. One or two surface for a shot at the raft. I hit one on the right and another from straight on. A third shoots out from under the raft. I land dozens of direct hits. Then rain starts up again, and I close up our home and rest. Is there anything out here except sharks, turtles, and rain? I make a mental note never to venture out into this part of the Pacific again. Of course, first we have to be saved...

Rain has fallen steadily for the past two days. The increasingly leaky roof adds to our misery. The outside coloring of the raft has gone from bright orange to pale orange and is now a light yellow. The miserable weather depresses us. We don't feel like playing dominoes or word games or even talking and remain ensconced in our inner thoughts.

Sim breaks the silence. "Bill, do you realize that, if we disappear, nobody will know how we died and what happened to the boat. They'll never know that we made it this long, only to die stupidly because no one searched for us."

"I've been thinking the same."

Sim continues. "Three weeks have gone by since our last call. If someone was going to look for us, it would have happened by now. We've had some clear days, enough chance for an air search."

"We must think of how to signal. We must get a message through. Perhaps a bottle..."

"A bottle. Who would ever find it?" She pauses then explodes with enthusiasm. "That's wild. It's great, let's do it."

"Let's give it some thought. But we must do something. My mother will die if we disappear. We are now almost forty days out of Panama. In another two weeks, we are due in Hawaii. Ten days after that, we will be truly behind schedule. People will surely launch a search. If they do, it'll be closer to the Hawaiian Islands, not here. I'm sure my mother knows we are in danger. She knew there was danger even before we left. Why, oh why, didn't I listen to her? My children will never know what happened to me. Do you know how difficult it is to go through life not knowing what happened to a loved one who disappears without a trace?"

I've never seen Sim so sad. I agree: "That's why we must send out a message of some kind."

Sim's despair builds. "And how will my babies ever get along if I disappear. Will the bank continue sending them money? Will the life insurance pay them? Meanwhile, what are they going to do? It may take years before they see a cent. And my mother, how is she going to survive without knowing about me? How? How?"

"Easy, Sim, before you blow a fuse. I left instructions at the bank to take care of your babies. The instructions stand until we return."

"I really don't understand you. You act so relaxed."

"And I don't understand what good it's going to do to get all worked up. There's nothing we can do about it. If we never show up, the bank will certainly go to court to declare us dead. I have no idea how the laws of Florida treat people who disappear. It could be seven years before they can settle the estate. Meanwhile the bank will disburse money to my dependents per my instructions and their best judgement as to real need."

Sim continues: "How will they pay the mortgage on the house? Will the mortgage insurance pay if we're not found? They'll probably lose the house to the Bank. Oh, my God. Why is everything so complicated? Why can't we die in peace and without worries..."

We hash the same subjects around for another hour until I suggest, "Why don't you read, it's almost dark." A semblance of peace settles over the raft, but Sim's apprehensions are far from over. I can almost read her mind, and I can feel new fears build in her stubborn head.

The easterly current picks up again after sunset. The raft moves steadily after swinging aimlessly all day. The wind is out of the southwest. Rain continues as I start to doze. Sim tosses fitfully.

SIMONNE:

When are we going to see the sun, to be dry and warm again? Will someone find us? When will God have mercy on us? When is He going to take us to safety, to our children, to our old life? Or do we have an old life to go back to?

Will this experience change us? If so, how? God will certainly become the keystone in our lives. We have learned to pray again. We have cleansed our souls before God. We've spoken candidly to each other for the first time in years. We try not to make future plans. How can we plan in these conditions? Death is our constant companion. Life as we knew it a few months ago, on land or on *Siboney*, is but a sweet dream. Whatever happens, we have made peace with each other and with ourselves. We ask God to forgive our sins, to accept our deepfelt repentance, and we accept His will. We place our hope in His merciful heart.

chapter seven

ABOARD THE RAFT "LAST CHANCE"
0800 TUESDAY JULY 4, 1989, DAY 20

The night has been the darkest and most dismal so far. Rain fell in torrents and sharks smashed the raft non-stop. Heavier rain started shortly after midnight and soaked us, our bedding, and everything in the raft not wrapped in plastic. Water leaked through the canopy in torrents. We cover up with the striped comforter and spread the sailbag over it to divert the water. The trash bag goes over the sailbag and diverts much of the rain water into the bilge which Sim periodically empties with the sponge.

At two this morning, a shark pounded the raft so violently and with such savage intensity that we genuinely feared our end was close at hand. At twice the speed of the others, this shark darted fiercely from one side of the raft to the other faster than I could follow. A phosphorescent wake followed its every turn, yet whenever I plunged at where I thought it would be, I failed to connect. How much more pounding can the raft take before it's holed and sinks?

Not one of my anti-shark ploys worked. Our theory that sharks stay away when it rains was thoroughly disproved. Time and time again, I plunged the fishing rod ahead of the ghostly shape hurling towards the raft. I never touched it. Ten, twenty, thirty violent blows made the raft spin. This shark was intent on destroying our little vessel. Petrified with fear, unable to deter the onslaught, we prayed as never before. Sim clutched her St. Michael medal through the attack and prayed so loud at one time that I had to quiet her less the shark pick up her vibrations and come after us.

Never has the dirty grey dawn been welcomed more devoutly

than it is this Tuesday. As though in pity with our plight, the wind wanes as the sun begins its climb hidden behind thick masses of clouds. Sim's eyes are closed. Rosary between her hands, she's deep in prayer. I have no idea at what time I slept, but I awaken to a marvelous surprise; blue skies with a sprinkling of white clouds lifts our spirit...and it's the Fourth of July. What is the gang doing back home? Picnics? Fireworks? Parades? And here we are, deep in the Pacific Ocean alone, surely forgotten, and lost. We're going to die. What is the Coast Guard doing today? Does anyone think of us? That we might be lost? In danger?

It's Tuesday, our twentieth day on the raft. Eighteen days have passed since we have seen signs of human life. We need bait desperately to start fishing. I'll grab one of Sim's birds if it comes within reach. We have lost a lot of weight. Sim is trim. So far, we have been burning excess fat. Before long, we will start losing essential muscle and, even worse, energy. Lethargy scares me. What if I am unable to make water? What if we run out of luck, and I'll be too weak to fish?

Sim notices I'm awake: "What a horrible night. I thought our time had come. In my prayers, I prepared to die. I was sure we would not see daylight." I can only agree, for I too had my doubts about the outcome of last night's vicious attacks. How can this raft withstand such punishment? How much more can it take?

On the positive side, the current is strong...we feel it...the raft jerks along, inches at a time...on its relentless movement towards shore...I have no doubt about that. And the sky is blue. Hope is blue, hope in the sky. A few days of decent weather would do wonders for our spirits. We lunch on a cracker with a touch of peanut butter. Three raisins make dessert. I savor each as I would an ice cream bar. By late afternoon, the current picks up from the west, and the raft settles back on its easterly course. Intermittent showers cut our visibility. Time stands still.

Sim has watched me fish. "We have some twenty crackers left. In three days, we'll be out of food. You've lost a lot of weight. I'm getting to like your beard. You have a full meal caught in it. There let me clean it."

"Leave my beard alone! I may need a snack in the middle of the night. I'll be fishing soon, but I warn you, I may have to catch a bird. The key to catching the first fish is bait. We'll wait another day but no longer. The longer we wait, the weaker we become. It's risky if we get too weak, and we're nearly at that point now." The truth is that I don't feel that hungry any longer which is a worse sign than hunger.

Sim is serious: "I'm sure something will come our way. Let's wait a while. I don't want you to hurt one of my birds. Did you see, "Beautiful" is back. This morning, he perched next to the raft and looked at me with those big yellow eyes. He is trusting and so sweet. He even pecked my hand. Please think of something else for bait. Don't touch my birds."

Sim has found solace with her birds. She continues. "If you kill one, all the others will leave. I can't stand the loneliness. This wretched emptiness. The birds are my only company and entertainment. The birds are God sent. They are my friends, and "Beautiful" is so perfect and so special. My own little guardian angel in disguise. You will leave them alone, won't you, Bill?"

She is so earnest, yet she knows that, if nothing else comes our way, she'll have to look the other way while I wring one of their beautiful necks. Our priority is survival, and to survive, we must stay strong and healthy even if it means I must kill a bird.

Our sunny day drags along. We play a half hearted game of dominoes until I'm called away to do battle with a dozen and more sharks. I then beat off the same two turtles who are still at it. How long do these dumb turtles mate, anyway? They've been at it for a week. "Ok, fellows, enough. Beat it," I scream as I beat the water with my pole. When they leave, we nap.

How do these monsters find our noiseless, minuscule raft in this vast ocean? We have drifted more than three hundred miles in the past eighteen days. The turtles and sharks always find us. What kind of homing signal do we emit? Is it Sim's eternal bickering? Or insane curiosity? Do they realize there's something edible aboard...?

Sim, who has been watching the water, says: "Bill, have you noticed there is an oil slick around the raft?"

"Yes, there is one right now. What's your point?"

"It has something to do with the arrival of the sharks. In the morning, after the first few slaps with their tail, the slick suddenly appears. It's not the raft. And I've looked carefully. We haven't floated into anything oily. The sharks must secrete it, like tom cats."

I have seen it too, and frankly I'm inclined to believe they, like tom cats, mark their territory. What else could they be doing? This belly up display and whacking of the tail?

When the sharks leave, Sim hands me the water maker. I drop the pre-filter into the water a foot under the raft, and with the body of the machine hooked under my right arm pit, I pump the twenty inch handle with my right hand. In this way, I rest one arm while the other works. I do twenty strokes with my right hand and ten with my left. When I tire, I hand the machine over to Sim. She makes water in a sitting position. She takes the handle in her left hand and holds the body of the machine against her bent knees. Sim is one of those lefties forced at school into becoming a rightie and still suffers from it. Often she has to stop and think where right or left is, such as in traffic. It drives me crazy.

We ignore the constant slap by sharks on the side of the raft as they are the smaller ones that reside under the raft. Suddenly, the filter jerks. Shark teeth have scratched the black tube. We stop for a few minutes then continue, ready to haul the filter up at any moment. In forty five minutes, we have two liters of clear fresh drinking water. The Evian bottles have ridges, about an inch apart, which help us measure our progress. We each do three ridges per turn. Two turns each and the bottle is full.

I chuckle quietly when I think of a couple of nights ago. In one of our pitch black, rough, rainy Pacific specials, she started to pee when I heard a loud oath in French. The can was bottom up and she had wet her bed.

We celebrate the Fourth of July with a quarter can of juice, one half of a cooky, and three drops of Hennessy for each. We sing the "Star Spangled Banner" and follow it with "America, the Beautiful." When we sing "From Sea to Shining Sea," anguish overwhelms us with such force that tears drown out our little celebration. The party ends prematurely.

Our thoughts go to shore and to how each of our family members are celebrating the day. Are they watching fireworks at Miami's Bayfront Park? The greatest Fourth of July we ever experienced was in 1986, aboard *Siboney*, in New York Harbor. We sailed from Miami to Cape May, New Jersey in nine days, stopped a few days in Atlantic City, then motored up to Sandy Hook. On the third of July, we took *Siboney* through the Narrows, into New York Harbor, and to an anchorage off Ellis Island. With thousands of other boats, we witnessed one of the most incredible two day shows the Harbor has ever seen.

While reminiscing with Sim, I have been scratching a large number twenty on a full sheet of paper. Sim looks over, but I manage to hide my artwork. She burns with curiosity.

At last, I'm ready. "Sim, make yourself pretty; it's picture taking time. This is day twenty and also the Fourth of July. A picture for posterity."

"Posterity. Do you really think there's any posterity for us? This is the end of the road."

"Bull. Hand me the camera." Enclosed in a ziploc, my Minolta has so far remained dry. I find a place for it on the opposite air chamber. We settle on a pose. I spring the timer as Sim holds the page with the twenty on it in front of her bare bosom. The camera clicks. Our raft bound Fourth of July celebration complete I settle down for a nap.

Sim startles me out of dreamland with a gentle nudge. She whispers excitedly: "A turtle. Just the right size. There."

I sit up. She's right. A turtle, with a shiny, light brown carapace and about twenty inches in diameter, swims towards the raft. We don't make a move so as not to spook it. While it approaches, I thread the fishing cord through the eye on the rod. At the end of the cord, I make a noose.

As the turtle comes alongside, Sim grabs a flipper then holds it firmly by its shell. I lean over her to put the noose around the turtle's neck and draw it up tight as Sim pulls the turtle out of the water. Flippers flail and its jaws reach out at Sim. She passes the flapping turtle through the raft and drops it in the water on my side. This is the first small turtle we have seen and the break we need to survive. Our prayers have been answered.

All four flippers thrash as the turtle struggles fiercely for its life. I push the pole deep into the water to keep its claws from damaging the raft. The slightest mistake on our part could make the difference between food and hunger. Worse yet, between life and death. As I wait for the turtle to die, I look up.

Skies are clear blue. A perfect day for a parade. It's now around three. The barbecue back home is going. Hamburgers, sweet corn, apple pie. But we'll have our own feast. Our first fresh food in twenty days. God has provided. He must intend to save us.

Thirty minutes pass, and the turtle continues to struggle violently. With an inexplicable force, it twists and snaps the pole in three pieces. I manage to catch one of the pieces and hang on to the line. Killing her is going to be harder than I thought.

"Sim, quick! Hold the turtle while I get the other pole ready."

Simonne leans over me and holds the animal. I prepare the larger pole. As Simonne holds the wildly tossing turtle, I put the other end of the cord through the eye on the larger pole, make another noose, and put it around the turtle's neck. I draw the cord up tight and push the turtle down. I've got it this time.

Another half hour passes. The turtle appears dead. The instant I loosen my grip on it, it thrashes madly and tries to escape. I know turtles don't drown easily, but I thought an hour should do it.

We are both tired, not to mention hungry. Funny, we have spent three days with almost no food, and we're not all that hungry. Now, with food at hand, we can't wait. It's time to cut this exercise short.

"Sim, let's bring it on board."

"Are you sure? It's still alive."

"Put the sailbag on my lap. I'll lift it up and put it upside down on top of the sailbag. You hold the line around its neck taught. Stay away from the beak. Cover its flippers with the bag. Ready?"

I flip the turtle onto my lap. It struggles wildly for air and life. It must weigh all of twenty pounds. Sim holds the bucket with one hand and the line around the turtle's neck with the other. I lift the turtle over the bucket with one hand. Claws at the end of the flippers flail wildly. I reach for the knife and saw away at its throat.

The turtle jerks and exhales air and blood with a gush and a gurgle. Blood sprays us and the whole inside of the raft. A whistling sputter surges from its windpipe. Sim flinches but holds the turtle firmly. Strength ebbs from our prey as its blood drips into the bucket. The intensity of its struggle lessens; its laborious breathing weakens. A spasm shakes the entire shell, and it dies.

I wanted to save Sim from this mess by drowning the turtle, but if we ever catch another one, we'll cut its throat right off. It's obvious now that turtles don't drown or asphyxiate easily. One of our more primitive animals, they've got to be tough to have survived through the ages .

Sim calls out. "Bill, watch out! Look, near the tail. What are those?"

"Remoras!" I hadn't noticed two three inch black eel-like remoras, similar to eels, fastened to the carapace near the turtle's tail. At the precise second when the turtle died, the remoras released their hold and wiggled free. They search for something alive to attach to with the suction device on top of their head.

"Quickly, hand me the can," I call out as the remoras slither on my lap in search of flesh. I push them into the can with the knife. "I'll keep them for bait." They squirm out of the can and head for Sim. She screams.

"Get rid of them. They'll grab onto one of us." I scoop them back into the can and throw them over the side.

Head down, the turtle remains over the bucket. Blood drains as Sim and I catch our breath and recover. I have never killed a turtle before. In fact, I've never seen a turtle butchered. General Electric stationed me at the Naval Base in Key West, Florida in 1952, on an assignment testing torpedoes. Most of the local eateries advertised Turtle Burgers. They were good, but that's as close as I've ever been to a dead turtle.

When blood no longer drips out of its slashed neck, I turn the turtle bottom up on my lap. I saw through the soft bottom carapace, lift one half of the shell, and cut away under it. I saw around the outside edges of both halves. In no time, the bottom of the turtle is loose and off. Vivid greens, oranges, blues, and reds cover the entire shell. All I can see are lungs and intestines.

Baffled, I question: "Sim, where's the meat? All I see looks terrible."

Sim is a good cook and meat handler. "Here. Try cutting there in the muscle that moves the flippers."

I follow Sim's finger and find dark pink meat, not unlike the dark meat of raw turkey. I slice off a piece and hand it to Sim.

"Ladies first." She takes the piece with hesitant fingers, looks it over with a skeptical expression, shrugs, and puts the piece into her mouth. I wait for her reaction. Her face explodes in delight: "Delicious," she says, turtle blood on her lips.

"Really? Let me try." I bite down. It has the texture of rabbit. Mmmm! I can't believe it. It's so good. It has a sweet and not a fishy taste at all.

We slice more pieces and eat without restraint. The meat is tender and tasty. Our hunger is such that we cannot stop. We slice and eat until we can no more. We rest, then eat more. I keep the last few pieces for bait. One of the two empty cans becomes the bait can. The other can is still the pee-pee pot.

We consider keeping the shell, but it's so heavy, and we know in this heat it will soon stink. How do we dispose of the shell and blood without arousing the shark population? I look into a clear, ripple free sea for sharks. There are none around. Strange.

We will dump the shell and the blood and then row down wind as fast as we can. I look again for sharks, then ease the shell over the side to windward without a splash. It sinks like a rock. I slowly pour the blood and pieces of turtle from the bucket so as not to splash the raft. I give the bucket a quick wash and signal Sim to start rowing.

We row steadily for fifteen minutes. We are exhausted but content. I look back to make sure no monster of the deep follows our trail. Our undersea world teems with life. All is clear. We put away the oars and drift on. We feel a sense of pride and achievement. We made it. We have taken a major step in our pursuit for survival.

Our stomachs fill for the first time in three weeks. Besides I have bait. We relax after all the excitement to enjoy the beauty of the day. The day is so clear, the sea so calm. It's so great to be alive.

The hot sun bores in on us. It even feels like the Fourth of July. We open the canopy. The sun and breeze will remove the dampness from our covers and clothing. Sim sponges drops of turtle blood from the arches and canopy. With our appetite satiated, we nap.

We awaken to a rare Pacific sunset, a perfect end to a spectacular day. The turtle has nourished not only our bodies but has lifted our spirits. With bait, we can fish. I can hardly wait to begin.

When I check my fishing pole, I realize that, if I want to fish tomorrow, I first have to re-bend the hook, my only one, which I straightened to use as a spear. But first, my paperwork.

I update the Log and work some arithmetic in my navigation workbook. Tomorrow we will pass the 500 hour mark on the raft. If we have drifted at one knot, we will have travelled five hundred miles. That's too fast. At half a knot, we would have traveled 250 miles. I am confident we've done better, particularly in the storms when each wave pushed us ten or more feet. We're somewhere between the two. I show my plot to Sim, who graciously agrees. I secretly add a few more miles to my estimate.

My best guess is that we've moved at an average of three fourths of a knot. In 500 hours, our run comes out to 375 miles. This puts us 750 miles from the Central American coast or another thousand hours if we maintain our speed...that's 40 more days. But we're bound to be found by a freighter or a search party before then. Someone has to be out looking.

Outlined by the last embers of a dying sun, a huge hammerhead shark circles the raft. Its dorsal fin cuts the water a raft length from the boat. We lie quietly until darkness is complete, and we can see them no more. We closed the windows at sunset less our predators recognize a movement or receive an instinctive signal to attack. The raft is so fragile that the slightest motion towards us would mean death.

Help has to be on the way. Today was a perfect day for an air search. Seas were calm, skies clear. Where is everybody? We fully expected to hear the welcoming hum of engines. But then, today is a holiday, one of the Coast Guard's busiest days. What form will our rescue take? But will they search this far from the US?

Our positive feelings are cut short by a rough scrape followed by an abrupt smash to the raft. The raft spins. Another blow. Did they smell the turtle blood and follow our trail? How much more can this raft take?

I fight back with the pole. The sharks will destroy the raft in short order if we allow them to batter it at will. The savage attacks ebb when we are well into night. We look out to our most beautiful night adrift. The sea is a mass of phosphorescence. Uncountable stars twinkle and flicker in the dark velvet dome of the sky. They are so close. As Sim reaches out to touch them, they bring back thoughts of her childhood...

SIMONNE:

We were in Opio, in the south of France, in the days following the war. We would spread old blankets on the garden in front of the old farmhouse and stretch out close to each other to gaze at the stars.

We looked in wonder at the heavens, sprinkled with so many millions of stars. There were as many and as near as tonight. My grandfather, a man of deep faith, became pensive and then said... "On nights like this, if you watch the stars long enough, your soul melts with the universe, and you'll see the face of God." All of us children believed him. On other nights, he would point out the stars and planets and call them by name. We made friends with them.

We got to know Orion with Betelgueuse and Riga, the dippers, and the bear around them. Sirius and the planets became our companions. Their names danced in our heads. We marveled equally at my grandfather's knowledge and at the mysteries of the universe.

And after much soaring among the star studded universe, we would come back exhausted, to fall asleep cuddled up near my grandparents. The smells of jasmine and fresh-cut grass and the heavy fragrance of our beloved fig tree, heavy with fruits nearby, surrounded us.

The dizzying majesty of our universe makes us feel so much more insignificant in this vast ocean. We search for solace. We are but a minute microcosm in this universe, but we are part of it; we belong; we exist. We are alive.

And how not to believe when God puts on a show like this. People on land...you can have all the fireworks you want tonight. We have our own private show, brighter than any man-made display. Thank You, Lord, for this. We feel Your love. Your existence is our existence. Our life is in Your hands. Give us strength. We will abide in Your will....it will be done.

BILL:

Light rain in the early morning shuts out the stars. Since dusk, the wind and current pushed us in an easterly direction, but now we're starting to lose both current and wind. The raft swings and heads more southerly.

Is it possible that not one of our loved ones imagines what has happened to us? If we die, and death is never more than seconds away, nobody will know how or where we died. They will make guesses and wonder about us for generations.

My MAYDAY messages didn't get through. The EPIRB signals weren't picked up either. Our children will never know how we met our fate. What can we do? Each of us, in our particular way, ponders our fate. Long after three a.m., we sleep, fitfully.

The night passes endlessly as so many other nights have passed. Hours mean nothing. Minutes are the real measure. Each night becomes seven hundred minutes of terror. Each minute is a lifetime at the edge of death.

Our fate is truly in God's hands. He has kept us alive through the past twenty days. He is going to save us. We have felt His hand. The turtle He sent gave us renewed strength and hope. Earlier, the slightest chore took all my concentration and willpower. I felt myself withering and drowsy. I was satisfied to lie on my back and to gaze out the window, convinced I was on the threshold of my end. The Lord sent the turtle at the most critical of moments. If He had waited another week or two, we may not have been strong enough to handle the struggling animal. When we eat breakfast of half a cookie each, our appetite isn't satisfied.

Sim smiles as she says. "I'm going to give you the morning news with your breakfast. Sometimes, I don't understand why we want to go back to our crazy world. There was a big shootout in Caracas between labor and the Government. Carlos Andres called out the troops and is killing people in the streets. Gromyko died, and Bush is calling for the Soviets to get out of Poland. Your buddy Reagan got thrown off a horse, and Gorbachev is in Paris. Everyone is calling him Gorby. Vive, Gorby, they cry. Of all the stupid things."

"Spare me the details. I'll have another cup of coffee and a doughnut. You're not wearing out the batteries, are you?" What a difference that little radio makes. I'm glad Sim spotted it before it floated away or sank in the cabin. Why didn't I grab the two ziplocs full of batteries that were under the bunk? She could've listened all night every night.

"No. I listen but five or ten minutes at a time. It's so consoling. I thought about home this morning. If we make it back, I want to make some changes in the house. On the other hand, the house may have sold. After all, it's been on the market more than four months. Well, whatever. It would be a blessing if it hasn't sold."

Now that we lost the boat, where would we go if we get back and find the house sold? We would be homeless. Cris would never sell the house without our OK. All we can do is hope for the best.

Are the children or friends concerned? They've had no report from us for 25 days. Could they find us if they searched? This ocean is immense. Where would they start?" Of course, nobody knows that the boat sank. They probably think our radio gave up. No one at home, not our family nor our friends, can imagine the worst. They are probably thinking that the wind has been contrary or lack of wind has us becalmed.

The time has arrived to test my fishing skills. With the help of Sim's scissors and the can opener, I bend the hook back almost to its original shape. My dolphin hook is three inches long and almost an inch wide. I position the yellow plastic skirt on the leader, tie the leader to the heavy parachute cord supplied with the raft, then feed the cord through the eye at the end of the pole.

I put a piece of turtle meat on the hook and cast. The line jerks and pulls tight. A triple tail shoots under the raft. I keep pressure on the line until Sim spreads the sailbag over my lap and the raft's air chamber. I pull the fish within three feet of the end of the pole, heave, and the fish is onboard and in the bucket. Sim throws a cushion on it, and we look at each other, then hug, cry, and laugh. We did it. Our first fish is aboard.

My Lord. That was easy. We are going to live. If only we didn't have the sharks to worry about, we might have an even chance. The fish struggles and almost escapes from the bucket. Sim puts all her weight on the cushion. We are so happy that we can't stop crying.

When we lift the cushion many minutes later, the fish flops out, the sharp spines along its dorsal fin barely missing the air chamber. The fish is as slippery as an eel. We struggle and catch it before it perforates the raft and shove it back into the bucket. A long hour later, the triple tail is at last dead. I put it on top of the camcorder case and move the plastic lid to my lap. Its 3/4 inch lip keeps the blood and scales from running into my crotch and the bedding beneath. I'm ready to filet our catch. Sim prays in French, giving thanks to the Lord for His mercy.

The fish appears to have three tails. The dorsal and anal fins are as large as its tail. Thus its name, "triple tail." I put one of our oars under the camcorder case top to stiffen it and cut along its dorsal fin. I free one filet and run the knife along the skin to remove it. The meat is white and firm. I hand Sim the first piece. I eagerly eat the second.

The taste is terrific. We gobble down each piece as quickly as I filet it. We are hungry, yet one filet fills us, so we keep the other for supper. As I am ready to throw the carcass over, a shark whacks the raft. I hit one with the pole as it comes around the end of the raft and bonk another as it swims straight in. In the distance, a turtle lifts its head out of the water to breathe. Will they ever leave us in peace?

I enjoyed my fishing interlude. It gives me a sense of accomplishment. I am the provider. With God's help, I will sustain my life and Sim's.

Our log entries become more succinct. Will anyone ever read them? We are alone. The odds for survival are slim...but I believe in keeping tradition alive and well. To the very end, we will keep up our entries into the Log. We will also maintain a semblance of decorum. We brush our teeth, comb our hair, and, of course, partake in the daily happy hour.

And now, happy hour and time to celebrate. Today is special. The fifth of July is Independence Day of two countries we love, Venezuela and the Bahamas. We first sing the Venezuelan national anthem, "Gloria Al Bravo Pueblo." We enjoyed many good moments in that beautiful country. *Siboney* sailed nine years through most of the Caribbean with the Venezuelan flag flying proudly from its stern. And that's where I met Simonne.

We often celebrated the fifth of July off Green Turtle Cay in the Bahamas. No Independence Day celebration is complete on Green Turtle Cay without a sip of ale at Miss Emily's. How far are we from Green Turtle Cay and Miss Emily's? Oh, to be granted but a few minutes of the past....

We pop open a bottle of Perrier after we savor two drops of brandy. The Perrier bottles have been high on our list of expendable items because of their high weight to content ratio. We finish the left-over triple tail filet and tidy up. Sim reads at last light.

"Last Chance" has held a steady southeast course all afternoon. Dark clouds blanket the sky as night approaches. The wind increases and seas build. We make good progress, probably close to a knot. All of my dead reckoning is gut given, and only if we make it, will I know how good it is.

The integrity of the raft worries me increasingly each passing day. The main air chamber tends to collapse in the middle which causes the floor to bulge. Air leaks increase from the hole I patched while both air valves refuse to seat and consequently leak. The many seams that keep the raft together are still intact, for if they start to peel, we're in big trouble. The raft is constructed of several dozen plastic panels glued together with each seam backed by a plastic tape. I still can't figure out how they glued the inside part of the last piece, but damn, I sure hope they've done a good job...used good glue...and it wasn't rainy the day they made the raft...

The outside of the canopy has changed from bright orange to pale dirty white which, in turn, has allowed the ultra-violet rays to eat away at the blue waterproofing on the inside. Why don't the raft manufacturers use a bright reflecting surface instead of the orange that fades? Probably a Coast Guard requirement that's a hundred years old. A lookout on a ship is more likely to spot something bright...that is, if there's sunshine...something we've had little of so far. I dare not breathe a word to Sim that the raft has lived at least a week beyond its designed life. I'll keep that piece of news to myself although I'm sure she's figured it out for herself.

How much pounding can a seam withstand before it comes unglued and starts to leak? If we develop a leak in one seam, others will certainly fail, a domino effect. A hole caused by a fish hook or by a fish itself or a piece of driftwood with a nail in it are real possibilities. It could happen anytime. With a hole of any size, even a pinhole, the raft will lose its buoyancy and begin to sink. We would have to pump continuously as the hole inevitably became larger. Sooner or later, water would inevitably seep in. The arches, hopefully still full of air, should keep the raft from sinking more than a foot or two. Maybe the four large and two small boat cushions would help keep us afloat. We would need to lie horizontally to maximize our buoyancy, and we would be constantly submerged. Sleep would be difficult, if not impossible. Fishing and making water would become real chores.

How long will we survive once we're in the water? The threat of hypothermia could be more real than the jaws of a shark. Immersed in the eighty degree water, the core temperature of our body will begin to drop after two or three days. First we'll shiver, but as our internal temperature approaches ninety degrees, our body will no longer regulate temperature. Shivering will stop, and we'll begin to get drowsy. Death from hypothermia, infection, fish bite, or drowning would be but a matter of time...days. I pray for Sim's sake that I don't go first. We've talked at length about most of these possibilities, but our minds refuse to accept defeat and death.

If we must die, I hope that it will be fast. Once the raft desintegrates, I imagine ourselves swimming for hours in panic and despair. Trigger fish will take penny size bites from each of our bodies. As we bleed, sharks move in. At first, they brush by tentatively to test us. On their second or third pass, they will bump us. Soon they will attack and quickly it's over. The raft sinks, and all trace of our presence disappears. Prayers, and the thought of our children, and our desire to live, fight these deathly images.

SIMONNE:

I pray for a more dignified death. I contemplate gliding down into the one of the seas' great abyss', slowly, like *Siboney*. Beautiful blue, gold, and yellow dorados and the singing of the whales and dolphins follow me...I recall the movie, Big Blue...and the attraction of the deep. What are we all searching for? Isn't it peace? Eternal peace....

chapter eight

0020 THURSDAY JULY 6, 1989, DAY 22

A loud whistle turns into a growl. Sim jumps up, certain it's another ship about to run us down. A solid wall of blackness falls upon us alike an avalanche. The sound increases and spreads, now deadened as we fall into a trough, then deafening as we rise to the crest of the next wave. Suddenly, we are in the midst of it.

Thirty knot winds gust to forty. Rain blasts the side of the raft. Great sheets of wind driven spray shoot through the closed window. The canopy fills with air to form a dome above us. Massive waves travelling at more than thirty knots threaten to overturn the raft. Water cascades through the canopy to bury us as we gasp for breath. Sim bails with desperation brought on by memories of the sinking *Siboney*. The water gains. She prays aloud for mercy. "Bail," I call out above the roar, "Bail, Sim, bail. We must beat the sea itself!"

I look at my watch and find it's one twenty in the morning. The storm rages on. Time stands still. We experience all the horror and terror of hell...a watery hell meant to last forever. Darkness is so complete I can see neither Sim nor the sides of the raft, but I can feel her desperation transmitted through the fingers that grip mine. I have always considered myself lucky. Good fortune has always followed me. I had wonderful parents, a great family, and a fun job. Right now, I can't shake the feeling that I've pushed my luck one notch too far. Death is upon us. No six foot vessel can survive long.

Waves batter us at sea level. Sharks attack from below. Wind and rain pound us from above. We cry out to the highest...Lord, have mercy on us. If this punishment continues, we will not survive until dawn. This is surely the end. We cry and are tempted to give up...to curl up and let the sea take us...but the sea will have to try harder if it really wants us. Rain floods through the canopy. We take turns holding the pole. Two giant waves born thousands of miles apart meet under us with a thunderous clap. My side of the raft lifts out of the water. Sim jumps upon me as we press to windward. The wave passes only to be replaced by another and then another. We pray with more intensity than ever before. Sharks again attack without letup. The rain keeps me from counter-attacking. Visibility is nil.

We can do nothing but pray. Lord, help us. Virgencita de la Caridad del Cobre, patron of Cuba, plead with God in our behalf. Help us. I close my eyes and see Her. And below Her is our raft, under Her arms, protected, cradled. The sharks leave, and at long last, we are allowed a little rest, a meager sleep.

Never has the gray dawn been so welcome. As though in pity with our plight, the wind drops as the day becomes lighter. We open the window to a pale gleam of light reaching towards us from a slowly rising sun. We are battered, bruised, wet, cold, and hungry. But we're alive. Our hearts reach out to thank God.

Our eyes feast on the one sunrise neither of us believed we would live to see. Each new ray helps our hearts grow stronger and our will to survive more firm. We breathe in this new day with its oranges, pinks, and reds, a display of colors to make a van Gogh green with envy. Whitecaps dance over the deep blue sea as we ride giant ocean swells that would put to shame the Big Wheel at any County Fair. We are alive, delivered from a deadly dark catacomb where we were held captive through eleven evil hours.

The force of the wind no doubt pushed us to the northeast all night at close to a knot. When we surfed, propelled by a breaking wave, our speed was more. Anyway, we have passed the 500 hour mark. Neither of us could have guessed on that first desperate dawn, with *Siboney* resting in its new-found cradle, we adrift for barely five hours, that we would continue to live as castaways for one hundred similar periods. We lived a full lifetime before that first dawn. Now we've reached a considerable milestone, and it calls for a celebration.

Before that, I must plot our 500 hour position; but right now, I'm too tired, and it's too rough to do anything. I have high hopes and a strange feeling that someone will soon find us. Twenty days have passed since we last saw a ship...twenty days drifting east towards the shipping lanes in and out of Panama. I row the raft in a circle whenever Sim kneels to look out. She always returns with the same report...no ships...no birds...no planes...we are alone and forgotten by all...we're forty three days out of Panama, twenty-six since our latest radio contact..WHAT IN THE HELL IS EVERYONE THINKING? WHERE DO THEY THINK WE ARE? WHAT IN THE DEVIL DO THEY THINK WE'RE DOING?

Around noon, I fish, but my luck in that department is out. I get several strikes but my hook is too big. Where in the hell were the bags of hooks when I needed them? Cast after cast bears no fish, and I begin to hoard my diminishing bait supply by baiting each successive toss with less and less bait. All fishermen have bad days and this one is terrible. I try one last cast. If it doesn't work, I'll save the remainder of the bait for tomorrow. I cast and lose the bait. It's a cracker and a dab of peanut butter for the crew today.

I stow my fishing gear, which consists of turning the rod back to turtle and shark bonker. I coil the line and hang the hook safely in a hole in the seam of the arch. What can I do to put food on the table? Soon we'll be out of crackers; we ate our last raisin, a mushed up sad looking thing I found towards the bottom of Sim's toilet kit. I found two soggy cookie crumbs and ate those too after offering them to Sim; like every mother, she insists on feeding others first.

We're short on food; the raft has gone weeks past its design life; the closest land is seven or eight hundred miles off, and to top it off, no one is looking for us. There is little doubt of that. Even if an air search is underway, we will not be located. They will search a thousand miles from where we drift. It'd be like looking for a Volkswagen between Miami and Seattle in a six hundred mile wide path. But then, we got ourselves into this mess; it was all my idea; why blame others? If we die, I am the sole culprit. Yet dying isn't the all of it; not one person will ever know how or where or when we died; we will have disappeared alike so many other seafarers throughout the ages...gone to sea never to return...in unmarked graves in an unknown sea...how many widows and sons and daughters and mothers have awaited fruitlessly for the return of a sailor from the deep...and have gone to their own graves never knowing the fate of their loved ones?

Just as I'm sure Sally has received my mental messages, Sim knows that her mother is aware we are facing certain death. As time passes, her suspicions will be strengthened; when six months or a year goes by without word from us, her heart will break from despair and the loneliness and the agony that she will never know what happened to her baby. When Sim suggests we send a message, I jump at the idea and right off have her dig under the covers for one of the empty Perrier bottles. On a sheet from the navigation workbook, I dictate as she writes a note in both English and Spanish:

HELP HELP HELP AUXILIO AUXILIO OUR SAILBOAT *SIBONEY* SANK ON JUNE 15. TODAY WE ARE 22 DAYS IN OUR LIFE RAFT. PLEASE, WHOEVER FINDS THIS NOTE, CALL COLLECT OUR SONS, CRISTOBAL AND ALEXANDRO GOMEZ DE ORTEGA, IN MIAMI AND INFORM THEM. TELEPHONE 305-667-7121 WE GUESS WE ARE BETWEEN COCOS ISLAND AND LAND. WE THANK YOU. GOD SAVE US. BILL AND SIMONNE BUTLER.

Sim folds the note until it fits through the neck of the bottle. HELP AUXILIO can be seen from the outside. Next she pleats several dollar bills and pushes them alongside the note in hopes that the sight of money will catch a beachcomber's attention. Sim screws the cap tightly and tosses it over the side. The bottle quickly falls behind, confirming that the wind and waves do push us along.

Later in the afternoon, the wind picks up from the southwest which prompts us to try a trick we learned several days ago when drying the sailbag. When we tie the sailbag atop the canopy, it fills and acts much alike a spinnaker. The raft picks up speed right off, and we leave it up until past sunset when the wind begins to die. Besides we can't risk losing it in the night, for it serves a multitude of functions. When I clean fish, I put it under the camcorder case to catch juices and blood that spill. At other times, we spread it over the air chambers when hauling in fish to provide protection against an accidental jab from a fish spine or a wayward hook. If Sim knew how many close calls I've had with the hook, she'd hook me in one of my dearest places.

On cool nights, we use the sail bag as a cover. Today it's delightfully dry after so many hours in the sun, and I throw it over me early in the night. Sim lies, as usual, naked and soaked with perspiration. The cotton cover and source of our sanitary napkin supply serves as our pillow. The striped cover remains under us as a mattress and wrap, but with each passing day, it becomes wetter and lumpier. Unless the night is windy and rainy, the sailbag is all we need for comfort. On colder nights, I wring out the wool blanket and spread it over me.

Rain begins with isolated drops, then builds to a pounding downpour. The canopy no longer keeps rainwater out, and we struggle to stay dry for as long as we can. Over the sailbag, we spread the trash bag which is not quite long or wide enough to cover us completely. The drips are continuous but a lot less when I raise the canopy with the pole. I jam it against my leg which works fine until I move or Sim moves or a heavy gust dislodges the pole and, at the same time, blows the trash bag off the sail bag. Then everything collapses. A bucket of water spills on us. I push my head further under the arch to escape the worse of the drips or at least keep them out of my eyes and ears.

In the midst of this medieval-type torture, I manage to sleep. I can never tell if Sim sleeps, for she remains immobile, hair soaked, hands on her chest, rosary clutched, saddened lips in prayer...prayers so intense she remains oblivious to the many drops that drench her naked body. Her Mediterranean nose reaches out to heaven...her heart and soul pleads with God for His ultimate sign of mercy...grant her life.

There is a positive side to the rain. There has to be a connection between rain and sharks. Sharks haven't battered the raft while it rains. I'll take rain over sharks anytime. Perhaps, in a heavy rain, the surface water loses its salinity, or does the pitter patter unnerve them? When the rain stops, the sharks return. I dip the pole into the sea for the remainder of the night. When I rest, the sharks attack the raft within seconds. Sim prays constantly. I look at my watch at intervals of under ten minutes in hopes an hour passed. The night becomes an interminable saga...a saga for survival which will not end too soon; if we are to die, may it be swift.

When a faint lightening of the skies announces we have once again lived to see a new day dawn, the wind has died and skies are clear. The sun, when it makes its appearance at eight amid a bright red eastern horizon, further confirms that we do move east. Where we sank, sunup was after eight thirty. Today the sun is up before eight. A half hour of sun time is seven and half degrees or 450 miles. That coincides with my dead reckoning. But I don't like red sunrises.

Sim lives her own sunrise as her body announces the start of a second period but three weeks since her last one. I was always under the impression that women tended to miss periods when scared to death. In her first period, not wanting to stir the attention of the shark population, we used one of our empty saltine tins to store her urine and soiled cloth. At the end, we capped the can and eased it away from the raft. Now we're much more blase. Sharks pummel the raft whether we throw fish carcasses over or not. Blood and fish entrails appear not to make them any more aggressive. All the same, I remind Sim to always throw her trash to windward, for I don't want the raft to pick up a taint sharks will pursue.

Sharks and turtles pester us all morning. I land several good hits on fast moving sharks, but there are so many of them that I miss half. When I look down, I see ten or more five footers at the ten foot level. To Sim's delight, several boobies perch on the raft this morning. The webbed feet of the mature birds are harmless. The younger ones have sharp nails. My Log entry for today Friday reads: TGIF-EXCEPT HERE ITS TSBF-TURTLES SHARKS BIRDS FRIDAY.

It's lunch time, and my stomach screams for something more than half a cracker. Our Fourth of July turtle has generated a gnawing hunger. I prepare the rod to fish and cut up the smelly three day old turtle meat into three small pieces. I cast and lose the first bait instantaneously. It's so rotten it barely stays on the hook. I cast again and lose my second piece. Sim has closed her eyes and pleads aloud...give us this day our daily bread...have mercy, dear God...

I'm desperate. My last, little piece of turtle meat was the most rotten piece in the can. I'd left it for last in hopes I wouldn't need it. When I lose it, the food chain will again be broken. We're back to where we were before we caught the turtle, with no ability to fish. The bait is so rotten it will not stay on the hook. I drop it gingerly in the water, and immediately I have a strike. The line becomes taut as the fish strains to escape. I give the line a hard tug fully expecting to lose it, but---, to my great surprise, a fish flies on board. With a lightning fast movement, Sim wraps it in the sailbag and bursts out both laughing and crying. We hug and cry without shame. Prayer is power. We have seen a miracle, nothing less. Sim looks up and exclaims with a burst of faith: "God, we do not deserve your generosity, but we accept it. Thank you!"

I plunge the knife into the head of the rainbow runner to kill it and quickly slice out both filets. In seconds, we dice them up and devour the tasty fish. The skin and inedible parts become bait. My next cast lands a five pound triple tail. Minutes later, another triple tail is on board and in the bucket with the first. Sim cheers, her attitude so much improved over minutes earlier. I clean and fillet what must total six pounds of fish; then we eat until we can no more. We save what's left for supper and bait. From now on, I will keep a larger supply of bait on hand.

Food and water will keep us alive. I cut up the best part of the filets for Sim as she has not taken to our raw fare and never eats enough to suit me. She's also a reluctant water drinker, so before I drink, I always pass the bottle first to her and insist she take a second and third sip. Our water intake has settled down to a fairly standard two liters a day with one full Evian bottle consumed throughout the day and another liter at night. Our bodies really call for no more.

The five spare liters of water fit under our feet while I keep the one in use between my hips and the air chamber. The empties create a storage problem, for when I turn, I usually squash one. The noise shatters Sim's nerves. I try all sorts of tricks to keep them out of the way, but nothing seems to work. There's still too much stuff aboard, and much of it is still soggy. We move the big black and white comforter, sopped and heavy, out from under us and drape an end on the canopy to dry. I dream of a dry bed, but I'm afraid that'll be a while in coming...if ever.

Where is everyone? I'm sure the search has started. We are now forty-six days out of Panama and would be nearing Hilo in Hawaii if *Siboney* was still afloat. Our last radio contact was 28 days ago. Is no one worried?. What are they doing? Where in the hell are the planes? And ships? Anything...

Wind and current die in late afternoon. The raft swings wildly and spins when the smallest shark bumps it, a baby shark that has been pestering us all day. They learn their nasty habits young. I'd rather be surrounded by tarantulas...

New sea birds join us. Our favorite is an all white bird the size of a sea gull with two long feathered tails. It has round black eyes and hangs suspended above the raft looking down at us. Frigate birds are our constant companions. A mother and young hover above us all day and, no doubt, all night. In the morning at first light, they are always there, a hundred feet above the raft. They soar carelessly, their sharp eyes ever on the lookout for a meal.

The dry bedding improves the mood aboard. Sim's reading fills our hearts with hope. This truly gorgeous day closes with a spectacular sunset as the sun plunges into the ocean. We gaze west until night turns the clouds ever darker shades of purple, then gray, and finally black. We give thanks for another day of life and pray for a quiet night. Stars appear, one or two at first, then hundreds. We look out our window, deep in thought. Sim breaks the spell: "Bill, will we make it?" I have no answer. The next eleven terrifying hours of darkness will only tell.

"Sure, sweety. The children, your mother, our friends must all be worried. A month has passed since our last radio contact. Someone will come looking for us. Soon."

Sim looks at me with her far away look. "Do you remember the voice I heard when we first shipwrecked? It said, "Forty days, forty days" over and over. I really think our punishment will be forty days long. We do deserve forty days of punishment, for we have deserted God for so many years. If that's so, we have seventeen more days. I know that only then will rescue come. We have to accept it." I'm surprised and relieved that Sim has now relaxed from her daily bouts of anxiety. Seventeen days with less tension is what I need.

Sim's incessant haranguing over our past relationship and our present situation wears the hell out of me. In the two hours prior to sunset, she takes off on her daily barrage rehashing topics I considered long dormant. Like the blond hairs she found in her bedroom after returning home from a long trip twelve years ago. I swore then and have over the past weeks insisted that I have never been unfaithful and have never ever taken and would never ever take another woman into her home. Ten days ago, with sudden death imminent, we played the entire scene over one more time. Her doubts will again surface, for she will carry them to her grave...or into the stomach of a predator.

The sharks arrive at ten and punish us non-stop until three in the morning. Tonight, for the first time in a week, my blows have no visible effect. I splash the paddle in the water until close to dawn when we finally sleep.

A shark awakens us on this Saturday, the 8th of July, when the sun is ten o'clock high. When I open my window, dozens of sharks mill under the raft. Never have we seen so many at one time. They are all four to six foot and appear to be silky sharks. One after another take turns slapping the raft. I repel them with pokes of the pole. After an hour, the entire mass of sharks move on.

Sim sits up with a jerk and cries out: "Bill, listen, an airplane. A plane, a plane!"

"Hey, you sound like Dadou. I don't hear it. Have you been nipping on the brandy behind my back?"

"It is an airplane! My God. An airplane. Listen."

Now I hear it. The faintest of sounds, but it is an airplane, propeller driven. Sim searches the skies while I row the raft in circles. I take out the mirror. The sound of the engines becomes louder then fades away. Sim searches the skies long minutes after.

Who were they? Where were they coming from? Are they searching for us? What else would bring a plane out this far? And where are they going? We must be getting closer to shore. That is the first sign of life, however remote, that we have had in more than three weeks. It's a good sign. Thank you, God. Thank you. You haven't forgotten us.

We spend the rest of the morning beating off turtles and sharks. What else? The lovers are back under the raft and at it again. Sim is unmerciful. The lovers are carefree.

What do turtles eat out here? Carrion, leftovers from dead fish are eaten by the fish and sharks if under water. Birds get it if on the surface. Turtles eat marine plants, but we haven't seen any plant life. They eat jelly fish, but so far we've seen none. What sustains them? Their giant shell must be a huge warehouse for food and air. I read an article in Smithsonian long ago which described an experiment with a turtle. One continued to live normally for a month with its brain removed. I couldn't believe it then, but I believe it now. They probably needed a high power microscope to find the brain in the first place.

Sim waits, fishing rod in her right hand. When the male turtle swims out for air, Sim shoots for its neck. The turtle paddles out a few feet, turns, and heads straight back to Sim. She deals out six more pokes. The turtle swims out and returns. The scene repeats itself every minute or two. I lie on my side with my back to Sim, intent on ignoring the proceedings. Sim prods me with the pole.

"Here, Bill, quick. It's on your side. I can hear it scratch the raft."

"I don't do turtles."

"You what? What does that mean? Hurry, take the pole. It's sinking the raft."

I remain inert and say: "I do not do turtles. Sharks yes. Turtles no."

"I can't believe what I hear. The man is crazy. He doesn't do turtles? We're attacked, and he doesn't move. Oh, Lord, give me patience."

The turtle is back under the raft. Sim boils over. She screams some nasty words in French and Italian both at the turtle and at me. I refuse to get excited. It bumps the bottom of the raft and scratches along the side a bit, but I can't see it's doing any damage. I am busy enough with sharks. The turtle will leave when it's ready.

When I decide to fish, I look down into our aquarium and into the nose of dozens of sharks that circle at different levels. I'll fish later. No use stirring things up.

Sim scrapes the toothbrush around the bottom of the peanut butter jar and spreads a thin layer on a cracker. We split the cracker two ways and wash it down with several gulps of water.

Sim turns white and clutches her chest: "My heart, my heart! Oh, Bill, I'm having a heart attack. Oh, my God. I can't breathe, I'm dying. Oh, my God!"

"You sound like Redd Fox, 'This is the big one, this is the big one.' I'd have a heart attack if I carried on like you. Let the turtles be, and you won't have any heart attacks."

"This is real. I **am** having a heart attack. Pain runs all over my chest. I can't breathe. Oh, Bill, help me. I can't breathe. Oh, Lord, help me."

"I think a little chest massage will help. Here, let me try."

"Keep your hands off me. I'm serious; I'm having a heart attack and you're making fun."

"What do I tell your mother after I make it to shore? 'Mama, your daughter died of a heart attack. A couple of turtles doing it got her over excited.' She won't believe it for a second. She'll figure I dumped you over the side for being a bitch. You get over your attitude towards turtles, and that's an order."

"I'm going to die. I know it. And you don't care. If I die, please, please don't throw my body over for three days."

"Three days! C'mon. You don't smell so great right now. Imagine after three days. You pop, kid, over you go."

Sim is serious: "Don't ever do that. Let my spirit leave my body. It takes three days for it to leave the body and rise. Promise you won't throw me in right away."

"How about two days? If you die just like that and if I can't revive you, it would be a shame to let all that good meat go to waste."

"Butler, you are atrocious. How can you talk like that when I could be dying any minute? Oh, it hurts! Ay ay ay."

"Perhaps if I could use a leetle tidbit for bait."

"Stop it, right there. Oh, I feel terrible!"

Breathing exercises finally relaxes her.

Some time after midnight, the wind increases followed by lightning and thunder out of the West. Rain pelts the raft until two or three when I fall asleep. Sim shakes me out of my slumber.

"Bill, listen. What is it? It sounds like a freak wave."

I hear it, like a rumble. It does sound like a huge breaking wave bearing down on us. Sim looks out and screams: "Bill, a freighter! A freighter! Coming right down on us!"

I struggle up and lean over Sim, who has lowered her window despite the wind driven rain. The bow of the large freighter looms high over the raft not two hundred yards away. Ahead of the bow, the now all too familiar bow wave builds and breaks with a roar. Navigation lights, like red and green eyes, look straight at us. My God, these people are going to run us down.

The rear of the stark white pilot house stands lit like a ghost against the blackness of the night. The ocean transmits the roar of the machinery through the skin of the raft and into our soul. It's now evident the ship will not run us down but pass close by. We could not have rowed out of its way.

"Help! Help!" We scream in unison.

"Sim, get the flashlight, find the flares."

"Here's the flashlight. It's too late for the flares. Besides it's raining."

"Then the whistle, get the whistle."

She finds the whistle and hands it to me. Sim yells as I blow the whistle and send SOS's with the flashlight oblivious to the pouring rain. The ship's bow is alongside, and the rumble of the machinery vibrates the raft. Diesel smoke fills our lungs. We search for signs of life. Where is everyone?

The freshly painted side of the ship passes mere feet away. The decks are empty. We look straight up at the living quarters, not a hundred feet away. We see every detail clearly, even the door knobs. There is no one on deck. The ship's stern comes into view, and on it, in large white letters, the home port of the ship "LIVERPOOL." We can't make out the ship's name in the dark.

I continue to blow the whistle and flash the light. Sim yells and waves her shirt which she has pulled off. The aft end of the ship is brightly lit. We watch in disbelief as the freighter speeds away into this dark and dismal night. We continue to yell as we hope against hope that we have been seen by someone in the pilot house or a crewman on deck who may have heard our cries of distress.

The ship's stern becomes a pinpoint of light, then blends into the night and vanishes. A light of hope gone by...a fading star in the surrounding blackness, extinguished by the drizzle. We are again alone. It passed so fast, so cruelly indifferent to our plight.

I find the compass and ask Sim to check the ship's course. She holds the compass up as I shine the light. The freighter's heading is 150 degrees. It steams for the Panama Canal. That means we're closing in on land although a course of 150 puts us way off shore. Where are they coming from? I generate a mental picture of the Pacific and come up with Honolulu. Shipping from the Far East will run closer to shore. From now on, we should have the flares at the ready all the time. But shooting one would've been a waste; there was no one looking out...again.

Sim collapses in my arms. We cry out our frustration and our anger. What has the Lord planned for us? Is this punishment not enough? How long? How long? we cry out. Soaked and depressed, we close the canopy and lie back down on our soggy bed. This was like a bad dream. How many more have we?

I look at my watch. It's four in the morning. It's the ninth of July, Sunday, and day 25 on the raft. We left Balboa 47 days ago. We have had no radio contact for 29 days. I'm sure a search party will set out on the next clear day.

The rain has become a light drizzle, and the wind increases out of the southwest. A southwesterly tells us we are still far off shore. The closer we get to Central America, the more southerly the wind will become. I remember that much out of the pilot chart. Besides that's the way it was on our way out into the Pacific.

Rain continues through dawn. The wind increases to twenty knots or more. It kicks up ever stronger waves. The canopy lets both rain water and the seas in. The overcast is so heavy we cannot tell when sunrise was or is going to be. It is now nine, so the sun is up somewhere behind the clouds. After midmorning, the skies clear and improve our outlook. Last night's ship hasn't been as hard on us as that first one, 24 days ago. We remain amazed that, in an ocean this vast, two consecutive ships practically run us down.

I fish early today and, with my second piece of bait, hook a three foot shark. Sim holds the pole while I pull the line through the eye at the end of the pole. When the shark rises to the surface, I find that my only hook runs through the shark's lower jaw. Sim lifts the shark out of the water while I grab it around the gills. The shark flails its tail wildly as Sim hands me the knife. I slash the shark's lower lip, remove my hook, and drop the shark.

I no sooner let the shark go than I realize we haven't eaten in two days. We've caught loads of sharks aboard *Siboney*, but I've never tried shark meat. I'm not quite hungry enough yet. Three small sharks chase my next piece of bait. I pull my line in and save my last pieces of bait for tomorrow.

The current stays strong all afternoon, the skies remain clear, and with three gulps of water, our bellies are full. Strange how we can fool our brain, or is our brain fooling us?

At sunset, clouds increase in speed, indicative of nasty weather ahead. Light, intermittent rain starts as soon as we button down the windows. Seas build again. Waves are nearly twenty feet and grow larger. Visibility is less than a mile.

Sim reads in the semi-darkness then grasps my hand and says with a faraway look: "Bill, I hope we make it because I don't want to die before I confess my sins to a priest. Do you think God will forgive me if I don't make a true confession? I have a lot on my conscience, mostly things I should have done and didn't."

"Easy, baby. If you have confessed your sins out here before God, he has received your message. You've been forgiven even if you don't make it to a priest but stop that talk. We're going to make it. Think positive."

"I try but it's so hard. I do want to turn my life around so much. How is it possible we stayed away from God for so long? He could have helped both of us through our troubles. I don't understand how I could have been so blind. I was so close to God when I was a child, and suddenly it was as if I forgot who He is. What a fool I have been. I needed Him so much..."

We've both missed enjoying the Lord's blessing for many good years; when we return, we'll remedy that. What we need now is help. While Sim prays, I'll send another message to Sally.

MT. VERNON, NEW YORK
0400 MONDAY JULY 10, 1989

Sally Smith tosses fitfully next to husband Brian. Their shaggy-haired dog Charm lies curled at the foot of their bed. She grunts whenever Sally thrashes.

Her eyes open wide. Her heart beats wildly. **Something is wrong.** The feeling of terror is inescapable. She sees a pitch black ocean. **Dad and Simonne are in a raft. There is deathly danger. We've got to do something.**

She jumps out of bed. Charm follows Sally to the darkened kitchen of their small fourth floor apartment. She looks up to God. I need help. What should I do?

Calls to the New York Coast Guard yesterday were fruitless. The Miami Coast Guard, on the other hand, were very helpful. They contacted their San Francisco office, who said they would check around to determine if anyone has come across *Siboney*.

She pours a glass a milk and returns to bed. Charm follows. Sally lies awake. **There is something deadly wrong. I know Dad is in trouble. I really know it. What can I do? What should I do? I'll give the Coast Guard another call first thing in the morning.**

chapter nine

ABOARD THE RAFT "LAST CHANCE"
0900 MONDAY JULY 10, 1989, DAY 26

Heavy rain eased us into our first deep sleep in two weeks. We awakened to an empty air chamber and a raft that barely resembled the customary oval. The floor sagged deep into the water. Our outstretched bodies floated on a bed shaped by the sea. What happened to our timer...the sharks? We've grown accustomed to their incessant pounding and failed to set a mental timer. Are we finally out of shark country? That would be fantastic news. Perhaps the salinity in the water has changed, or have they tired of harassing their plastic toy?

Today is Monday and the beginning of our fifth week adrift on this great Pacific Ocean. Our children are at this moment either in school or at work .Are they not worried? It's July 10 and our twenty sixth day on the raft. Is help on the way, or have we been totally forgotten? In two days, we'll complete our fourth week. Never in our wildest imagination could we have imagined that we'd be out here this long. Where is everybody? I've sent mental signals to Sally every night, sometimes in the wee hours of the morning. Am I getting through? I feel contact, but am I really getting to her? When I open my eyes, Sim gazes out the window.

"Good morning, sleeping beauty. Are you interested in the morning news? Fidel sentenced Ochoa and three others to death in Cuba. Menem took over in Argentina. Arabs attacked an Israeli bus. Fourteen dead. Bush is in Poland. And the big fires are still going strong out west." Sim continues: "I suppose that, with all that going on, everyone is too busy to hunt for two lost sailors. I really cannot believe that no one is searching for us. It's not possible that two people can go off the scope for thirty days and nothing, absolutely nothing, happens."

"Speaking of nothing happening," I say, "I've got something happening, and we'd better plan on how to do it quick."

"Use the bucket. Don't put it off. Go on."

"I need music and Playboy. If you hum, that'll do it. I've got my own little centerfold, a bit bedraggled, but still bellisima."

"Stop your baloney and get it over. When you're finished, I want you to cut the matted hair on the back of my head. Now, do your thing and be discreet, will you. My gosh, I haven't seen anybody do it in their pants since my kids were babies."

"Slow down, kiddo. There's no chance I'll do it in my pants...voila...you see, no pants. Besides do you think it's that easy after three weeks of nothing. Give nature a break. Ok, here I go. Hold the bucket." I struggle up to my knees and sit on the wobbly bucket as Sim holds me with one hand and steadies the bucket with the other. I strain. The cramps are terribly painful but nothing happens. A long time later, I give up and crawl back into my bunk exhausted. Sim fills the bucket with the dozen things it normally holds...knife, fishing reel, gloves, cord, and the gun case with the scissors, nail file, and the can opener.

Sim berates me: "I cannot believe it. All that fuss for nothing. You are a catastrophe."

"You didn't hum. C'mon, I tried hard enough. I almost fainted, you yoyo. What should I have done? I'm so full of it, it hurts. That was a bad drill."

"Do something useful like cut my hair. Cut it short, here, like this, inside the matted parts." I chop off big matts of Sim's hair which I pile on her lap. I think I over did it, but I'm no Vidal Sasoon.

I fish early. We are both starved for our increased ingestion throughout the last week reawakened our appetite. The bait, in a tin can next to my feet for three days, is so incredibly smelly that I gag with the first whiff. I dump the entire rotting glob onto the filleting board, evil juices and all, and pick out the best pieces as the nauseating stink fills the raft.

With my second cast, I land the same shark I caught yesterday...sliced lower jaw and all...what a persistent little rascal. I jerk it out of the water and hold the violently writhing beast by the gills until I can cut off its head. Once I remove my hook, I throw the head out as far as I can which brings on a wild fight among the trigger fish until the inevitable black shape bullies its way through the morass and gulps down all that's left.

With the head of the shark removed, Sim relaxes but still keeps an eye on me. I throw the old bait away, clean the board of the dark smelly juices, and gut the shark. Whenever we caught one back in the Bahamas, we removed the jaws and dropped the body over the side, for we always had better fish to eat. The meat runs along the length of the shark and is divided into four sections; each separated by a membrane. I cut a bite sized chunk and try a piece. It's chewy, not without a vinegary taste. Though I'm starved, it's not really that appetizing.

I cast with my fresh bait and instantly hook a rainbow runner. I quickly fillet and feed it to Sim. Pieces of meat around the head become fresh bait. In no time, I have a two pound triple tail on board.

"We're back in business," I proudly exclaim to Sim.

"You're terrific. I love you. Thank you, Lord, for your bounty and generosity," Sim says with traces of fish on her lips. A tear runs down her cheek generated by genuine awe at the series of miracles that have kept us alive.

Instead of waiting for the triple tail to die as I've done in the past, I place it on the filleting board and hold it firmly with my left hand. With the knife, I cut along its dorsal fin, then run the knife along the central spine until the filet is loose. After the other filet is removed, I toss the carcass into the morass of triggers and sharks and watch with sadistic joy the ensuing battle. At sea, the big guy usually wins...not unlike things ashore. I wash the scales and blood off the filleting board and stack the fresh fillets on the paddle. With the paddle on my chest, I stretch out alongside Sim, and I feel for the meat with my fingers, then cut small pieces, less than a half inch cube. Simonne gets most of the triple tail, and I eat the shark. She's as tough to feed as a finicky child and refuses to eat all that she needs to survive. I gorge myself yet leave plenty for tomorrow's bait.

The wind picks up, and seas build to fifteen feet even before we finish lunch. Low, fast moving dark clouds quickly bring rain as visibility drops to less than a mile. What continues to bother me is the absence of larger sharks. I keep my concerns from Sim, but I keep wondering why. Did the shark I hooked send out vibes to his brothers to watch out for the bad guy on the raft? A shark hasn't touched the raft since late morning. To the patter of rain, we nap and awaken at last light.

On our customary evening look around before sunset, we find a heavy black cloud bank rolling in from the southwest with the portent of nasty weather on the way. No sooner do we button down the windows than heavy drops begin to fall. Seas quickly build to twenty feet, and breaking waves again begin their repetitious collision with our fragile craft. Is there a wave out there that will overwhelm us? A huge vertical wall of water that will but for an instant mark our burial place with a mighty swath of white foam? Or will we be allowed to live?

Sim reads at last light. Rain falls all night as the seas quiet...the night is quiet...too quiet. Where in the devil are the sharks? And there are no turtles either. Something strange is going on, but what is it? We pump air every two to three hours and pee about as often. Sim, bundled in her corner of our miniature home, listens intently to the radio for a long while. We're both awake long before dawn.

After first light and with the sun about to emerge, I lean over and say: "You were on the radio last night. Any headlines?"

"Ochoa is in deep trouble in Cuba. They ratified his death sentence. I wonder what's the real story there. Big sex scandal in Japan...Prime Minister and a geisha...big fires out West still raging. Why don't they come out and get some water from out here." How much less lost do we feel as we stay in touch with world events though castaway in this so empty part of the world. How would it be if we had no contact with the outside world? We're alone though not entirely. The escape and peace Sim receives through her little radio has helped keep her going, but the big question is...how much longer will the batteries hold out? When will we pick up a news item about a search for two souls from Miami lost in the Pacific? Or is no one worried?

Today is our twenty seventh day on the raft. Tomorrow we reach the four-week mark. Someone has to be searching. Not today though, for with weather like this, planes will definitely not be flying. A passing ship wouldn't see us even if they ran us down like the last two nearly did. We spend most of the time deep within the troughs. If a ship that passes a few feet from us doesn't see the raft and the raft was bright orange then, what chance do we have with a vessel a half mile distant? Besides we're convinced that today's ships post no lookouts.

When dawn finally arrives, it finds two sopped souls lying on soaked bedding in a soggy raft. Rain poured through the canopy all night, and it seems as if Sim bailed continuously. Most of the water runs to the lowest part of the raft which is under my rear end. For it to flow towards Sim, I have to lift my bottom and arch my back to concentrate my weight on my head and feet, both perched on the sides of the raft. I hold up my cushion to expose the bottom of the raft as Sim pushes on the floor and soaks the rotting sponge, then squeezes it over the can. She then patiently waits for more water to trickle down from the cushions, the foul weather gear, and the covers and repeats the process. A fussy homemaker, she keeps going until she gets the last drop which is, of course, impossible. I grumble from my awkward position for her to hurry which, of course, does no good.

What would our life be like up in the Northern Latitudes? If the boat had gone down off Japan, we would not have survived and shiver with the thought. On the other hand, we might have been found sooner by one of the many Japanese fishing boats. Where in the hell are all the fishing boats? The seas around us run with life...perhaps when it calms...

We saw the ship that passed several nights ago much too late. By a horrible chance of fate, Sim had taken a good look thirty minutes earlier and had seen nothing. That's the price we pay for the comfort and safety of an enclosed raft. With the front and back of the raft permanently closed, we can only see out the sides. But I had rowed the raft around and given time for Sim to get a good look from the top of a swell in every direction. If we had looked in time, we could now be steaming towards Panama in a warm clean bed. As I reflect on our bad timing, Sim looks out, jumps, and calls out:

"Bill. A ship. A ship. Coming to us. There, can you see it? Oh, Lord, be merciful, help us! Let them see us this time."

Sure enough, a small white freighter heads our way. It's still a mile away but on a heading that will take it right by us. Sim quickly grabs the three flares from her toilet kit and hands me one. I remove the outer layer of protective paraffin as Sim unzips the canopy and brushes it aside.

The morning is hazy, but the ship is so close there is a good chance the watch will see one of our flares. The approach angle is perfect and I wait for them to get closer. Once the wind angle is right, I strike the cap igniter against the head of the flare...nothing happens. I try again. Then again. On the third try, the flare bursts into life. Hot blue red flames shoot out one end as pieces of slag spurt into the sea. I hold the end of the wooden handle far out over the water, for a single drop of molten slag on the air chamber would sink the raft and spell our end. Hot flames burn my fingers, but I refuse to let go.

A dense cloud of smoke billows towards the sparkling white ship as it approaches at more than fifteen knots, perhaps twenty. A fifteen degree list to port is unusual for a ship at sea and makes it look like it's lame. We search the decks for signs of life, but we see no one...but then, who would be out strolling on a dark, drizzly morning like this? My flare sputters and dies. In seconds, the ship will be at its closest.

"Sim, quick, give me another flare," I cry out. "He's still heading our way." Sim has waved a shirt and shouted for help all the while. With nervous agitation, I prepare the second flare. It ignites as the white ship speeds up to us. The cloud of grey smoke from the first flare crosses the bow as the second flare begins to burn brightly. Dense smoke carries amidships and across the bridge as the white ship passes alongside. If they don't see it, they will surely smell it. The door to the bridge opens and Sim detects movement. She waves the white T-shirt tied to the end of the fishing rod even more desperately. The door closes, and the small white freighter flies by. Minutes later, it is but a blur in the southern haze.

I kneel, stunned. I have just burned two flares out of our total of three. Now we have but one flare left. Why did I shoot the second one?

Sim is adamant: "He saw us, Bill. Someone on the bridge saw us but decided not to stop. Oh, Lord help us. Why did you shoot two flares? No one will ever see us now!"

"Hand me the compass," I command.

The white ship's course is 120 degrees. Unquestionably, it heads for the Canal. But from where? Hawaii again? We're in the shipping lanes. We go twenty-four days without sighting a ship, and then we see two ships in two days.

I wasted two flares. Visibility was bad, and at the speed they were moving, it was obvious the ship was racing somewhere. They saw us but couldn't stop. Their schedule for transiting the Panama Canal would not allow time for a stop. When I voice my concern, Sim cries out and calls them criminals. In the old time, she says, laws were more strict; the Court in the Hague would have hung them high and dry. I don't know about that.

Regulations at the Panama Canal are so strict that, even in our case, had we missed our schedule, our fine would have been $300 compared to the $100 it cost us to go through. The white ship had a transit time, perhaps was running a little late, and was racing to Panama. To hell with the son of a bitch.

I try to hide my distress and frustration from Sim, who is upset enough as it is. Every ship that passes without sighting us further confirms my feeling that we are invisible. Our best chance is at night when we can fire a flare except that now we have but one. To hell with ships. On top of it all, we've again lost the current and the wind has died. Waves continue from the south. The raft swings aimlessly.

It's time I fished. With my first cast, I catch a blue runner. When I throw my line out next, I accidentally snag a huge sea turtle. I reel it in slowly so as not to excite it. I turn the turtle with the pole to put its menacing beak far from the raft. I hand the pole to Sim and grab hold of its left front flipper. The hook is somewhere underneath. With one eye on its beak and the other on my hook, I follow the line to the hook, twist it, and pull it loose. The turtle jerks then swims off. Whoa...that was close.

Now that we are in the shipping lanes, we have to increase our vigilance. To do the job right, we should take a look every half hour, and even then, we'll miss some ships. A ship goes from horizon to horizon in less than a half hour, more like twenty minutes, but will spot us only on the approach. Our best chance is still at night...but we have but one flare...damn me for missing that bag of flares...

This fact suddenly dawns on Sim: "I can't believe you wasted two flares on that ship and not only two flares but two out of a total of three flares. Now we have one left. One. Do you know what that means?"

She takes a short breath and continues. "We're not going to make it. I know it. We should prepare ourselves for the worse. No one will look for us. Those stupid ships that pass cannot see us. We don't know where we are or where we are going or where land is. God has given up on us. It's all over, Butler."

"That was dumb," I admit. There was too much daylight for the flare to be seen properly. The light rain had cut visibility even further. We could see them clearly because they are large, but they couldn't see us. How could they? The raft is smaller than most waves, and we vanish within the swells for long periods of time. And no one runs ocean going ships any longer. Far from land, even we have left *Siboney* unattended many a time. I would set a ten mile intruder zone on the radar and go to sleep. How many stranded sailors did we pass as we slept?

Sim is right. I should never have shot off that second flare. Even the first flare was a mistake. These flares work best in the dark. There was too much daylight, and then there was the drizzle.

Sim squares off. "You're not going to touch that last flare, Butler, not without talking to me first," she orders. "Do you understand the significance of being down to one last flare? How in the world did you miss that bag of flares on the bunk? It was right there. I saw it. It must still be floating around somewhere."

"I really don't know. It was dumb of me."

"Too many more dumb moves will get us killed. Oh, Lord, have mercy. Help us. Do something. Send us a ship or a plane...push us to land."

The raft swings as rain begins again. The drizzle becomes a downpour. Sim removes the psalms from the ziploc she carefully stows under her headrest and reads before darkness encloses our little world.

Several bumps and a scratch announce the arrival of one of our flippered foes. It's foolish to go after them in the rain, so Sim prays. I repeat my newly found words to the Lord's Prayer over and over, content despite everything. Heavier rain begins at two in the morning. We lie on our backs, sailbag over us and the plastic trash bag again covering the sailbag. A dozen drips fall simultaneously from the canopy while we struggle to keep the trash bag in place. I push my head further up under the arch where I can keep the drips from dropping into my nose and ears. I can't see Sim but can hear her sputter. Soaked before it started, the rain thoroughly sops us. Sim bails.

This is the second day with no shark activity. It's not normal. After more than three weeks of intense shark activity of a sudden...no sharks. What's going on? The sea isn't like that. There must be a reason, but I can't imagine what it is.

I pray the sharks have all left for good. Don't hurry back. They probably left Mr. Turtle behind to make sure we don't get bored. A turtle has been with us for hours, bumping and scratching. Sim tried a couple of shots an hour ago but missed and ended drenched. She now tries to yoga herself to sleep.

Dawn welcomes us with more rain. I peek under the canopy and find a string of low black clouds again approaching from the west. Great. A good storm will push us to shore, and everything aboard is soaked so what's a little more water. The log book, our writing tablets, and the camera are the only dry items on the raft at the moment. Through most of last night, I kept the Log dry on my chest, under the plastic trash bag.

The constant rain have caused the warts on my leg to grow large and black. My back is a mass of open sores brought about by lying for days with a T-shirt soaked in salt. Sim says my back looks terrible and spreads lotion on the worst of the sores whenever I sit up to fish. When I turn on my side to give them a chance to dry, Sim complains I take up too much space...damn it all and damn her too...she's a great companion, but her incessant negative attitude wears thin...why can't she be a bit more positive?...we're going to make it...I don't know how...cramped and uncomfortable as we are...but we're going to make it....

We've tried every combination of positions but none work for long. On our side, I fold my knees into Sim's. While it feels great to get off my back, I can't hold the position for more than twenty minutes without getting a cramp. This is about the time it takes for Sim to fall asleep. When I must finally turn, I awaken Sim, who gets completely out of joint. So much for four man rafts. Next time we'll get a ten man raft...NEXT TIME???

I can hold back my stomach cramps no longer. Since my last try, I have never been without pain, and I announce: "I've got bad news again. I've got to go."

"Bad news! That's terrible news. Why don't you jump in the water and do it? It's raining, Butler. Your timing is bad. Can you hold it?"

"I can't. I've had terrible cramps all morning. The moment has come."

"Ok, get it over with." Sim empties the bucket and sets it on one of the small cockpit cushions. She holds it while I climb to my knees on the wobbly floor. I live the most horrible hour in my life. Several times, I come close to a dead faint. Sim supports me throughout the ordeal. Never, ever, have I felt such excruciating pain. Tears roll down my cheeks. I collapse on my cushion thoroughly exhausted yet relieved. I hope I never have to go through that again. Totally drained and dizzy, I quickly fall asleep.

When I awaken, the weather has cleared. Sim has pumped as the raft is solid. In the middle afternoon, feeling much better, I fish and quickly catch our limit. I clean the first fish and throw the carcass as far as I can. The usual horde of trigger fish head for it, but they suddenly scramble and swim in the opposite direction. Then I see why. A great white shark with a head two feet in diameter swims casually up to the fish and gulps it in a flash.

I freeze. No wonder sharks haven't attacked the raft for two days. That great white has been under us all that time. I dare not mention a word to Sim and continue to clean the fish while I look over the side for any motion. The great white is no where in sight, but what do I do with the blood and fish juice? That great white has been casually munching on all those carcasses I've thrown over the last couple of days. I now don't dare throw any others over the side...or will it get stirred up if I cut off his snacks? Will it then snack on us? My Lord, what next? This is without a doubt our most dangerous moment so far. This unpredictable, wanton killer could turn on us at any moment...the end may be moments away...

I empty the bucket and dump the two filleted fish and all the juices in it. Sim wonders why I'm messing up the bucket, and I tell her it's because I plan to use the whole fish for bait. She looks at me with a skeptical look yet doesn't argue. I get the impression she'd rather not know.

I feed a rainbow runner to Sim, then divide the three triple tails. We end up stuffed with what may well be our last meal. While I fished and filleted, Sim dried the bedding and put order into our makeshift home. The foul weather gear came out from deep beneath us full of water. Each piece weighs close to twenty pounds. Also out and drying is her life jacket which has been out of sight for the past several weeks, buried under the cushions.

From one of its pockets, she removes the ziploc with our passports, cash, travellers checks, and credit cards. We normally travel light on cash and heavier in traveller's checks, but the situation in Panama, prompted us to go a little heavier in cash. On arrival in Panama we found there was little to buy except for the basics which were fairly inexpensive. In the Free Zone, we did find excellent French wine which now rests in 14,000 feet of water. Perhaps in 1000 years, a descendant of Cousteau will uncork it.

In the ziploc, we find the two thousand dollars in cash and three thousand in travellers checks are clean and dry. They all get a bit of sunshine before going back inside the pocket of the life jacket together with a set of family snapshots, passports, and American Express card. Can't get shipwrecked without one...

As night falls, the weather clears, seas abate, and the current increases. The wind blows gently from the southwest. I like the combination. This has all the portends of a fine evening except for that great white. What does it have on its Machiavellian mind? Is it waiting for some signal, a faint vibration, a sound, a smell...what? But then, it's been with us for two days and has only come close to feed. Let's hope it doesn't touch the raft. Otherwise...I dare not think further...WHAM!

The violent whack spins the raft. I bounce up like a coiled spring. Is it the great white? When I look out, I'm met with one of the happiest sights ever...the regular sharks are back...I would scream with joy except Sim would wonder what's going on. Pole in hand, I wait for the next pass. I can't see the shark, but I see its trail of phosphorescence as it swims by. I stab at it as it slides alongside the raft along with four or five similar shapes. The pack is back. I relax with a sense of immense relief. I know how to deal with this bunch. The great white has moved on.

Sharks batter the raft all night. A large turtle swims under the raft and stays with us. Neither of us sleep. Sim prays. In the more violent of the attacks, she holds her St. Michael's medal between her fingers and asks him to protect us, to free us from danger. At two in the morning, things quiet down, and she listens to the radio while I try to snooze.

We pump air more often. Intervals are down to an hour and a half. Where is the air leak? Could a seam be opening? That would be the definite beginning of the end. Once one seam goes, the others will soon fail too.

God have mercy. Please save us. I splash with my paddle. Sharks hit us whenever I stop. I splash without stop all night. At five, I give up, roll over, and sleep. Sim takes over.

When I open my eyes, daylight greets me. Sim's awake.

I throw her a kiss. "Bon jour. Any news this morning, madame? Ah, is the coffee ready?"

"Just a few headlines. Lawrence Olivier died. China says it will not have mercy for the ring leaders of the riots. The new President in Argentina says he's going to squeeze the Argentineans and their economy. Good luck to him. Bush is in Hungary. He gets around. That's it from the news room. And the coffee...those who sleep late in this pension miss breakfast."

At nine, the sharks begin their attack. Later a turtle swims by to check out Sim's attitude. She becomes frantic and strikes at it with all her energy ignoring my pleas to relax. She genuinely hates turtles and pokes at them whenever they're within range. The turtle swims out ten feet, turns around, looks up with those crude black ringed eyes, takes a breath, and heads back towards Sim.

The scene repeats itself again and again. I'm afraid Sim will have a real heart attack if she continues. Her honest aversion to turtles and her conviction that they will tear the raft apart are beyond reason. This same turtle has been pestering us for almost two weeks and has done no damage. "Sim. I'm going to fix the turtle so it'll go do something else."

Sim looks at me with a quizzical look: "What are you going to do?"

"Pass me your scissors. The big ones."

Sim has two pairs of large scissors and hands me the one with a long sharp blade. I wait for the turtle to swim to my side of the raft then nudge it closer with the pole as I gently turn the shell towards the raft so that its head, with the dreaded beak, faces away from us. That beak could easily cut the raft in two.

With its left front flipper in my left hand, I gently lift it up out of the water and away from the beak. I plunge the scissors deep into the turtle's neck with a twisting turning motion. The turtle reels and lunges at my hand with the ugly beak. I quickly release the flipper and pull out the scissors. With a violent splash, it swims away. Adios, you devil...we will not see him again.

Sim couldn't see what I was up to. "What did you do?"

"I gave it a scissor job. It won't be back."

"Poor thing. That's not fair. I don't want to hurt them, just scare them away." Maybe so, but this devil has left us forever. So I hope.

We put our sodden bedding out early today to take full advantage of the rare sunny weather. A day this clear is perfect for an air search. The planes should be out today, and we must keep an extra sharp lookout. If we see a plane, should we use the last flare or save it? Save it for what? If the great white returns, it may be too late. If the Coast Guard won't help, why don't the children find an airplane? The Bank will provide the money. Gus can be the Captain. But then, where should they look? We've been adrift four weeks. We're seven weeks out of Panama, forty-nine days, and if we hadn't sunk, we should have been approaching Hawaii. That's where they will search. They have a tough equation to solve before even getting airborne. We did talk to hams in California a few hours before we sank, but how would they locate them? Meanwhile we have been on the move; at three quarter knot, we've drifted nearly five hundred miles.

A waft from the bucket reminds me that it's time to deal with that stinking mess. I cut several pieces of bait, then dump the rotting lot over the side and wash the bucket. Triggers and sharks scramble for the scraps. The great white is nowhere in sight. My noontime fishing expedition is a bust, for I use up all my bait and catch nothing. The fishing cycle has again been broken. That was dumb of me. Why didn't I postpone fishing until the fish were biting? Or save more of the carcasses?

Sharks and turtles return. We recognize individual turtles by their color, size, and markings. One with a red splotch on its shell, probably from a collision with a freighter, has been with us for two weeks. Another has a broken shell. Today's turtle is new, caught in the same strong current that pushes us east. Each nudge takes us closer to a landfall still too far off to calculate. The light breeze from the south and a bright sun dry the bedding. As night sets in following a brilliant sunset, we catch sight of a filling moon, a sight that fills us with hope and dreams. Our family could be looking at this same moon at this same moment; if it were only possible to bounce a rescue signal off it to one of them and get some action...

The whack of a shark jolts me out of my musings. I grab the pole and look into uncountable tiny mirrors, each ripple reflecting moonlight like a giant fireworks display, ever changing but constant in its brilliance. I can see nothing beyond the surface of the ocean. The raft receives two more jolts. I paddle and turn the raft away from the moon, but I still can't see a thing. Four hard whacks follow. Moon, why are you doing this to us? You have always been good to us. How we've yearned to see you, and now we must pray clouds cover you, or else the sharks will surely destroy the raft.

The sharks leave us around two and we're allowed a short nap. When I turn, Sim listens to the radio. She calls to me: "Bill, radio reception is good. Shall we do it?" I had asked Sim to call when she picked up two or more strong stations that didn't fade out right away. Hopefully, we can locate the source of a radio signal by rotating the radio until the signal disappears.

I tell Sim: "Ok. You tune to the station and I'll do the fix."

She passes over the radio and earphones. "Here's Radio Sandina in Managua, Nicaragua."

I put on the earphones and turn the Walkman until I can no longer hear the broadcast. Sim, with the compass in one hand and the flashlight in the other, awaits my signal. I rotate the radio until the station disappears and place it over the compass.

"Thirty degrees," I call out. "Ok, Sim, get another station."

We repeat the process with a station in Costa Rica, which bears sixty degrees. Thirty degrees to Nicaragua and sixty to Costa Rica puts us many hundred miles off shore. We have probably traveled almost five hundred miles and have five or six hundred more to go. But we are moving in....first the sun, now the radio confirms it. We'll check these two stations again in a week.

The current holds steady all night. A brilliant day greets us when we awaken. It's Bastille Day, July 14. The sharks gave us a break last night, and we fell asleep seconds after their last whack. "Vive la France," I call out when I first notice Sim's eyes open.

"Thank you, dear," Sim says with a faraway smile. "Wouldn't it be wonderful to be in Paris today? We could have stayed with my relatives. It's nine here, so in Paris, it's three in the afternoon. The parade must have ended. I heard Bush and Gorbachev and dozens of other fat bananas are there."

"Wow, we could have been on the Champs d'Elysees with the bands and all the people. This is the party of the Century."

"Yes, and here I am, stuck with you out in the middle of nowhere. Not really that bad a place were it not for all those sharks and turtles. It's good that I love you...otherwise I would only have two choices: kill you or myself."

"It's good that I love you, or you would be out there swimming after all those nasty things you've said. Vive la France. Look what I have for the party."

"A Heineken. Where did you find it?" Sim is semi-shocked. As stowmaster, how did this item slip through her inquisitive eyes?

"Zee skeeper has zee private stock. Except that's it for this jaunt." I had kept it hidden under my head inside an old stinky sweatshirt bought in Balboa. The can has started to corrode and would not have lasted much longer. I offer Sim the first sip. Two sips later and we're both high. Tipsy, we delve into the events that led up to the storming of the Bastille and of all the momentous events that soon followed. Simonne sings the "Marseillaise" twice, and amid shouts of "Vive la France", our celebration ends.

The beer can quickly empties, and we break out a saltine each for lunch. I drink a large glass of saltwater, then wash the nasty taste out with a gulp of fresh water and a cracker crumb. This is our second day without fish. I will snag the next bird that comes close whether Sim squawks or not. Two days ago, when a small booby perched on the canopy, I moved my hand slowly towards it until I touched the web of its feet. I will first grab the feet of the next bird that comes along, then quickly put a hand around its neck to keep the long hooked beak from cutting into me.

Then I'll either stretch its neck or twirl it. Our Spanish cook at our home in Cuba twirled them over her head. Seconds later, the chicken was dead and simmering in boiling water to loosen its feathers. I will twirl the bird I catch, then cut off its neck with my knife. I can already hear Simonne's horrified squawks. Am I up to it? We can afford to wait a couple of days but not longer. Besides Sim will let out a double squawk if I eat one of her bird friends on Bastille Day.

At noon, we enter a trash line, usually a sign that land is not far off. Could there be a river nearby that empties into the ocean? The line runs north and south which we traverse on our easterly drift once again confirming the wind does push us along. We cross pieces of colored plastic, leaves, and small pieces of wood. When Sim spots a larger object ten feet from the raft, we row towards it and find it's a pumice stone, three inches long by two wide and one inch thick. It has little stones imbedded all through it and is so strange that we keep it. If this is truly a land-borne trash line, then we're a lot closer to land than the radio signals indicate. On the other hand, it could be munched up ship trash. But the pumice stone...where did it come from?

Simonne picks up faint radio signals in the late afternoon. Though she can't make out words, for it's more like a rumble, she has no doubts it is a shore station. When she first listened four weeks ago, she heard absolutely nothing until midnight. AM radio waves have a range of 100 to 200 miles, depending on the power of the station. When we cruised the Bahamas, we lost all of the Florida stations when we were one hundred miles out. As we get closer to shore, she should pick up stations earlier in the day...and if she doesn't...we'll know we've drifted into the westerly current....

We make two liters of water, skip supper entirely, and await nightfall and the arrival of sharks. Whoever is the timekeeper in shark country never fails to signal. At ten PM sharp, the attacks begin. A light cloud cover helps block the moon, but there is still enough light coming through to keep me from seeing our nemesis. The sharks are particularly vicious tonight and strike the raft with machine gun precision.

I plunge the fishing rod into the water while lying on my back. As a precaution against losing it, I've tied a six foot length of cord from the pole to my wrist. I hear the midnight chirp on my watch as I fight off an urgent urge to sleep. I never stop moving the pole in and out of the water, for the splashes do keep away all sharks except the bad ones. Sim prays all the while.

Once, before I tied the pole, I'd fallen asleep with the heavy end on my chest. When I moved in my sleep, Sim caught the pole as it started to go over the side. Now I keep the pole tied all the time which creates a problem when Sim needs it in a rush to beat off a turtle. What would we do if we lost our first line of defense against sharks and turtles? Besides the pole is part of my fishing gear. We could never survive on drinking water only for long.

Sim prays, rosary in her hand, eyes fixed on the canopy, face tired and forlorn. Our hands still joined, I pull her towards me to give her a kiss. We hold each other for the longest time. Today is day 31 aboard "Last Chance," Day 53 out of Balboa, and Day 34 since our last radio contact with land. Is no one searching for us? Does no one care? On the other hand, we alone got ourselves into this mess, and alone we will find a way out. No one will come looking for us. If they do, they'll never find us. We're invisible.

We share a cracker for breakfast. Then while it's still cool, we make two liters of water. Sim has the morning report: "Bush and Gorby enjoyed the party in Paris. There's a Soviet Sub on fire off Norway. Do you think the kids will make a connection? Probably not. Leona Helmsley is in deep trouble with the tax people. Her trial's going on in New York....the world goes on without the least concern over our fate. We are so insignificant. Why should anyone worry?" Of course, if Trump or Michael Jackson had vanished, it would be another story.

"Forty days," continues Sim, "Our punishment is forty days. At that time, God will send someone to save us. Moses went up the mountain for forty days, and Jesus stayed forty days in the desert. We have forty days of Lent and the Moslems have Ramadan. Yes," she says with a distant look, "We must wait for the fortieth day to pass. You'll see."

"Sim, I think you're right. C'mon, cheer up. Let's celebrate our anniversary; can you believe you've been in this waterbed with your lover for an entire month? Isn't that the greatest? You always wanted a long honeymoon."

"What honeymoon are you talking about?...with sharks and turtles and a shaggy, fish smelling raft mate? It's been a little crowded. But really, one month? How much longer will the raft hold together?"

"The raft will last until we reach shore or someone finds us. If no one saves us, we'll save ourselves. We've travelled at least five hundred miles so far. Another few more, and we're home. Let's eat a can today," I continue. "It's almost Sunday and an important milestone. Not too many people drift around the Pacific Ocean or, for that matter, any ocean for a month."

Sim digs under the bunched comforter that makes up her head rest and comes up with a small can. She hands me the bent can opener which I force back into shape. It doesn't quite remove the lid, and I need to use the knife to pry it off. Simonne takes the handle of the toothbrush and ladles a white paste into my mouth. My spirits light up with the first bite. It turns out to be cream of mushroom soup. We savor each tiny morsel until we finish half of the can. It takes all of our self control to stop and leave half for supper.

With our hunger partially satisfied, we play a game of dominoes. I win. When we tire of that, we play twenty questions while the afternoon slowly dwindles away. I stump Sim with the castle in Disney World, and she gets me with the Miraflores locks of the Panama Canal. We stop playing when rain water leaks through the canopy and the wind increases to more than twenty knots. Thirty foot swells roll under us like express trains. Six foot breakers ride their tops and wash completely over the raft. We hang on for dear life in our seaworthy little craft. Before night sets in, we finish the mushroom soup, pray, and prepare for the night.

By the time midnight comes around, we have seen everything: sharks, turtles, rain, wind, and huge breaking waves. On the plus side, we have a strong current. The weather is out of the southwest and isn't improving or changing. Sim now prays for high wind and waves like I do as she realizes we need speed to reach land

and safety.

Time is our enemy. Every day that passes increases the chances for disaster. I haven't mentioned a word to Sim we're in the wrong raft. She still thinks we're in a "top of the line" life saving device...

"Bill! What was that? Quick! Look!"

I try to open my eyes, but they're glued shut. I pick at the hardened ooze and work my eyes open. I'm in a daze. In fact, I have been dreaming, unusual for me. "What's going on, Sim?"

"Something is in the raft. It flew in the window. Here, it's over here. Take the flashlight."

I switch on the flashlight and feel around. My hands tighten around something slippery and long. "It's a flying fish, Sim. We've got bait for tomorrow." It could also make delicious ceviche. On the *Siboney*, we always had three or four on deck in the morning. We scaled and cleaned them and marinated them in lime juice. "You've never tasted anything as good as flying fish ceviche." I tell Sim. "Pass the lime juice, I'll show you."

"I hope a dorado doesn't decide to jump in," she exclaims. "It would tear the raft apart." Dorados spring ten feet into the air and, when they land, give the ocean a mighty slap.

I put the flying fish into the bait can and turn back to Sim. "Do want to hear my dream?" Sim nods, and I recount my dream:

"We are on a raft much like this one. It's a clear blue day. When I look out, I notice we're in Biscayne Bay. It's Sunday morning, and the Bay is full of boats of all sizes. Sailboats and powerboats pass close by. People on board wave at us but keep going. I can't imagine why they don't stop. We wave and yell, but it doesn't do any good. They can't hear us.

"Several boats from Matheson Hammock Marina motor up and stop. Our friends say hello. We chat for a while and they drive off. I don't know what to think. They act as if our floating around the Bay in a worn out raft is normal. Shortly all the boats leave, and we are again alone.

"And that's the dream."

Sim nods. "I had a Biscayne Bay dream myself several nights ago. It took me hours to fall asleep that night. It always does. I couldn't find a comfortable position. While I tried to sleep, I prayed to God to save us. I thought of my babies. I cried and drove myself into a complete mental mess. All the while, you were snoring. Finally, I got so tired that I fell asleep and dreamt. I still don't know what to make of it. It was so vivid and in full color."

She has me curious.

"I was on a boat. *Siboney*? No. It was, but it wasn't. I was on Biscayne Bay, in Miami, near the Rusty Pelican restaurant. I can see land. Then, suddenly, it's not the Bay anymore. I am on the high seas. Where? I don't know. The water is dark green.

"A strange looking boat comes our way. It looks like a square houseboat. As it passes, I notice it's black and has large windows, like a house. I can see furniture inside. On the roof of the houseboat sits a man. A large man, like a Viking. He has a red beard and a wide fur hat. He looks wild. I hear a voice say, "This is der Schwarze Ole," which in German means black.

"The man sits with his booted legs over the side; his right elbow touches his right knee. He looks down at us but does nothing. The boat passes. We scream and call. The boat doesn't stop.

"We see several other houseboats coming, like a procession. The first is English; I can see inside. There is a fireplace and flowered sofas. A white haired mother and an older son are having tea; they chat with each other, oblivious of us. There is no time to call. They continue on their way and disappear.

"Another houseboat approaches. This one is French. I hear voices; I see people. Children are laughing. A piano plays and food is on a table. It too vanishes.

"Then comes the last house boat. It has a German flag. This time, I can see inside a large rustic room. Five little girls are there, sisters, all dressed with pretty flowered dresses. Blond tresses hang from their heads. The father sits on stairs that come from above. He has a little nursery rhyme written on a banner in German. It says something about his five little daughters and how proud he is of them. There is much joy and happiness. This houseboat also leaves, and again everything is quiet and empty. The water is dark and green. I am alone and I wake up."

I shake my head. "That's a first class dream. It's strange that we both had dreams involving Biscayne Bay. Will we ever see it again?"

Sim is earnest. "There's a message there. In my dream, four boats passed us. The first was Scandinavian, the next English, then a French, and the last German. They all flew flags, but none of them saw us. On the raft, a Norwegian ship passed by on the second day; an English ship passed us a week ago. Two more ships, a French and a German will pass by, but none will see us."

She continues dreamily. "The second houseboat had the man singing a nursery rhyme in German. I'll hum it for you. I used to sing it to my Cris when we lived in Germany. It's so soothing, optimistic, loving, so consoling. God sent me this dream to lift up my heart, to give me hope." Tears stream down her cheeks while Sim hums the tune.

A thundering wave drowns out her last few notes. Another great mass of black water capped by deep froth collides with our fragile vessel. The windward side of the raft collapses from the weight of the water. Sim bails madly. Will we live to see another dawn?

chapter ten

0830 JULY 17, 1989, DAY 33

The storm raged throughout the night. Bolts of lightning highlighted towering breakers that attempted to overwhelm our battered raft. In the midst of the maelstrom, sharks and turtles located the raft and attacked without letup. Our black, water-filled world was a scene from hell. Salt and rain water mingled to find and soak our last shreds of dryness. Air loss increased under the harsh punishment. We pumped and bailed in a mad struggle to keep the raft afloat, ever ready for the unexpected and the expected...sudden death from either bolt of fire, rogue wave, or wild predator.

A hellish roar and a rendering smash carry the raft into the chasm of a trough. "Last Chance," on its beam's end, threatens to flip. Instinctively, I lean heavily on the high side and pull Simonne over with me. The sea passes over us while bucketfuls of sea water burst into the raft. We hang on as the wave spends its energy and speeds on, oblivious to the bobbing bit of plastic in its way. The raft slides down into the abyss made by the escaping wave and then rises to face the next onslaught. That would have been a wet wave even for *Siboney*, my dear *Siboney*, which now rests forever in her cold, black, wet grave. We sailed together through rough weather and calm seas. My sons even sank you three times, and you popped back up, stronger than before. You have a long history and now you are gone.

Dawn catches me by surprise. The raft is soft which means Sim slept too, an unusual event, and that the sharks left, also unusual. When she dozes, I do my best to stay awake to keep sharks and turtles away, but she's had terrible luck with that. No sooner does Sim drop into a deep sleep than a shark slaps the raft with the force of a freight train. Instantly, she's up, terrified, and unable to snooze for another half day.

The morning, though heavy with rain, is more welcome than a bright, sunny day back home. We open the leeward window to escape in a some small way the confinement of our miniscule habitat. Dull gray seas sweep underneath and speed away. We follow each as they roll down wind and long to speed with them to their inevitable collision with land.

We start a new week this Monday, July 17, our thirty-third day on the raft, half way into our fifth week. That we are still alive and healthy is a constant source of amazement to us. Sim's lost 30 pounds, most of it excess fat. Anyway, we've talked about losing a few pounds for years. I wrap my hand around my upper leg...my thumbs completely overlap...weeks ago they barely touched. Most surprising, we haven't had a cold or infection of any kind. Where are the customary boils of the castaway?

We have a dozen and a half crackers left and one rusty can with who knows what in it. If it's more of that diet Veg-all, over it goes. I will use the flying fish today as bait.

Noon brings calmer weather as seas subside and skies clear. In the distance, a school of fish jump out of the water and leave a wide froth on the sea. I put out my line with a piece of the flying fish as bait and get no takers. There are no fish anywhere near the raft, so I stow the fishing gear. Together we make two liters of water, eat a cracker each, and then start to nap. A loud splash and the sound of heavy breathing startles us.

Sim jumps up and calls out: "Dolphins." Several circle as one of them slides under the raft. It's three times as big as the Flipper variety, and they're grey with light spots all over. Let's hope they chase the sharks away as legend has it. Dozens of small fish leap out of the water to escape their fast moving jaws. Frenzied trigger fish jump wildly while the dolphins plunge from school to school to feed. I continue to watch the activity out of my window as Sim tries to rest.

School fish dart desperately over the ocean in search of safety. They dive under our raft with the dolphins in hot pursuit. The water surrounding the raft boils as the dolphins come up for a brief breath and dive again with a violent kick of their tail. Hundreds of fish bump the raft as they try to escape. A white froth surrounds us as the trigger fish leap out of the water. They're so close and so many. Can I snatch one?

I put on my gloves and empty the contents from the pail. Sim has her back to me and appears to be half asleep. A fish almost jumps into the raft. I lean over and grab at one of the black shapes, but it wiggles away, too slippery to hold. On my second try, I wrap my hand firmly around a fish and lift it into the raft. It's black with a tiny mouth. I drop it into the pail. In seconds, I put three more fish in the bucket. One jumps out and onto Sim's feet.

Sim jumps up with a: "What's that?"

"A fish. I've been fishing. I caught three fish."

"You used the flying fish?"

"Madame, watch my hands. Faster than the eye." In minutes, I plop three more fish into the pail, now almost full.

"You're fabulous. Oh, I love you. I'm so happy." Tears stream down her cheeks. "What are they?"

"Trigger fish. Not the best eating although they are a delicacy in the Bahamas and in some of the Caribbean Islands." From the looks of it, we have an unlimited supply. They are like piranhas and will bite at anything including cloth and, of course, human flesh. Their skin is tough as leather. "I hope this dull knife will cut through their hide," I say to Sim. "Dig out your nail file, and I'll sharpen the knife before I begin."

I set up the camcorder case on the paddle as my filleting board and press hard to saw through the hide of the first fish. I open it all the way around and remove the filet complete with hide. I do the same with the second filet and toss the carcass far from the raft. Dozens of its school mates quickly remove all the remaining flesh. As it drops deeper, the dull grey shape of a shark moves in and gulps what's left. I remove the filet from the skin and toss the skin over the side. Fish again scramble. I cut the filet into half inch cubes and offer Sim the first piece. She savors it and declares it not too bad. We finish seven filets and leave the rest for bait. Stuffed for the first time in days, I pass Sim the water bottle, then retire, my day's work done.

Rain starts before midnight with a violent squall from the east. It kills the last of the west wind and pushes us away from land at an alarming rate. The current is light, the raft swings, and not far away, Sim hears a whale blow. This thirty third day has been full of surprises. On to day thirty four. Oh, dear Lord, be kind...have mercy....

We awaken abruptly at eight in the morning to a dozen quick whacks. A large pack of greenish grey sharks attack the raft from all directions, their big bulging eyes full of mischief. I land my first hit on a five footer, then bonk three more in a row. Left behind is their unmistakable oily wake.

"Sim, I can't believe what I'm seeing. Look. Two of the sharks have tags. One has a round white tag, and the other tag is long and red."

Sim's reaction is immediate: "I'd like to meet the son of a gun who tagged them instead of blasting them to pieces. That's criminal. To be eaten by a tagged shark. Who would ever believe it!"

"The sadists probably recapture them to check their stomachs. Oh, look here..this one has a French Passport and blonde hair...."

"Stop joking and beat them off. They're going to destroy the raft before too long. How many in the pack?"

"They're hard to count, but there are at least twenty, and they are all about the same size. Did you know that from birth sharks pack together in groups according to age? Otherwise, the bigger ones end up eating the little ones."

"Butler, you are the great living encyclopedia. Anything else, Cousteau? Answer the big question. Why do they continue to attack the raft? You say to spray, but why? I'm not sure I buy that."

"There's not much floating in this part of the ocean. These sharks must be males intent on leaving their mark. Many animals do the same. Even humans mark although we are a bit more subtle."

Their attack pattern is always the same; they turn belly up as they come abreast of the raft, then run their belly along the side and spray. At the last moment, they instinctively whip their tail, possibly to spread their oils. I stab at every shark that approaches within reach. If I hit one behind the eyes, it flips its tail with a splash, then circles five to ten feet below the raft. Sometimes it comes up for another poke, but usually it stays deep only to be replaced by a more adventurous brother. After an hour, the pack leaves as quickly as it arrived. I don't get a chance to settle back down when a loud breath announces the arrival of a turtle.

As it heads straight in, I pass the pole to Sim. "Your turn, sweety. Turtle ahoy on the starboard bow."

The sea boils with trigger fish as I prepare to fish. They await my next cast, their gurgling mouths spitting water, their black beady eyes on my every move. When my bait but touches the water, dozens of trigger fish leap for it. Before they grab the bait, I jerk it up and drop it ten feet away. The triggers rush to the new spot. Before they arrive, I jerk up my hook and drop it in the original place. Much of the time, I lose my bait to a trigger fish that leaps out of the water and sucks the bait right off the hook. The trigger fish have small, hard mouths that are solid teeth. Wide open, the mouth of an average size trigger is no more than the size of a dime. When it strikes a bait, it either sucks it in fast or grabs a piece of the bait with its teeth and pulls it off the hook. When a triple tail is in range, I drop the bait right on its nose. More often than not, the triple tail spooks, and a trigger steals the bait in an event that lasts no more than a second.

Before I lose all of my day old, mushy bait, I put on my gloves and quickly catch three triggers. With fresh bait, I cast back and forth again to lure the shy triple tails closer. One swims in. When I drop the bait on top of it, it strikes and, with a hard jerk, runs off with my line. I pull the line taught and in seconds board a two pound triple tail. Two more triple tails quickly follow, one a monster of five pounds that barely fits in the bucket.

I drop the next bait over the side and, without noticing, let out too much line. Quickly I feel a tug and I return with a hard pull. The line tightens. Sim grabs the pole and pulls the extra line up to the eye. She holds the pole out from the side and takes line in as I haul. I look down and freeze. It's a big bull dorado, at least a forty pounder. Sim holds the pole far away from the raft while I arrange the sail bag to cover the air chamber and my lap. We prepare for the inevitable fight for which dolphins are well known.

I pull on the line and Sim takes it up. Surprisingly, the dorado isn't fighting. We don't really need this fish, for we have more than enough food for today. Perhaps I can get my hook back and release it. I ease the line, in hopes it'll jump and spit out the hook. I pull on the line until the fish is inches below the surface. I can see it clearly: big blue, silvery yellow, and strong. Why doesn't it battle for its life? My mouth waters. Since we left Panama, I've hungered for dorado.

"Ok, Sim. Here it comes. I'll lift it onto my lap. You drop the pole and cover it with the sail bag. We've got to keep it off from the side of the raft at all costs. Ready? Now!"

I heave, and the dorado is on my lap and covered by the sail bag in less than a second. We put our weight on it and look at each other with amazement. It can't escape now. We laugh and shout. Sim passes me the knife, and I stab the beautiful animal a dozen times about the head. It quivers and dies seconds later. Its shimmering colors turn to a dull blue at the moment of death.

We look at each other speechless, unable to believe what we have done. This bull dorado weighs at least forty five if not fifty pounds. Two castaways landed it on a flimsy raft in the middle of the Pacific Ocean. This has to be a record of some kind. And it'll stand forever because no one else will ever do anything this crazy again. With three triple tails and now this dorado, we have far over fifty pounds of fish on board.

"I'm starving for dorado so I'll filet it first," I announce. "First, get the camera and take a picture of the big fisherman." I push up against one end of the raft with the dorado lengthwise in one hand and the five pound triple tail in the other. Sim pushes herself up against the other end of the raft and snaps.

I slice a filet from the tail, cut it into small chunks, and promptly pop a chunk into my mouth. The meat is mushy, not like the usual dorado, and the taste is strange. I try a piece and hand some to Sim, who gags.

I ask: "What's wrong?"

"That fish is bad. Feel the texture; it's not firm like dorado meat. And it tastes funny. Bill, that fish is bad. It's sick."

I cut a piece towards the head, and the meat there is also bad. It appears to be old and tastes rotten. This dorado had to be on the verge of dying when I caught it. It was unable to compete for food and hit my tiny piece of bait. I recover my hook from deep inside its stomach which means I would have had to kill it anyway. I drop the dorado over the side where it sinks like a brick.

I prepare the big triple tail and make Sim eat a few bites, but the rotten dolphin meat has killed our appetite. When we're finished, over half of our food remains. Why did I ever go for that last cast?

Evening is upon us. Sim reads as wind and waves again pick up, and by the time night falls, a good breeze blows out of the southwest. Waves build. Great. Let it blow.

I look over at Sim: "Are you awake?"

"Awake. You're a real comedian, or do you think my name is Bill Butler? I pray this terrible wind and big waves stop. I can't take it any longer. Some of those waves bash the raft harder than a shark. How much more punishment can this raft take?"

"Only five days to forty," I remind her. "I hope that little voice called it right. I'm ready to bail out."

"Speaking of bailing, give me a hand. Move your behind and hold this cushion up so I can get to the water." Sim bails strenuously. When I push down on the floor to make a sump, trigger fish bite my hand through the fabric. Water drains from the bedding and foul weather gear to fill the sump.

We begin our sixth week wet and despondent. There is no wind and no current. We have seen no planes, no ships, no birds, and no land. Sharks batter us, and turtles try their best to mate with the raft. The raft has lost much of its integrity. We pump air every 45 minutes to keep the air chambers from bending in half.

"Bill. A terrible thing happened last night. A United jet crashed in Sioux City, and there are a lot of dead. That's terrible. Think of all the poor people who died. Horrible, horrible. Just before the plane crashed, they were all praying in the cabin, no doubt like us, pleading with God to be saved."

"And we're still alive. I can remember back to our first day or two on the raft when you worried about staying afloat for a week. Here we are, after five full weeks, doing not all that badly."

"You are a zombie. We're drenched to our bones in a rotten, leaky raft lost in the Pacific, battered constantly by wind, waves, and sharks. Butler, wake up, our situation is critical."

Sim's negative attitude depresses her and bothers me: "We're alive, kid. There are a lot of good people in Sioux City who aren't. Let's thank God for taking care of us as well as He has. Think positive. We're going to live; we're going to make it...perhaps not in the next few days, but we'll make it. God will help us if we help ourselves and maintain our faith in Him." Sim, rosary clutched, prays. Her focus is far off. Tears stream from her tired eyes.

Thoughts of her mother and children plague her, so sure she is that she will not again see them. I find nothing to say of comfort. Sometimes silence is the best therapy.

Late in the morning when the rain stops, we put the bedding out to dry. The sea continues to flatten, and the sun makes an earnest try to shine through several layers of clouds. Our spirits improve. At one, I fish, and I catch two trigger fish, and with fresh bait, I quickly land two triple tails. The second triple tail pulls loose of the hook and jumps around loose until Sim pins it with a cushion. The hook isn't on the line and has to be lost. Later, when I filet the triple tail and cut its stomach open, I find our only hook deep inside surrounded by a gullet full of small fish. What luck. What would I have done if I lost my only hook? I can't count on catching too many fish by hand.

We eat until we're stuffed, pump up the raft, then snooze. Later Sim reads; we finish the triple tail and fall into Sim's favorite subject and one I try to avoid: our excellent chance of dying. I can't argue with her, for most of Sim's points are valid. We've defied the odds this far. Will our luck continue?

It's better than for many in the Sioux City crash. Many good, God loving people aboard that airplane died while we continue to live in an environment thousands of times more perilous than the one in which they lived until those last few seconds. Like an air crash, when we go, will it be all over in seconds? We are being allowed to live but for how long? Another week? Another month? We must continue to pray to the Lord for help and His mercy. I see no other way out.

The current picks up speed during the night and pushes us to the southeast. When the current is strong, the raft defies the wind and waves and lines up with the current. The long side of the raft points in the direction we move. When the current lessens, the raft will swing through twenty, thirty, and up to ninety degrees to either side of our course. With no current, the raft drifts perpendicular to the wind. With these daily observations, I plot our daily dead reckoning position. How close am I?

"Preparing for night" is part of our established evening routine. Sim puts the flashlight, flare, compass, and radio next to her head. I tie the air pump next to the valve. Our eye glasses and watches dangle from pieces of fishing line above us. The pole rests lengthwise next to me ready for instant use. We each have a paddle close at hand. A bottle full of water lies next to my hip ready for the night's consumption. Sim reads just before last light.

When morning dawns, we find the boobies have left us for good this time. Storm petrels weave their nervous way inches over the waves in search of an unwary baby flying fish. Above two frigate birds soar, observing, waiting, hoping. Today is Alex's eighteenth birthday. Simonne has been on a guilt trip...I shouldn't have left him alone to face the rigors of the world...I'm missing this most important of birthdays...what is my poor baby doing? I hope he's not alone...I'm a terrible mother...

"Happy birthday, Sim. Let's celebrate." We sing "Happy Birthday" while tears roll down Simonne's cheeks. We top our party off with a drop of brandy each. There is still a half inch left in the bottle, and we've been nipping on it for a month.

Sim saddens: "My poor baby, I wonder what he's doing all alone. I hope some of our friends invite him over. He's probably lonely and worried to death over the fate of his mother. I hope his father called from Spain and his brother invited him out to dinner or something. Poor baby, how could I have abandoned him? I am the cruelest of mothers, leaving a young baby alone like that."

"Baby, he's bigger than I am and better able to handle himself than most twenty five year olds. This is doing him a lot of good. Away from you, he'll learn fast how to solve his own problems. You mother him too much. When you see him next, he's going to be responsible and mature."

"When I see him next? Will I ever see him again? Don't you understand, we're not going to make it."

"You're dead wrong. We've been adrift thirty eight days. If that voice you heard is right, we have but two days to go. Our test is about to end. God isn't keeping us alive only to let us die. He teaches and waits for us to find how we should live the rest of our lives."

Sim nods: "You're right. I should have more faith."

I try for a change of mood: "Let's have a little game of dominoes to celebrate. Shall we play games?"

I find it easier to sit up now that I've lost my paunch. Before we start, Sim washes my back with fresh water and spreads cream on the worst of the open sores.

After mid-morning, a heavy black cloud out of the east develops into a full fledged squall. This new dimension further confuses the waves and kills what little wind was starting to build from the south. With no current and an easterly wind, we'll soon be back where we sank. Oh, dear Lord, have mercy on us.

The squall lasts less than an hour, and as the sun struggles to reappear, I hand catch two trigger fish for bait. Then I land a large triple tail and stop, not wishing to load the raft with fish we can't eat. I put it directly onto my filleting board and quickly remove both filets. The top of the camcorder case, full of blood and insides, spills over onto my crotch before I can empty it over the side. There's everything in it now...blood, scales, pieces of fish. Sim picks scales off my belly, legs, and bottom. How I dream for a dip in the ocean. The trigger fish would skin me within seconds.

A light southwest wind starts to build in the middle afternoon. The current returns, skies clear, and the sun shines. That it shines as well on two infatuated turtles makes the day less than perfect. Under, around, out, and back again, the male chases the female; the female tries by every means to remain chaste; he does his best to keep the ocean full of baby turtles. Sim gets terribly worked up. She says words in Italian that sound highly improper. I lay back and hope I'm not next on her hit list.

The day is bright and clear, and as I scan the horizon, I study the makeup of a string of white clouds to the east; "Sim, look, there, to the east," I point. "See those clouds, the ones that go straight up. Those are land clouds. Heat generated on land funnels moisture up and forms that type of cumulus. A cloud that hovers and does not move down wind is indicative of land. Often it hangs downwind from the center of the island. Keep your eyes open."

The cloud does not move. We watch it with hope in our hearts and a prayer on our lips. Land...never have I yearned for land more than I do now. Land, with people and green trees and birds singing and gardens with flowers.

Sim's thoughts go back to our garden at home, our now empty house, the palm tree growing by the canal, of the cardinals at the feeder, and of her young son just turned eighteen, alone in the world....

MIAMI, FLORIDA
2315 TUESDAY JULY 18 1989

The Butler residence, empty of all furniture, rocks to the sound of a live band and over a hundred screaming teenagers. Alex is celebrating his eighteenth birthday. Mom and Bill are far away on their dream trip, sailing around the world.

Alex invited forty of his close friends to a full-blown birthday bash. These friends in turn invited their friends. Each paid $3.00 to get in. Alex planned to have a good time and end up with money in his pocket to finance the balance of his summer vacation.

Haphazardly parked cars line the streets leading to the Butler home for two blocks in every direction. The quiet residential neighborhood has never seen so much activity. One of the boys parks his car inside a neighbor's driveway. The neighbor threatens him with a shotgun. Another neighbor notices the scene and calls the police. Minutes later, several cars full of skin heads pull up and crash the party.

The Dade County Swat Team sends in their full resources in reply to the phone alarm. They surround the house while a police helicopter hovers overhead. Their searchlight lights up the scene. The police enter the house only to find nothing out of order. Outside the crazies have other ideas. The police decide to stop the party, and the children quickly disperse. Alex's eighteenth birthday party is over.

0700 WEDNESDAY JULY 19 1989, DAY 35
ABOARD THE RAFT "LAST CHANCE"

I'm so relieved the trauma of Alex's eighteenth birthday is behind us. Sim's been next to impossible to live with. What that kid needs is a chance to fly on his own.

Our night passes quietly. Dawn brings us a beautiful day, our thirty ninth adrift. Tomorrow is day forty. I hope the voice Sim heard was right about being saved in forty days.

This is perfect weather for drying. We drape our bedding over the canopy, one corner at a time. We dry each edge, careful it doesn't fly into the briny. By mid afternoon, all the bedding is back in place and enjoyably dry. Sim rearranges our stores, and we lie back to enjoy the fine weather, the peace, and our dry bed.

It's peaceful except for a nagging, whistling sound. Air escapes from the patch I fitted on our first day on the raft. Whenever a wave washes over it, water covers the leak and makes it whistle. Air leaks faster than a week ago. Sim's remark earlier today of, "I don't like the sound of that leak" started me thinking.

In fact, I've wanted to check the patch for several days. Sooner or later, I will have to adjust the two patches to reduce air loss. The repair would have to be done on a calm day, such as this. Why not try to fix it now? We have an hour or two of light remaining. Sim will not want me to touch the patches. I'll have to convince her a step at a time.

"Sim, I think I'll take a look at the patches."

"What do you plan to do?"

"Just look at them!"

She looks into my eyes: "You're not going to take them apart?"

"No, never. I just want see if there is anything loose."

"You shouldn't do it."

"I'm only going to make sure everything is OK."

"I am not sure."

"Look, it's losing more and more air, and unless we do something, we are going to end up pumping air every few minutes."

"See, I knew it. You want to fix it. Bill, you're not going to take the patch apart; that's final."

"I wouldn't do anything without telling you. I'll just check to see if they're loose, that's all."

"I don't know. Let's think about it."

"It'll be days before we get a calm day like this again. I should take a look at it now."

"Let me think about it."

"Holy mackerel, think about it. It'll be dark; the weather will pick up, and we'll be pumping every ten minutes. Ok, think about it. But get ready to pump."

"Do you promise not to take anything apart?"

"I said I am only going to take a look at the patch to see how it's holding. If the wing nuts are loose, I'll tighten them. If we wait any longer, it'll be dark, and we may as well forget it."

"How are you going to do it?"

"First, we have to let the air out of the arch facing the patch."

"Let the air out of the arch? I don't like it."

"Don't worry. I'll let out only enough so I can lean over and reach the patch. It'll just take a minute."

"OK, but be careful. And no crazy things."

"Relax, baby. In a few minutes, I'll have it fixed."

We haven't taken air out of the arch or, for that matter, put any in since we first filled it after we sank. It has held air perfectly, a constant reminder how easy our life would be had we not torn the raft when leaving *Siboney*.

"Sim, let's go. Let some air out of the arch."

Sim unscrews the air valve and air slowly whistles out. She closes the valve, then reopens it to allow more air to escape. I can tell she is worried.

"Ok, Sim, that's good. Let me see if I can get to it."

I turn on my knees and lean over the arch and canopy. I reach the patches easily. Each patch is an oval disk, about an inch and a half by three inches, made up of two parts. The part that goes inside the tube has a rubber gasket and a screw stem. The other half fits outside the tube and fits against the rubber gasket. A wing nut runs down on the screw stem and, when tightened, seals the patch.

Both wing nuts are tight.

"Bill, what are you doing?"

"Checking the wing nuts."

"You promised not to do anything!"

"Don't worry. I'm just looking at it to make sure it's tight."

As the original hole was too large for one patch, I aligned the two side by side. Air escapes from the space between the two. Three weeks ago, I dismantled the inboard patch and moved it closer to the other patch. While the patch was off, the emergency internal sleeve had kept us buoyant. The adjustment had worked.

Sim is anxious. "Bill, what are you doing?"

"I'm making sure the patch is tight. They are slightly apart. The plastic I put in last time isn't doing the job. That's where the leak is."

"Bill, don't take it apart!"

"Hey, don't worry, have patience."

I jostle the inboard patch. It would leak less if both patches were closer. I need to loosen it.

"Bill, how is it?"

"Fine. Just a few more seconds."

I loosen the wing nut one turn, but the patch is still too tight to move. I turn the nut another half turn. It's still too tight. I ease it again. Then a bit more.

"What are you doing?"

"Relax. I'm just checking the patch."

"What do you mean? Don't you dare to take the patches apart. Promise."

"No problem. I'll be finished in a minute."

I loosen the wing nut another partial turn. Without warning, the wing nut flies off with the top of the patch right behind it. There's a sudden rush of air, and the raft collapses. The air chamber becomes limp and sinks. I stare momentarily at the gaping hole and the three pieces of the patch in my hand.

Sim screams: "What's happening? My God! My God! We're sinking! What have you done?"

"The patch came apart. Pump! Fast!"

Sim had plugged the pump in as a precaution and dives for it as she prays loudly: "Holy Mary, Mother of God. Save us!"

My knees push the floor of the raft deeper, but I have nowhere to move. The air chamber is now an empty piece of limp plastic. Half of the patch is inside the air chamber, but the rubber gasket has slipped off. My knees push the floor deeper, and water pours over the side.

Sim, under the collapsed arch, pumps furiously and prays aloud in French. I take the patch out of the hole and reseat the gasket. Water rises over my feet. The hole starts to go under. I pull the tube up and insert the patch with my left hand. Water fills the raft. Within seconds, the raft will sink from under us.

I fit the inside half against the other patch and put the top half on. Luckily, the parts are on a wire welded to the end of the screw. I can't lose them. Water reaches my waist. Sim treads water, still pumping. I hoist the corner with the patch to keep the air chamber from filling with water.

Sim, submerged, cries aloud: "My God. We're sinking! Oh, Lord save us."

"Sim, relax. Pump! Don't stop! Don't harass me."

"Are you crazy? We're sinking. What have you done? Oh, Lord, have mercy on us!" She pleads with God in French.

"Sim, don't make me nervous! Pump, for God's sake!"

Sim hasn't stopped pumping. More water pours over both sides of the raft. Empty water bottles float away.

"Have you fixed it? Bill, we're sinking. Fast, fast, be fast. Our Father who art in Heaven...."

I struggle with my nervous fingers to complete the job before it's too late. The top half must go on exactly in line with the bottom half, or it will not hold air. My waist is under. I shift my weight. The patch is going under again, but this time I can lift it no further. The air tubes are entirely empty. Seconds remain before the raft sinks all the way.

I fit the top of the patch in its place, spin the wing nut, and tighten the assembly. I drop quickly and spread my weight over the entire bottom. The sides of the raft rise several inches above the water.

"Sim, I'll take over pumping. Bail! For goodness sake. Bail!"

Water floods the raft. Everything is underwater. I pump frantically, but the air chamber doesn't fill out.

"Sim, how does it feel? Is it getting tighter?"

"I can't tell."

Sim bails while I pump air. Ever so slowly, the air chambers expand, and the raft regains a little of its buoyancy. The bedding and clothing, so carefully dried earlier today, are all soaked. Night closes in on us. Sharks batter the sides of the raft. We could have been in the water right now...

Sim can hold her anger back no longer: "You bastard. You tried to kill us. I told you not to touch it. You're a murderer. A terrorist."

"I thought the emergency air chamber was full."

"You're stupid. You almost sank us. Another second and the raft would've sunk."

I can find no honest excuse for my mistake. Seconds separated us from death. Should the raft have filled with water, the tube with the open hole could have sucked in water. There would be no way to empty it.

The single inflated arch would not have kept us afloat. It was an almost fatal, inexcusable mistake. I feel like an idiot. Sim lashes at me with fury. I take it because I know I was wrong. Otherwise, I'd choke her and throw her to the sharks.

Once the main air chamber is rigid, we inflate the arch and close the canopy. Will my hurried patch job hold? Soggy bedding lies in lumps under us. It had been so dry, drier than we've seen it weeks. Now they will never dry. The saltwater will rot them like our T-shirts.

Sim fumes silently, her pressure valve about to blow. I came within seconds of sealing our fate. I honestly saw the raft plunge towards the deep. My knees sank two feet. The patch came together with no more than a second to spare. At the last moment, when our fate hung in balance, I felt the hand of the Lord guide mine. I could never have done the job alone. Thank you, dear Lord. You have helped us at the time of most need...don't leave us...

Simonne hasn't stopped bailing. On her knees, she has searched out water in the bilge. Together we wring out the bedding which Sim then piles on top of me to continue to sponge the remaining water.

Sim rages silently as she spreads the wet bedding underneath our trembling bodies. She arranges the comforter over the cushions then bunches up a corner as a pillow. We lie on the cold and soggy comforter, exhausted and shaken by our near brush with death.

Our body heat slowly warms the comforters, and we manage to snooze until heavy rain awakens us. Water pours through the canopy. Sea water continues to drain to the sump created by our behinds. Sim bails while I pump air. Air has held for an hour which is surprising considering how fast I put the patch back together. I may have to adjust it again...but....

Simonne bails throughout the night. She uses a sponge when there isn't enough for the can. To bail is an escape for her ire. Dawn is upon us before we know it, and her bombardment starts. I've been readying myself all night. She organizes her thoughts, prepares her missiles, and lets fly....

"Why did you do it? Why? Can you only answer that single simple question? Why?"

"I thought I could improve our lifestyle, keep from pumping so much."

"You have improved our life style alright! That is if you enjoy living in a soaking bilge. You've done a great job improving our life style. Now we are pumping more often than before. You've soaked everything on board in salt water. We have lost our tooth brushes and toothpaste, and God knows what else floated away. Improve our lifestyle. Hah!"

Sim barely breathes before she continues: "You are a criminal, Butler. You tried to kill me yesterday. How can anyone be so stupid is beyond imagination. Why couldn't you leave the patch alone? From now on, you touch nothing, not one thing. Do you hear me?"

"I can't avoid hearing, you're yelling so loud. I thought the inner tube had air in it like it had when I fixed the patch the first time."

"You thought. Your sick thinking almost got the two of us killed. I thought this raft was tough after it got us through all those storms and shark attacks. You have now proven it's just a piece of junk. A small hole in the air chambers and it's over. That's all I need. I couldn't sleep before, imagine now!"

I can't argue. It was stupid of me. I should have first made sure the inner tube had air. Or better yet, I should've left the patch alone. Now I've killed what little confidence Sim had in the raft.

Meanwhile I pump air, and Sim bails. I make two liters of water. When the sun shines through, I try to dry our bedding, but it's an exercise in futility. Then I wring water out of the foul weather gear. Not much success there either.

Sim lashes at me. "Toss that over board. I have never seen foul weather gear that absorbs more water. If I fell overboard with it, I'd go straight to the bottom."

"We've got to keep it. We might need it to keep warm."

"Butler, you are sick. Don't even bother to explain how that soggy, heavy jacket is going to keep me warm. I worry about you. Your brain is no longer functional. Maybe it's from eating too much trigger fish. Help," she screams, "Get me out of here!"

I look for a hole in which to hide. I refuse to argue, and honestly, I have no argument. Somehow the Log book and workbook stayed dry, for they were on top of the camcorder case at the opposite end of the raft which floated higher because of a trapped pocket of air. At least we saved something. I enter my debacle into the Log.

Life must go on. I fish. I first hand grab three triggers for bait. I cast for a triple tail. I use every trick I know to bring them in. Hundreds of trigger fish follow my every move. I tie a trigger fish carcass by the tail and hang it under the raft as a diversion. I cast out quickly as the triggers busy themselves with the carcass. They catch on to this ploy and cover both spots. When sharks move in on the dead trigger, I pull it out quickly. Another bad idea...I had better watch myself.

Today trigger is the only thing on the menu. I had so hoped to improve Sim's disposition with a better meal. Simonne tries to dry the covers all afternoon. As evening approaches, our gear is ever less soggy. Her readings have an increased meaning today. We thank God for saving us. Two or three seconds more and the raft would have sunk. Thank you, Lord, thank you. I pray myself to sleep.

Simonne interrupts her prayers only to bail and help me pump air. I awaken to pump the air chambers full, then continue to doze. Sim can't get to sleep, her blood still pure adrenalin. The night is endless. Sharks arrive at two and batter the raft for an hour. A turtle and more sharks bother us until the wind shifts to the south.

Sim screams into the night. She howls like a wolf in a pathetic plea for help, for reassurance. I listen to her cry long into the night. By the time skies lighten, the wind has built to a good blow. "Last Chance" scuds along. Both current and winds propel it eastward. An occasional wave showers water under the canopy. Low, fast moving clouds sweep past on a collision course with land, now possibly no more than two hundred miles to the east. This is day forty one on the raft for us, the twenty fifth of July. At nine o'clock tomorrow night, we will have been adrift one thousand hours...that's sixty thousand minutes....

I keep my calculations in my navigation workbook. By some minor miracle, it's still dry as is the Log. I keep both in a plastic bag next to my head. I have been doing some mental navigation. One thousand hours at one knot yields 1000 miles. That would put us closer to the coast than our radio signals indicate. One thousand hours at three quarters of a knot totals 750 miles. That would put us 350 miles off the coast, a very plausible answer. One thousand hours at a half knot would have us six hundred miles off the coast. Radio fixes and the strength of radio reception tell us we're closer.

An average speed of three quarters of a knot over the past forty two days, when considering both current set and the effect of wind and waves, should be very close to actual. That means we have three hundred and fifty miles to go. At a speed of three quarters of a knot, we will need 500 hours to reach shore. Five hundred hours are twenty days. Lord have mercy on us. Can we make it? Can the raft make it?

How could this flimsy raft hold together that long? Closer to shore, we will again be in the shipping lanes. Sooner or later, some alert crewman will see us. Also we should spot the commercial fishing fleet. Why haven't we seen a single fisherman? Are there too many sharks to make commercial fishing interesting?

Sim sits up and looks out. Her face lights up. She yells.

"Bill, a ship! Up there! About a half mile. It's big!"

The ship steams at high speed a quarter mile to the north. It heads west. They have transited the Panama Canal and are on a great circle route to the Far East. High waves and lack of sun kill any hope of being seen. I still haven't had a chance to use our mirror for signalling.

Sim turns away from the ship. "How many ships does this one make?"

"There's the *Ter Eriksen* and the one twenty four days later, then the white one and now this one. Four."

"We're going to see more ships from now on. We must keep watches. The one on watch must paddle around every fifteen minutes to scan the entire horizon."

"Aye Aye, captain. What do we do when it rains? Or at night with only one flare?"

"We pray and hope." I can't get Sim to focus on the upside of our future.

In minutes, the ship is but a dot on the fading horizon. It came to save us, and we did not grasp the opportunity. We didn't signal; we didn't wave. God will not save us unless we meet Him half way.

Sim's dejection shows on her face: "I wasn't looking. God did mean to save us in forty days. Oh, Bill, why didn't I look out in time?"

"Sweetie, He will save us; there's no question about that. He sent that ship as a signal, but we are not yet ready. He meant to show us He could save us at any time. We need more time."

"More time? Oh, Lord, how long? How long? Have mercy on us. We have begged for forgiveness; our reconciliation is complete. Why continue to test us? There are so many bad people in the world that really deserve punishment. Why us? Why have you singled us out for this terrible punishment? Save us, Lord! Save us soon! Don't wait until it's too late. Do it now."

"Easy, baby, remember who you're talking to. He will save us in His own time and in His manner. Your frustration every night with God is not helping. He's up there waiting for you to come around to Him. He's not going to save you until you place yourself in His hands and quit your complaining."

"Forty days is enough. I can't take it any longer. It's too much, too much! I know that we both went our own ways without thinking of God. I know my shortcomings, my sins, my lack of gratitude. Oh, God, don't be cruel and vengeful. God, have mercy on us, take us back, please! Please, please let it be over soon, soon." Tears flood down her cheeks.

She's gone too far. "Stop that," I bellow. "He will not save you with talk like that. God waits for you to put yourself one hundred percent in His care. The way you're acting, there's little hope He will save you. And He won't save me either since I'm stuck alongside you."

"Enough of you, Butler, playing the saint. You are a bigger sinner than I am, so be quiet. You, of little faith and much less devotion. Where do you suddenly get all your faith? It's weird. It's inconceivable that you should preach to me. You. All of your life you've been known as Bad Billy Butler."

"Bad or not is not the point. I believe one hundred percent that God will save us. I will wait until He is ready to get us out of here. And you are not. You want everything to happen, now, now, now! Life doesn't happen that way."

"Well, I feel good when I complain and cry out to heaven. At least, there is a dialogue. And God being God, He understands. Job also complained. I know I'm impatient. I'll try to improve."

I put my arm around Sim as we lie naked on our sodden bedding. Soon we are asleep.

The southwest wind blows steadily. Ten foot waves mounted on twenty foot swells wash under and over us. Mountains of water hurry by to some shore far away. Take us with you, oh wave. A wave passing under us now will reach shore before nightfall. We, on the other hand, will have drifted a mere fifteen miles by nightfall. I'm becoming impatient too.

If we only had a vessel that could sail. Or a raft that could skim the waves or one we could row or steer. If we had the dingy, we could jump in and sail away. We'd be on shore in three days or four. Yet, in the dinghy, we could sink and never reach a safe haven. The raft is slow but steady and more or less safe if I stop fooling with it.

The two a.m. express arrives on schedule. The shark batters not only the raft but the marrow of our nervous system. I poke the six foot silky shark twice with the pole and never faze it. I pray to the Virgin de la Caridad del Cobre, asking her to help take this demon away. Seconds later, the shark departs. Thank heavens for prayer and thank you, Virgencita.

At four in the morning and then minutes before dawn, other sharks attack. They hammer the raft and threaten to split it open. I row for hours with a steady splash. The ploy works at times. Often it makes no difference. When it quiets, I sleep.

I awake to the presence of a third person in the raft at the far end of the raft, near my feet. It's so dark I can't see my toes. I sit up, eyes now open wide, heart pumping madly, and grope for our visitor. But where is he? There is no one. We're alone. It's just Sim and I. I lie back down, now convinced the entire scene was but a dream.

I snooze, for I know not how long and again awaken with the same feeling. This time, however, it's no dream. Someone is in the raft. Our visitor is near my feet. My heart beats like a bongo drum. We are not alone, of that I am sure. I lie, eyes wide open, and search the darkness. What is it? Who is it?

I'm unable to sleep after that and listen to the rain. The wind continues to pick up as we remain on our easterly course. Sleep is now impossible. Breaking waves roar in from the south and toss us about without mercy.

God wants to save us and has helped us every day to survive. The voice Simonne heard so many weeks ago was right on. "Forty days," it had said...we had to spend forty days on the raft...help would come on day forty-one. The ship passed minutes after four in the afternoon on day forty one...and we missed the boat. We didn't trust our inner feelings that told us to keep an extra keen lookout. We dismissed that inner voice. Another error.

We weren't keeping a strict lookout as our near sinking was still on our minds. And what about the vision? Was it a warning to stay awake and look out?

The sun slowly makes its appearance. Clear skies promise a dry day. Simonne, listening to the radio, is far away in her own world.

She takes the earphones off. "Every day I can hear stations later in the day. A week ago, I received only static starting at six in the morning. Now the sun is up, and I still hear Costa Rica and clearly. Here, listen."

The signal isn't perfect but it's not bad. I hear music. We can't be much more than two hundred miles away, possibly less.

When we hear a station right through the day, even at high noon, we'll be within a hundred miles. Today's signal lingers until ten, then fades away. Land remains hundreds of miles to the east.

"I heard a couple of news items. Fidel says he is going to stick to the hard line. Khashoggi, the big Saudi millionaire, is in deep on the President Marcos Philippine theft case. He's out on a ten million dollar bail. Chicken feed for him. There was a plane crash in Libya, all dead."

"What ever happened with that Sioux City crash. Did anyone survive?"

"Yes, but over a hundred died. They still don't know what caused it."

At noon, I catch six trigger fish with my hands but zeroed out with the hook. There are hundreds of trigger fish under the raft. All wait inches below the surface for anything that moves. One bit me yesterday when I got my fingers too close to the water. They bite Sim when she dips a cloth in the water to wash herself. Her daily rub down with salt water is followed with a few drops of fresh water.

A trigger fish bites through my glove as I cut it open. Several of the tenacious little devils have nipped me after both filets are out. Yesterday, I caught one trigger too many, and when I threw it back in, the waiting triggers thought it had been filleted and attacked it fiercely. They killed and devoured it in less than a minute.

Trigger fish meat is firm yet not tough. Sim now says she prefers it to the other fish I catch. With lunch over, we move our bedding around to dry. My shirt airs on the canopy, stiff with salt.

We pump air every forty minutes, so my repair didn't help. The empty peanut butter jar contains forty or more strips of paper which Sim uses to wrap the plug. Sim remains in charge of raft air chamber tightness. After two hundred strokes, the raft feels hard as a rock to me. I call over to Sim with a "check it," and she comes back with her usual, "not yet." I've failed to convince Sim that higher pressure will make the air leak out faster.

We pump air day and night every forty minutes. Deep sleep is a long forgotten luxury. I sleep longer than Sim, and often she has pumped alone. Even back on land, I seldom have trouble falling asleep or staying asleep. Sim is like a watchdog; a mere whisper has her awake and alert. She says she sleeps like a mother does, antennae out, ready to jump at the smallest cry.

Another ship passes close by at four in the morning. This one heads east, towards the coast. It must be bound for Puntarenas. Sim sees it when it's abreast, too late for a flare. We're beyond disappointment at these near misses. Sim, an hour later, picks up a Puntarenas radio station. These are two positive signs we are closer to shore.

A calm, clear morning greets us as we rise and fall to the tune of twenty foot swells. Simonne has been looking out the window rather intently since dawn. Has she seen something? For days, I've watched dark shapes on the horizon that look like long hills, and when I'm at last convinced it could be land, they disappear. Sim continues to look in the same general direction. I keep my eye on Sim for any change in expression.

Sim is the official lookout. I am more awkward, heavier, and can't see well without my glasses. Two to three times each day, she turns on her knees, pushes above the canopy, and scans the horizon. I grab a thigh to steady her and, jokingly, give her a little push towards the side.

"Bill Butler," she declares, "don't you dare!" With a "How could you think such a thing," I give her a second nudge. My hand reaches all the way around her leg. She has lost a lot of weight. Gone are her mighty thighs and her big bosom.

The morning passes quietly. We produce the usual two liters of water. I stretch out again while Sim returns to the window. She looks always in the same direction. I see her lips curve, and with a triumphant look in her eyes, she turns towards me.

"Land," she calls out.

"Are you sure?" I don't really take her seriously.

"Land. Land! I'm sure of it!"

"What kind of land? What do you see?"

"It's far away. Like a small hill. There are two hills. But far away."

"Where? Let me see it."

I struggle up and follow Sim's pointed finger. Swells are more than 15 feet and waves two or three, a calm day for the Pacific Ocean. To see it, I have to wait until we are on top of a swell and then look in the right direction.

I see nothing. I wait for the top of another swell and give up. "I can't see it," and lie back down.

"It's hard to see."

"What does it look like, exactly. Here, draw a picture of it in the work book. Hold the page at arm's length and trace the land to the exact size."

Sim, sitting now, keeps one eye on the island. She holds the log work book up and draws the contour of what she sees. Her sketch is about three quarters of an inch high and one inch long. She draws one hill to the left, which is north, a quarter inch higher than a hill to the south. I get up a couple of more times but fail to see it.

"Sim, check the bearing of the mountain with the compass. That'll make it easier for me to spot."

The compass is always hard to find. I can never fully understand how, in such a confined space, something as large as the compass can vanish. I find it under the life preserver and hand it to Sim. She trains her eyes on our tiny speck of hope.

She calls out. "It's 120 degrees. Let me see. Yes, 120."

"OK, now let me take a look."

Sim paddles the raft around so my side faces east. I hold the compass up and find 120. I wait for the raft to climb to the top of a swell and see it...a single mountain with two uneven bluish peaks. It's land, it's beautiful, and it's about 30 miles away.

We take turns looking at the island throughout the afternoon because an island it must be. It's larger than when we first saw it. Our hopes run high. The sun sets on two happy castaways. Sim is ecstatic. This is her happiest moment since Panama. As darkness falls and she reads, we dream of a sandy beach on a faraway isle.

I cannot recall what islands lie off the Central American coast except for Isla de Cocos. I know there are several small ones, but they are all close to shore. But this can't be Isla de Cocos. Isla de Cocos is to the north and behind us. This island bears south of east. Besides how can we be in sight of it when all the boobies left us weeks ago? Where else could they have flown? I fall asleep with this quandary on my mind.

We have a day or two before a landfall. How exciting, castaways on a deserted island. Or is it mainland? Two high hills on a lowland. That would be better yet....

Wind and waves ease during the night, but both are still from the south. If we are to reach the hills, we need wind out of the west. Thanks to the strong current, our course has been east all night.

Sharks are particularly nasty tonight. Our faithful two A.M. visitor bashes the raft with vengeance. This shark alone is intent on destroying us. Since it first appeared three weeks ago, we have travelled more than two hundred miles. How does it find us, night after night?

Nevertheless, our night is full of hope. Land is at hand at last. We are travelling to the east. A ray of promise shines over us for the first time since cast away forty five days ago. Even the sharks that batter our raft bother us less tonight. The weather is calm and clear; stars are out. When it dawns, land should be closer. Our hopes and spirits soar. I fall asleep with Sim's prayers in my ears.

Saturday, the twenty ninth of July, dawns clear and bright. We have been awake for hours, desperate to catch a glimpse of land, land that offers us our first real hope in seven weeks. When it dawns, will it be closer? Are we heading for it? First light holds off for an eternity. Darkness yields to true dawn when the eastern horizon erupts bright red. We look; the island is there and it's closer than yesterday.

Sim's excitement equals mine. "Let's row," she calls over to me. "Let's row, come on."

We jump at the thought and deflate both arches. We pass a line under the raft and tie the ballast bags against the bottom of the raft which should make the raft easier to row. I tie the pole to one of the paddles, and it now becomes an oar. My paddle is a flat piece of plastic six inches wide and twenty inches long.

"Sim, you set the pace, and I will follow to keep the raft headed towards land."

We row surrounded by a flat, calm ocean and crimson sky. We float easily on the long oceanic swells. Today's sun is about to emerge. We're alive. Dear God, thank you for everything. We don't deserve your mercy.

We pull on the oars with unknown strength. Sim leans into her paddle without stop. I push water to keep up with Sim. The open raft gives us an exuberant sense of freedom. We are one with the world. Visibility is perfect. After fifteen minutes, we rest and take in our vista. Life is so great. Our world so beautiful. The sun emerges from behind orange clouds. Light fills our eyes and hope overflows from our bodies. Excitement saturates our spirit. We are alive after six weeks adrift, and land is at hand.

If we were to drift with the canopy down, we would not miss a single passing ship. We have so longed to take in the true beauty of our surroundings. We row, our eyes attached to the two hills ahead that loom large and inviting. Twenty minutes later, we take another break. We row but the raft barely moves. The island, clearly outlined against the bright eastern horizon, stands out clearly, still afar. I wonder how high the peak is. Is it a hill or a mountain? Is it an island or mainland?

After another thirty minutes, we give up. The island is more than fifteen miles away, and it's obvious we'll never reach it rowing, at least not from this distance. We must conserve our energy...save it for what might come up. If the wind and current push us closer to within a mile or less, then we'll row. But it's hopeless to try from this distance. The wind picks up from the southwest.

"I've got a great idea," I exclaim. "Let's sail."

"You've tried that before and it didn't work. What makes you think it'll work now? How do you plan to do it?"

"We'll inflate the bow arch and let the wind blow into the canopy. I'll row to keep the raft stern to the wind. Simple. It should work."

"It's not going to work. Besides I get scared when the canopy is down. Suppose we tip over."

"Simonne, look, there is no wind. The sea is calm. What's going to tip us over?. What do we have to lose? Let's try it for a while. Come on, Sim, how else will we ever know if it'll work? What do you want to do? Stay out here for the rest of your life?"

"OK, go ahead. But it won't work."

I inflate one of the arches and row the raft around so the breeze blows into the inflated arch. I steer towards the sun and the island. An hour passes. We haven't moved.

"I told you so." Sim says, but I can tell she was hoping it had worked.

"Ok. It didn't work."

"Besides I don't like the ballast bags tied. The wind is picking up. Look at those waves. Come on, Bill, quit playing around."

"All right. all right." With my near zero credibility, it's useless to argue for more time. We re-rig the canopy and untie the ballast bags. The raft catches the current, and we lie back down, more frustrated and exhausted than ever.

Simonne draws the contour of the island to scale as she did yesterday. The contour hasn't changed, but it's almost twice as high.

The exercise has made us hungry. We will open our last rusty can at lunch. I jiggled the can yesterday to determine its contents. It sounds like it's part liquid and part solid.

Looking back, it's probably as well we didn't bring more cans. We would have eaten better up to now, but all the remaining cans would be nearly terminal. In Miami, we meant to remove the labels, mark each can, and dip them in varnish or paraffin. Who would've guessed then we were destined to drift in a small raft across the Pacific?

At one in the afternoon, Sim fishes the can opener out of the gun case. When I pick up the can, I find it's leaking. The can was fine yesterday. Sim looks it over and says:

"Last night, when I told you I heard a swish of air, I was so afraid it was coming from the raft near the window. Well, it was the can when it popped. I felt something sticky on my hand when I poked around early this morning. What a pity, we might have eaten it yesterday before it popped. No, it was already bad then."

I open it anyway. It's a can of pears. The pears smell and look good. A light layer of foam covers the syrup. Sim, official sniffer on shore and at sea, sniffs. The pears smell fine. I dip a finger into the juice and into my mouth. It tastes fine. On closer inspection, Sim cocks her head, shakes it, and points over the side. I shake my head. No, no, it looks good to me...I'll just eat one or two....

"Baby," says Simonne, "I know it hurts, but we cannot take any chances. Right now, we are healthy. We haven't been sick. It's a miracle. If we eat this, we take risks that could be fatal. Suppose we get botulism? I don't even want to think about it. Let's not take a chance."

Over it goes...our last can.

I slip on my gloves, and in minutes, six trigger fish fill the bucket. I remove the twelve filets and pile them on the paddle. I cut small pieces and pass the choicest chunks to Sim.

I've become a trigger fish connoisseur. The biggest ones are the tastiest. The bad part is that I lose most of the big ones because I can't get my hand around them. I always taste a small piece of the filet before passing it on to Sim. Identical trigger fish taste different, and some parts of the filet are better than others. The part of the filet closest to the head is the best. I cut the tip of the filet for Sim, then separate a piece with bones and toss it into the bait can. I eat the rest. Sim will eat the tips from four or five filets. I eat until I can no more.

While I fished, the raft leaked air faster than before though it always has lost more air whn I fish. After lunch, we pump air every 20 minutes. I tighten the string around one of the valves, but that doesn't help. Sim checks for anything that may be rubbing against an air tube and finds nothing. We listen for the hiss of escaping air. We hear nothing. What can it be?

Before sunset, we take a bearing on the island. It's now 105 degrees compared to yesterday's 120 degrees. We drift down on it from the north. If we stay on this track, we'll pass to the south of it. The current pushes us east, and the wind swings from the south all the way to the west. Tomorrow, we will be closer and better able to estimate our approach.

As the sun falls towards the western horizon, it takes with it a cornucopia of reds and purples. The sunset reminds us of heaven and hell as depicted in old religious paintings. Our Hell is about to end, and soon we'll be on an island in heaven. We witness the most spectacular sunset so far. We enjoy every ray, every changing cloud, every reflection from every wave...our hearts full of hope and expectation. Tomorrow should bring us closer to land and safety....

Sim sits while I prop my head up with an extra boat cushion. We watch in silence as day evolves into night.

Land. Land is a double edged sword. Land is safety, a beginning, an escape from our predators. To reach shore will be to live again. Through the past forty days, death awaited each day as the sun set. True odds have been against our living to see each new day. We must reach this shore. When we get closer, we'll row until we collapse.

Once on shore, we will find a way to live. We'll wait for a boat. If it's a large island, it may have stands of bamboo. I could make a boat...a catamaran or a cross between Kon-Tiki and the Polynesian outriggers. We have a knife to cut the parts and rope aboard to lash it all together. We can do it. If by chance it's Isla de Cocos, there will be people on shore who will help us.

On the other hand, arrival on a windward shore at night could be tricky. I dream of gently gliding towards a soft sandy beach, the moon full, gentle breeze edging us on. I'll jump over first, lead the raft in, and then hold Simonne's hand as she joins me in our new found haven.

What would happen if we arrive on a dark stormy night? Rough breaking seas could push the raft towards rocks, a half mile from solid footing. The raft could tear and sink under us. We swim in heavy current. Predators circle ever closer. We search desperately for a hand hold on the jagged coral as it tears our flesh. Blood gushes as we climb higher towards a minute rocky outcrop far from the island. Our raft lies on the bottom.

I awaken from my wild imaginary wanderings with a shudder. It's so very dark. Simonne prays, and I follow with my now revitalized Lord's Prayer. I pray more intently tonight than I have in forty years. Tomorrow we should be much closer....

◄╼chapter eleven╾►

0830 SUNDAY JULY 30, 1989, DAY 46

A new day, Sunday, dawns on two wide awake castaways. Sim scans the horizon window, expectant. She clasps the compass in her right hand as she awaits for our island to emerge from the shadows. We expect to see it large, verdant, and close at hand. Though seas are calm, the ever present twenty foot swells hide it. She sweeps the eastern horizon in the few seconds we ride atop a crest. Yesterday, the island was twice larger than when we first saw it. Today it should be again as high or higher. Yet current and wind have been weak.

Sim's voice falters. "Bill, I can't see it. It's not there." She turns on her knees, gets her bearings, and concentrates on a small piece of horizon. Silently, she surveys the rolling seas for sign of land. Of a sudden, she calls out.

"There it is! Oh, Bill, it's the same size as the first day. We're farther away. The current has pushed us the wrong way. How can this happen? How can we go backwards?" Tears run down her face as she collapses in my arms.

I was afraid this would happen. The sea is relentless. Punishing. It's ever full of surprises. Days ago, becalmed, I had a feeling we were not going east. Without a landmark, I couldn't tell. Sim's heart is broken. She had built up so much hope; I had too.

"I knew it. We are not to be saved. How can this happen?" Sim's profound distress is contagious. "How many other days have we travelled in the wrong direction? What's going to happen to us?"

"I really don't know." It's no use making up stories or playing the macho. "We lost the current. Pray it returns."

It cannot be Isla de Cocos. I'm sure we passed it two weeks ago, the day when all the birds flew off. If the two hills are part of the Central American land mass, it will not matter much where we head. If it's an off-shore island, we will drift past it and to the mainland. That is, if the current returns. Or if the storms out of the west return. Lots of "ifs"....

This could be one of the islands off Panama. If I remember correctly, the coastline swings east after Punta Mala. Noriega uses one of the islands as a prison where he tortures political enemies. We heard all about it when in Panama. I shudder. What will happen to us if we drift towards it?

I study my raft-made chart of the Pacific. My dead reckoning tells me mainland Central America could be under two hundred miles to the east. Isla de Cocos is behind us, unless we have been drifting backwards. How many other days have we not drifted east?

I draw up a picture of the Pilot Chart to recall how the current runs in this part of ocean. From way out west up to a hundred miles off the coast, I am sure the current runs east, towards the coast. After that, I can't remember what happens to it. It must go either north or south. My guess is that it runs south, towards the Panama Canal.

Visible proof that we have gone ten miles or more in the wrong direction sets the mood for the day. We have had no propulsion of any kind for two days. No wind and no waves. And worse yet, no current. I make an entry in the Log: distance travelled in the last 24 hours...7 miles west.

When seas are high and the wind blows more than fifteen knots, breaking waves propel us down wind. Often a single wave pushes us six feet in two seconds. Days ago, as we sat becalmed, she had prayed and prayed for wind. A monster of a storm materialized out of the West. We hung on for dear life through the night. In the morning, while it was still rough, I had pleaded "Sim, baby, next time, don't pray so hard for a storm."

I toss out a paper. It stays inches away from the raft for several minutes until it sinks out of sight. There is no wind and there are no waves. There is no current, or if there is, it doesn't flow to the east. We remain becalmed all morning.

"Sim, please pray for a storm. You and all our good friends in Miami who prayed for fair winds have overdone it. We'll never . get out of this stuck in a dead calm."

Not all news is bad. We had a miracle from an entirely unexpected quarter. The leak in the air tank had been increasing daily. Yesterday, towards evening, we had to pump every half hour. Around midnight, we fell into a deep sleep. When we awakened three hours later, we found the raft had hardly lost any air. Today we have been pumping every hour. We have no explanation to what happened last night except that someone up above is looking out for us.

I cannot find a comfortable position. When I lie on my side, my legs or elbows always get in the way with one part or another of Sim's anatomy. She complains loudly.

"Bill, get your elbow out of my liver."

"Move your leever."

I get punched. And I move my elbow.

During the afternoon, the wind picks up from the southwest. We are on the move again.

I fish ten triggers. I gorge on twelve filets while Sim eats three. We make two liters of water. Three other liters are stored under the cushions.

Sharks batter the raft. I beat them off until rain starts. Heavy drips soon soak us and our bedding. But who cares?

I take a bearing on the island: 120 degrees. This means we are drifting north of it instead of south as yesterday's bearing indicated. Heavy black clouds hasten nightfall. When the rain stops for a few minutes, I take a look around. My God. A shark three times longer than the raft circles ten feet from the raft. I don't say a word to Sim. I curl up next to her and hold her tightly and pray. As total darkness sets in, I look out again. The big shark and all the small sharks have disappeared. What surprises do we have in store for tonight?

Rain pours through the canopy and on us until dawn. We cover ourselves with the wet sailbag and the trash bag and huddle to stay warm. As this forty seventh morning aboard the raft dawns, we know not what to expect. Will we be closer to the island? Will we see it? Or will heavy overcast cut visibility?

A light breeze from the southwest greets us this Monday, the thirty first of July. What was not soaked yesterday got it last night. I keep the Log Book near my head in our driest place. I know not how much longer the pages will remain dry enough to write on. Sharks were not a problem last night. That big shark may still be around.

The skies slowly turn lighter. Soon we'll know. Did we again drift backwards? Sim has been at the window since first light. She calls out with a happy ring to her voice: "There it is! Bill, it's much closer!" I peer out. Sure enough. The island is there, large, looming blue in the hazy morning light.

"Get a bearing."

"It's..it's..160 degrees. Let me check. Yes, 160."

"That's not good at all. That means we are passing it to the north. If the current runs south, we could reach it. This wind from the southwest pushes us away."

"What do you think?"

"It's too early to tell. Can you see any features, rocks, beaches?"

Sim reports: "The contour has changed. There's only one hill, but I see nothing on shore."

I shudder at the thought of an approach on a coral laden, rocky outcrop. If there is light, we could row around the reefs. The ballast bags would surely catch on the rocks or coral. If the approach is in the dead of the night and these Pacific nights are the blackest anywhere, what could we do? We'd try to row steadily offshore to await daylight, that is, if we could. We'd be safe on land, our odyssey over. It's a large island, five or ten miles long. The peaks are high, perhaps a thousand feet. People certainly live there. Boats must visit regularly. We'll wait for a boat to take us to the mainland. Or I'll make a boat, a sailboat. The striped comforter would become a sail...

We could live on the island for months as we build up our strength. We can make water. There's bound to be food. Simonne is a wizard at spotting edible tubers and fruit. Taught the old ways by her Italian grandfather, she could certainly keep us fed. There are bound to be bananas. We still have a few soggy matches, but we can surely find a way to make them work. We can make signal fires. Bill Robinson and Simonne Crusoe. What fun! Come on, wind. C'mon, current. Take us to our new home!

There is no other land in sight. Sim is right. It is an island and an island far away from the mainland. Near the northwestern tip, Sim spots a fishing boat. It's too far away to signal. What island is it? Isla de Cocos? Never. We passed it weeks ago. We are much, much closer to the mainland. Sim holds the work book at arm's length. The island is now more than four inches high compared to a half inch when we first saw it three days ago. If we hadn't drifted west, we would almost be there. With luck, in a day or two, we'll make it, God willing.

I hurry up my fishing expedition before rain begins again. After lunch, when Sim sits up to look for the island, she sees something else: a twelve foot hammerhead shark. We embrace tightly and stay out of sight. Hammerheads eat everything: plastic rafts, watermakers, dirty castaways...I don't dare play poke-the-shark with him. We pray he swims away. We remain quiet for hours. We dare not make a move.

Wind and waves increase. Water splashes through the canopy. Sim bails. Looks like another wet, rough night ahead. Wind picks up out of southwest by west at 15 knots. If it doesn't shift, it will push us north of the island.

Sharks attack fiercely all night. On one hand, it's good news. The monster left. I try to repel them, but poor visibility keeps me from scoring any solid hits. I splash the pole in the water. This keeps the sharks circling several feet under the raft with only the most intrepid rising closer to the surface with mischief in mind.

Dawn is slow to arrive. I look at my watch constantly only to find mere minutes have passed instead of the hoped for hours. Sim has been at the window for the past hour in search of shipping and for a telltale light on the island. We have to reach shore soon. The raft has lost its integrity. As waves pass under us, it folds in half. We've lost a lot of weight even with our heavy fish diet. Neither of us have had a bowel movement in the past four weeks. Is this normal?

"I see it," she calls suddenly. "Pass me the compass."

"Are we closer?"

"Yes! Yes! It's big. And we are very close. It's at 220 degrees. Yes, 220."

I get up to look. Rain clouds shroud the top half of the island. It's not more than four or five miles away. Trees line the hill. What can we do to reach it?

"Sim, let's row."

She is ready at once. Once again, we tie the ballast bags up against the floor of the raft to reduce drag. We row furiously for over an hour, but the current is too strong. We make no progress and give up. We cannot waste our strength.

The island grows smaller as all three forces, wind, waves, and current, push us away. It's definite; we've missed it. Safety so close at hand yet unattainable. Neither of us can talk..our thoughts follow a variety of paths...but they all end up at the same bottom line...will we ever be found?...will we ever make a landfall, or are we to roam the seas forever?...a mythical, ghostly raft to be found years from now with nothing but bones....

We return to our everyday chores. We make water and fish triggers. Sharks attack the raft all through lunch. They don't attack while I fish. I wonder why?

Later in the afternoon, I snooze and Sim is the lookout. I hear her gasp. I open my eyes and feel the raft rise. It goes up for a few moments, then drops back.

"Sim, what was that?"

"A whale shark."

"A what?"

"I'm sure it was a whale shark. It was huge. It's head was ten feet wide or more! Its mouth was as wide as its head. It was brown and had white spots all over its body. My God, it was more than fifty feet in length!"

Fortunately, whale sharks are not carnivorous. They feed on plankton and other microorganisms. What next? How do we get out of this aquarium full of monster sea creatures? Today it's only a gentle giant but tomorrow what?

The slack current allows the raft to swing to the whims of wind and wave. It reminds us of our lives. We also have drifted aimlessly in a life without direction. On the raft as we drift, a strong new current begins to reshape our lives. At first, the current was weak and we swung with indecision. As time passed, a strong spiritual stream has taken hold of us. Every day brings us closer to

God. A new strength grows inside of us.

Sim reads my thoughts. "Do you think we'll reach the island? What can we do? This raft isn't going to make it much longer." She looks up. "Oh, Lord, why are you testing us in this way? Isn't forty eight days enough punishment? How much longer must we suffer?"

"Simmer down, baby. God will save us in His time and in His manner. We are in His hands. He will save us."

"Saved when? Why doesn't he save us now? Perhaps we have been so bad that He doesn't plan to save us at all. He's torturing us, and in due time, we will die. I'm sure of it."

She calms and I reflect. This island can't be that far off the coast. If we miss the island, in three or four days, we will be on the mainland. Besides the closer we get to land, the better chance we have of seeing a fishing boat. They can spot us much easier than a freighter. They're closer to the water and go slower. And they have lookouts watching for fish.

Frigate birds follow our every move. Fishing boats normally head for birds. New varieties of shore birds have joined us. The coloring of the boobies has changed from the ones that slept around the raft five weeks ago. Where the earlier ones were white, these are dark brown. The black portions of the first group are now white in the new comers. Interesting. I suppose Darwin or Audubon have covered the subject. As night approaches, all the sea birds leave to roost on land. If we could only fly away with them. A hundred conflicting hopes and fears race through our heads. I fall asleep as Simonne tries to pray.

Sharks attack the raft all night. I fight them off until rain starts around seven in the morning. I open the window, pump the raft up, and fall asleep in seconds.

Sim shakes me awake. I open my eyes to bright daylight.

Instantly, I prepare for an emergency. "What happened? What's wrong?"

"What's wrong? You spend all night sleeping while I have to bear all the attacks from sharks and turtles, pump air, bail, and listen to it rain. All you do is snore. It's not fair. I need company."

"Am I hearing correctly? You have shaken me awake to inform me that I am sleeping too much. Is that what you are saying?"

"It's not right that you sleep and I can't. And when you're sleeping, I feel so lonely. I can't stand to be by myself. I can't bear it," she whines, tears streaking her cheeks.

"I should toss you over the side. After I make most of the water and put all the food on the table and pump most of the air and spend the night fighting off sharks, I get harassed when I finally grab a little sleep. I cannot believe what I'm hearing. Get me the log book; I want to make an entry."

Her face falls. "Forgive me, baby, I felt so depressed and lonely. I know we're going to miss that island. I so hoped to reach it. I was so sure we were going to be safe on shore. When it became obvious we will get no closer, I just got crazy. Will you forgive me?"

"Never, unless you give me a big kiss and then put some of your lotion on my back. It stings all over. How is it?" I roll over on my side.

"Terrible. You have ugly open sores from your shoulders to your waist. I'll clean them." She sprinkles several drops of fresh water to wash the salt out of my wounds then spreads the last drops from a near empty bottle of cleansing lotion. My back feels much better right away.

"Did you see the island? Where is it?"

Sim has taken a bearing. "It's way behind us, fifteen or more miles and bears 240. It's gone."

"Your news isn't all bad news. Now we know we are back in the current, and we are making time to the east. We know that we will hit the coast of Central America. Let us now forget the island and keep our sights to the east where our new hope lies."

I pull out the Log Book and review our entries since we first saw the island. We spotted it first on July 28, day 44, at a range of 25 miles. This is day 49, and the island is 15 miles astern. We've drifted 40 miles to the east in 5 days, and that includes a day or more drift to the west.

The day is dark and dismal, and heavy black clouds shroud the island in a veil of rain. Rain squalls again soak us. I take advantage of the cool, rainy day to make two liters of water.

When the rain lets up, I pluck eleven trigger fish out of the ocean and into the bucket. Sim insists I fish only for trigger fish. When I cast for triple tails, I may get nothing in an hour, and all that time, she has to pump air into the leaking air chambers. The truth is, I enjoy my fishing interludes.

The trigger fish have destroyed my hands with their tiny painful barbs. I've counted more than thirty trigger sting marks on my right hand alone. On my little finger, near the first joint, I have a dozen barbs. This is the finger that wraps around under the fish when I grab it. My thumb and index finger are also full of the telltale red stings.

Night arrives early, and we settle down to another interminable nightmare. I flick the flashlight on for a second whenever my watch chirps and a dozen times in between. The striped comforter under us is so lumpy and wet and stiff I can lie in one position for no more than a few minutes. To turn is agony, for the sores on my back scream. I move the bedding aside and rest on the bare plastic cushion for an hour, but it turns out to be less comfortable. At long last, my watch chirps. It's six A.M. Two more hours to dawn.

When I awaken next, Sim has the window partly open and peers out. I close my eyes. If there is any news, good or bad, it will come soon enough. The outside corners of Sim's lips point down in her typical look of despondency. News will not be good. I had better be quiet. She turns and notices I'm awake.

"The island is nowhere in sight, but then visibility is but three or four miles. I'll check again in a couple of hours after the rain lifts. The weather will clear soon and the southwest wind is picking up. The current is also strong."

"You're a great first mate. Skipper sleeps in, and mate has the morning report on the bridge. At least, you didn't shake me awake again."

"I should have, the way you were snoring, except I thought the racket would keep the sharks away. It did attract a turtle who probably thought it some kind of mating call."

"Turtle? Where is she? Was she good looking? I'll take anything now that my raft mate has sworn celibacy. I'm going deaf and blind and I get no pity. Say, I had a super dream. Do you want to hear it?" Sim nods.

"We're on this raft in the Pacific, and it's a clear, sunny day with medium sized waves. A big sports fisherman, like a fifty foot Hatteras or Bertram, heads for us. The Captain is big and fat and there are several tourists on board. They see us and stop next to the raft. The fat man calls out and asks what's the matter. I tell him our boat sank; that we're shipwrecked. He guns the engines in neutral.

"I plead with him to save us. He yells down to hurry up and jump in if we want to, but to leave the raft. He's in a fishing tournament and can't wait. I argue that it'll only take a second to pull the raft aboard. He says no; there is no room and to hurry up, or he'll pull away.

"We jumped on board and go with him to Isla de Cocos. We swam on a sandy beach, ate well, and partied with a group of people. Then he left in a hurry and said he would be back for us later. And I woke up."

"Sounds like one of my dreams with the unhappy endings. Now that we've missed the island, what happens?"

"We head for shore. The weekend is coming up. People come to these waters from all over to fish for big blue marlins, sailfish, and tuna. The sport fishing gang should be out Saturday and Sunday. The commercial fleet probably heads for shore on Friday and heads back out Sunday night. We must keep a sharp lookout."

Sim nods. "I've been dreaming of food," she says. "Do you remember that little restaurant on Madison Avenue where we had the blinis after visiting the Metropolitan Museum? I dreamt we were there, sipping that delicious cold white wine and eating blinis. Oh, I'm so hungry for real food."

"I told you never to talk about food. Blinis. I'd give anything for a blini. I never ate one before that day. When we get back, I'll take you to New York for a blini bust."

The morning passes with light banter, water making, and a nap. I catch my usual dozen trigger fish, serve up lunch, and nap again. When I awaken, Sim looks out and the rain is over.

"I see the island. It's the same size as when we saw it on that first day a week ago, and it bears 260 degrees, almost due west."

"More proof that we are moving in the right direction. There is land to the north and east, and the current and wind push us in that general direction. All we have to do is keep the raft afloat until we reach shore. We have food and water and nothing else to do but to husband the raft. We'll make it, sweetie, we'll make it." Poor Sim, hair matted, gaunt, pale, looks away to the east. She tries so hard to believe what I'm saying.

Our small feathered visitor is back. The same small black sea bird has slept aboard every night for a week. It alights for a rest and flies off when I fish or if Sim chases a turtle. As night begins to fall, it lands on the canopy. It leaves before first light.

The bird is all black and about the size of a sea gull. Its webbed feet are pink and delicately soft. We see its little feet through the canopy. This one has been good company. When we open the canopy, the bird gets uptight and stares down, watching our every move.

This morning, I watch our little dark sea bird preen. It pushes its beak into its preen gland, picks up oil, spreads it first into wing feathers, then works towards its tail. I sit up. The bird takes no notice of my motion. Can I catch it? Its feet are no more than two feet from my head. If I could move my hand under it, then come up quickly, I can grab it.

What will Sim think? Her eyes are closed. She's probably praying, thinking of her children. It'll liven up her day. I decide to go for it. Carefully, I study the angle of attack and wait until the bird is busiest. With a thrust, I grab its feet. Surprised, it struggles and squawks as it desperately flaps its wings. Sim sits up with disbelief. I grab the bird around the neck.

"Do you like my birdie? It's going to be lunch today. How would you like me to prepare it?", I tease.

"Bill Butler, don't you dare. He's one of my friends. He's been with us for a long time, and he trusts us. You're not going to harm him."

"No? Watch. I can't decide whether to wring its neck or stretch it. Which is better? We can sure use a change in diet."

The bird's squawks can surely be heard back on shore. Its wings flap wildly, and just when Sim is absolutely convinced I'm ready to wring its neck, I release the baby bird which flies away at top speed. Sim hits me with the ultimate nasty look, but things soon settle down to our usual boring routine of inching along at a rate that's impossible to perceive.

Evening comes quickly. Sim reads the six psalms which increase in meaning as we move closer to the realization that God's help is our only hope. He has performed so many miracles for us already. He has decided we should be saved but that the cementing of our faith in Him needs more time. Sim has come a long way from the time a few weeks ago when the sighting of a ship and its disappearance behind the horizon would cast her spirits into black despair. She then questioned the heavens and argued with God over the why for our punishment. "Why is He doing this to us", she would say. "Why not to Noriega? Why not to all the crooks and war mongers, killers, and monsters? There are so many in this world. What have we done, Oh, Lord?" she cried over and over. "Have I killed? Robbed? Have I hurt someone on purpose?" She tormented herself terribly and searched her soul for sins and pled out loud for forgiveness.

Now she has made peace with God. She knows that if He has kept us alive this long, He intends to save us. She no longer prays for help but prays for others..for the sick, the lonely, the poor, those who have forgotten God. He has singled us out. This trial is His way to bring us back to him. We are important to Him. Hope is in our hearts. We come back to life. We'll make it.

It is now totally dark. The raft rocks gently in a rolling sea. We feel the current push us ever eastward. We pray, then lapse into a light sleep, our hearts full of hope. Later the two a.m. shark awakens us on schedule. I no longer try to hit it with the pole. My prayers get better results.

The dawn of a new day is, at long last, upon us though a high cloud cover hides the sun. Sim is up and scans the western horizon for the island, fearing it may turn up closer. She sees no land. Its bearing yesterday, August 3, was 260 degrees, nearly west.

With all the excitement created by the island, the increased air loss problem has caught the back burner. We pump every hour if we are quiet and every half hour when I fish or move around to poke at sharks. Sim has checked her side of the raft and as far around the canopy as she can reach but has found nothing. I've run my wet hand over the outside of the air chamber particularly where I jabbed it with a fish hook several days ago. I'd hooked a triple tail which suddenly got away, and the hook imbedded itself in the air chamber. My heart skipped about six beats. At first, I dared not remove it, but when I did, luckily the hole didn't go through.

Up on my knees, I hang over the side. I follow a line of bubbles near the water line to a thin sliver of a break in the fabric behind the air cylinder support. Sharks slapped the cylinder around until it broke loose, but not before it wore through the fabric. I tie the two flaps that hold the cylinder in place and stuff rags over the hole which slows the leak.

The shark pack is back, and they attack for most of an hour. One of the first hard whacks loosens the rags around the hole, and I can hear the whistle made by the bubbles. Now that I know where it comes from, it's suddenly louder...like a ticking time bomb. I hang over the side and rearrange my rags. One rag has fallen away and the others are thoroughly rotten. I tie odd pieces of string around the other rags. As I work, Sim pumps air non-stop.

We need a patch and we've used up our only two. Besides those patches are almost two inches wide so I would have to open a two inch hole in the air chamber to insert the inside half. We'd be heading for the deep again before I got it all put together. Besides Sim would have a heart attack with only the suggestion.

To plug the tiny hole, I need a screw, and I ask Sim if she's seen one around. Sim quickly pulls the fishing reel out from under her head with its two long screws that at one time held it to the rod. The line on the reel keeps me from removing the long screws. I must empty the reel. I loosen the drag and pull on the line, but the reel has corroded and the drag hasn't released. I pull harder, and a few inches of line eases out. Fifteen minutes later, I have taken no more than ten feet. With 300 yards on the reel, this little job could take days.

I cut away at the line on the reel with the knife, and in no time, I've got a major snarl. Impatient now, I hack away and snarl it even worse. I use the knife as a saw and throw over the side all of the strands that come loose. I try to remove the screw by slanting it to one side, but there is still too much line on the reel. I cut more line off and try again. The screw still will not come out. I give it a tap with the knife handle and force it out. To my dismay, the screw isn't stainless steel but chrome plated brass. When I forced it, several threads were damaged. It's now useless.

To get the second screw off the reel, I cut away another large wad of nylon line. Once safely out, I put both wing nuts on the good screw. I prepare two gaskets from a pair of leather gloves and will cut two washers from the camcorder case. I plan to push the head of the screw into the hole, followed by the washer, then a gasket. On the outside of the hole, another gasket and washer, will be followed by the wing nut.

I make an oval washer, 1/2 inch wide and one inch long which will have to slip into the hole in the raft which is under an eighth inch wide. I cut the top washer about one inch in diameter and make a hole in the middle with the scissors. I assemble it all on the screw: oval washer, smaller gasket, gasket, round washer and wing nut.

I work all day on my project. Sim has helped me cut the leather gaskets but has said nothing. Night is upon us as I finish. I'll make the repair in the morning when I'm rested. The night is typical; we bash sharks, pump air every forty minutes, and turn over and around dozens of times in search of a comfortable resting spot. However I lie, my bed is rock hard, freezing cold, and sopping wet. Miraculously, I sleep.

Saturday, August 5, Day 52 of our voyage in "Last Chance," dawns quietly. Except for the two A.M. "freight," we had a relatively quiet night. Seas roll gently under the raft, and a light, southerly breeze keeps the temperature in the raft near perfect, at least for me. Sim and I have two different body temperatures. She heats earlier than I do and strips down to bare skin while I'm still wrapped under a cover.

The day is perfect to fix the air leak. The patch is ready to go, and Sim begins to pump as I turn onto my knees and lean over the side. I unlace the flaps that hold the compressed air cylinder, untie the maze of string that hold the rags, and feel for the hole.

Sim worries: "Bill, be careful. Don't make the hole any bigger. Don't do any damage. Do you hear me?"

"Yes, dear." If I'd listen to Sim, we'd never try a thing.

"Don't yes dear me at a time like this. We could die."

"Si, mi amor. Hand me the patch, pump, pray, and be quiet."

"You're impossible!"

As I push the head of the screw into the hole, a loud hiss

makes my heart skip. I hesitate. Sim had said not to make it worse, but worse it will have to be to get the screw and washer in. I push a little harder, and the air hiss is again magnified. What have I done? Is this the right way to do it? Suppose I open the hole, and the fix doesn't work? I give it another shove, and the head of the screw slips in. Now it's the washers turn. The head was a quarter inch wide..the washer is a half inch. Oh, my God, will it work?

Sim gasps loudly as air gushes out and creates a noisy sea of bubbles. I can't get the washer in without first cutting open the hole. I draw back and look down at the bubbles and think. What do I do now? Whatever I do, it must be fast and it must be sure.

Sim, busy pumping, can't help hear the escaping air. "What's happening? Can you fix it?"

"I'm almost finished," I lie.

"How much more?"

"I'm almost through."

In reality, I'm in a dilemma. I don't dare open the tear any further. If the fix doesn't work, what will I do then? I try to relax and think.

"Bill, I'm getting tired. Have you fixed it? I hear a loud noise. What have you done?" Sim pumps faster to stay ahead of the escaping air.

"I'm almost finished." Damn. I don't dare open a bigger hole. I better leave it alone. I pull out the screw head. A loud hiss confirms the hole is larger than it was before. I hand the assembly to Sim.

"Hold it."

"What happened? I thought you had it fixed. My God. Listen to that air coming out. Bill, what have you done? Oh, Lord, have mercy on us. He's done it again!"

"Everything is OK."

"What do you mean, Ok? I can hear the air coming out. It's worse!"

"I'll have it fixed in a jiffy."

"HELP!" she screams.

I work feverishly. I lace the flaps back up and stuff all of my rags between the hole and the flap. The leak is definitely a lot worse than before. I rearrange the rags a dozen times. Nothing helps.

"So, what happened?"

"I couldn't get the patch inside."

"I knew it. You made the hole bigger. You did it again. You really want us dead. Not even God can save us if you keep hindering His efforts."

"The hole is the same size. Listen. It's the same as before. No problem."

"No problem, he says. No problem! My God. Here we are, surrounded by hordes of sharks, lost in the Pacific, in a raft with a new, manmade monstrous air leak, and the man says no problem. You're dangerous."

"What do you suggest? Are you planning to swim for it? Go. So long. Can I help you over the side?"

"You're detestable."

"It's probably genetic. Perhaps brain surgery can help when we get back."

"Get back! The captain says "get back" in one breath, and in another, he does his best to kill us. Bill Butler, you're not going to touch another thing on this raft. Nothing. Are you listening to me?"

"Am I listening? They can probably hear you back on the island. Ok, that's it. No more repairs. You do it."

We settle back down. I should have thought the problem out in more detail. At the moment of truth, I failed to follow through with my plan. If I had opened a slight slit in the tube, the patch would now be in place, the air loss contained, and Sim calm and quiet.

I make two liters of water while Sim keeps pumping every 15 minutes. This cannot go on. I have to do something but now I am shaken, scared. Every time Sim looks at me, I recoil. But she is right. I need to be extra careful. A false move now and nothing can save us. I know she would like me to fix the leak, but at the same time, she fears the outcome.

I prepare to fish against Sim's protests. Not a trigger fish is in sight. I chum and the bait remains untouched. We never had that happen before. Other fish race around, nervous. Earlier this morning, in the distance, we had noticed a school of fish breaking water. They jumped as if they were either feeding or trying to avoid being part of someone's lunch. I throw out a few more pieces of bait as chum. Several triggers swim within reach. In twenty minutes, I catch ten. As we lunch, we find out why all the fish are so nervous. A pod of large Pacific dolphins feed nearby.

We count five large dolphins, three times heavier than our Florida "Flipper" variety. These are ten feet long and are dark gray with small darker spots. With powerful thrusts, they zoom around feeding busily. "Shark pack" circles at the ten foot level, never far from the raft, but careful to remain out of the way of the dolphins.

At three in the afternoon, all hell breaks loose. The dolphins start to feed in a wild frenzy. They go crazy and drive their thousand pounds at high speeds in search of the two hundred pounds of fish they need a day. It appears they are intent on getting today's ration from under our raft. As the afternoon progresses, the dolphins feed more aggressively. The sharks join the frenzy and also zoom inches from the raft in their quest to swallow whatever is in their path.

Their prey, mostly trigger fish, badly in need of shelter, head for the raft. We become the center of activity. Sharks and dolphins bump the raft without stop. A foaming sea of fish surrounds us. What should we do? What can we do? The situation has quickly turned deadly. We still pump air every 15 minutes.

The creatures become wilder. Incredibly, the sharks and dolphins work as a team, each exciting the other into more savage bursts of speed. We, in turn, become more tense, for instead of dispersing, the battle field is tighter as the afternoon grows. We pray for darkness in hopes the sharks and dolphins will take their fill and leave. They seldom feed at night, but when night at last falls, the frenzy continues at full tilt. Large masses of phosphorescence speed under us. The raft is battered and made to spin. I yell and splash the pole, but nothing works.

We lie down and try not to panic. There is nothing we can do but pray. The dolphins are tireless and have turned the sharks into wild feeders. Small fish leap out of the water to escape the frenzied jaws. The fight drags on late into the night. My mind races to come up with a way out...there is none. My watch chimes...midnight.

Suddenly, the raft shoots straight up. We're on a bucking bronco. The raft shakes fiercely from side to side. We're tossed up, down, right, left, and forward in violent jerks. I hold Sim tightly as I try to fathom this new crisis. What has us in its grip? I fully expect to see a set of great, bloodthirsty teeth emerge through the floor of the raft. Sim prays at full voice and beseeches her favorite saints for help as never before. We're thrown a foot up with each savage thrust. This is surely the end. Time stands still. Whatever it is, it does not release its hold. This poor raft is doomed. We hug each other tightly, convinced our end is close at hand.

The raft explodes from a violent convulsion. I brace for the sudden rush of water. But the raft is quiet. It's over and we're still afloat. It had to be a shark caught in one of the ballast bags. A dolphin would have torn the entire raft to shreds.

Moments later, we're thrown into the air by another savage thrust. Sim screams. I hold her tightly in one arm and grab the pole in the other. We're pushed around furiously, propelled through the water by an invisible, turbulent force. All movement stops as it started. We're still alive. Oh, Lord, what test do you have for us next?

chapter twelve

0200 SUNDAY AUGUST 6, 1989, DAY 53

We log in August 6, Sunday, day 53 adrift, at two in the morning. The battle around us continues to unfold. The wild ride two hours ago still has us badly shaken. Sharks and dolphins jostle the raft, and by the size of the phosphorescence, even dorados have joined in. We hang on and pray as never before. Is this the end?

Why are we still alive? Why didn't the shark in the ballast bag destroy the raft? It's nothing but another miracle. What a great God we have. We squint into the darkness. Breathing and splashing confirm the melee is at peak. Two more hard bumps shake the raft. Then we feel a hard rasping thump along the floor of the raft. Sim cries out.

"Bill, they did it. They holed the raft."

"What do you mean?"

"There's water coming in. We're sinking!"

I get ready to tell her she's wrong when I feel the rush of cold water. Water rises quickly over the cushions. Sim pulls up a cushion, and I hold it as she bails frantically. The night is too black to search for the leak. We must wait until dawn. Sim bails without letup while I pump air. Now we have two serious problems. I turn on the flashlight and find an empty Evian bottle which I cut in half. With the larger container, Sim keeps up with the leak if she doesn't stop.

The scrape we heard had to be a dolphin. Its dorsal fin sliced a hole in the bottom. What luck, it didn't tear the air chamber. Or is the floor of the raft coming apart at the seams? I dare not speculate further. We must await morning. Exhausted, I fall asleep at once.

Sim bails non-stop for three hours. At five, I take over. She curls up on the spot and falls into a deep sleep. I dip the bottom half of the Evian bottle into the bilge and toss the water over the side. I bail a full container every three or four seconds. It's hopeless to look for the damage. It could be anywhere. Outside there is no activity. Damage done, the monsters have all left like the whales that sank *Siboney*. Damn them all!

I bail right through sunup. When Sim awakens, she separates the cushions in the middle of the raft and finds that the leak is coming from the bow. She moves the gear piled on the first cushion to the opposite end of the raft. She lifts the cushion and finds no damage under it. She picks up the second cushion.

"Here it is," she cries out. "My God! The tear's four inches long and the water pours in. Can we fix it?" With the cushion removed, water gushes in faster, bubbling inside the raft. I bail furiously.

The gash is a foot or so from the bow and near the center of the floor. A dolphin, in a high speed pass, cut a corner a bit close. Sim presses the two sides together to slow the flow but cannot keep it together. I let air out of the air chamber to make the bottom of the raft less taught.

"Let's try to sew it closed, Sim. Do you still have that needle and thread? I'll hold it while you look."

Sim digs into her toiletry kit and pulls out a shiny darning needle and a package of threads. I thread the needle with six strands then push the blunt needle through the fabric while Sim holds both sides of the tear together. The can opener is my pusher. I get the first stitch through and tie it off.

Two stitches later, two strands tangle and break. On the next pass, all the threads tangle. I cut the thread and leave the stitches in.

Sim bails while I cut a two foot length of the parachute cord supplied with the raft and unravel it. When I have the needle ready, Sim drops the bailing can, pulls up both sides of the tear, and holds them together to slow the flow. I push the needle through the holes I had opened, and the tear comes together as I work my way down to the aft end of the raft. Eleven stitches close the hole though a trickle of water continues to flow into the raft. At least, we will not have to bail non-stop.

The raft is a total mess. Cushions, bedding, gear, all sopped, spread in every direction. Worse of all, the Log book got wet.

"Sim, let's reorganize the cushions."

"What do you mean? What crazy idea do you have now?"

"Water will continue to leak into the raft. If we leave the cushions as they are, we'll be swimming in water all the time. Besides there will not be enough room to bail."

"And how do you want them now?"

"We'll put one on top of the other on the long side of the raft. In that way, we'll stay drier, and we'll have a groove in the middle to scoop up the water."

"I don't like the idea."

"Why?"

"We'll fall off. It'll be uncomfortable. I don't like it."

"Ok. Then get ready to swim all the time. And how do you plan to bail? The cushions cover the entire bottom. One on top of the other is the best solution. There will be a space between your cushions and mine."

"Let's think about it."

"Think about it? Until when? Until after we're neck deep in water for a week?"

Somehow we find a way to lean back and rest a bit. Sim bails every 15 minutes. I hold a cushion up as she dips under it. If she waits twenty minutes, water rises over the cushions and soaks my shirt. On the other hand, we've been soaked for weeks, alternating between salt water and rain water.

I insist: "Come on, let's do it."

"Ok. But I don't like it."

Instead of four cushions crosswise on the floor of the raft, we place two lengthwise on each side of the raft. Two smaller cushions, each a foot square, support our head. Our feet rest on life preservers, jackets, and wet bedding.

Our gear now sits directly on the raft floor, and an eight inch space between the cushions is perfect for bailing. I take advantage of the cool weather to make water. Sim offers to help, but she's busy enough bailing four times an hour and pumping. I soon have the water made and fish caught, filleted, and served. We settle down for a quick lunch.

We find it hard to adjust to the new cushion arrangement. With the wider of the cushions on top, we have more surface to lie on. But the top cushion slides off every time we move. Our situation gets worse by the hour. We can no longer huddle to keep warm.

Bilge water rises over the cushion several times each hour and resoaks my shirt. My back sores sting like thousands of needles. And to make matters worse, rainfall continues.

Sim stayed awake and bailed every fifteen minutes all night so afraid she is that we will sink. I have been unable to convince her that the cold water lapping on our bare behinds is a fail-safe, early warning system. We drift along quietly. The seas are so calm and quiet I can clearly hear the hiss of air escaping from the hole behind the rags. We've got to do something about it.

"You're not going to touch any part of this raft again. Ever again. Are you listening?"

"Yes, dear." How can she read my mind in the dark?

"Don't yes, dear me. Have a little respect. If it wasn't for me, you'd be dead."

"Listen," I say. "What's that?"

Sim looks out the window. "Dolphins. They're back. Oh, Lord. How long? How long will this continue? There are two, no three, four, five. Oh, no, they are the same ones! Not another day like yesterday." A dolphin blows next to the raft; it's almost whale size.

Sim is tired and distraught; "They really want to destroy us and the raft. I know they will not leave until the raft is in pieces. And you didn't cut loose the broken pieces of the ballast bags. I told you they were hanging down all torn and could entangle a shark or dolphin. But no, you ignore my suggestions. It's OK to tinker with the patch and almost kill us, but when real maintenance needs to be done, you do nothing. You are a pain."

"Just pray, will you?"

"Pray, ha! I'll probably pray that the dolphins swim away with you and leave me in peace and quiet."

"You'd be bored in no time. Give me a kiss."

"Give you a kiss? You have thirty days of rotten fish hanging on your beard. I'd probably get salmonella. I'd rather kiss a jelly fish. Besides we have work to do. Let's try to fix the air leak. It's too dangerous to have all those problems together. We must resolve them one by one, or we won't make it. Why can't you arrange the rags like you did on the first day?"

She is right, but I didn't need her prodding. I know we have to repair the air leak, but I need to relax before I try. I nod off. When I awaken, Sim snoozes.

At noon, I fish, but our usually teaming aquarium is void of life. The dolphins surely have scared them all away. The trigger fish remain calm when dozens of sharks swim within their schools, but when dolphins appear, they panic and vanish.

An hour later, I try again but the ocean is still empty. The sea is glassy. There's a light wind out of the southwest. A current out of the West pushes us east. I make two liters of water. Will I be strong enough, in a week or two, to continue making water?

The Log Book is sopped and now weighs several pounds. It contains a record of our voyage until day 52. Today is the 7th of August, day 54 on the raft. We're 75 days out of Balboa. The trip to Honolulu from Panama should have taken no more than 60 days. We're 15 days overdue. Is no one worried? If they are, why isn't anyone looking for us?

"Sim, where's my camera?"

"You must be kidding. Your camera went under days ago."

"Where is it?"

"Under your feet."

I dig my Minolta out from under a pile of foul weather jackets. It's exactly as Sim said, soaked inside of the protective ziploc. I should have removed the film with the shots of the big dorado and the snap on the Fourth of July. Over the side and into the depths it goes after I remove the film. The film is soaked, and when I rewind it, the emulsion peels off.

The trigger fish return late in the afternoon, and soon after, dinner is on the paddle. Sim eats better now than she did weeks ago. While we eat, the continuous gurgle from the air leak reminds us that soon we should do something about it. Sim bails every fifteen minutes. She manages to get the water to drain to a spot in the raft where she can bail easier by shifting her body around. When I bail, the water is everywhere except where I want it. When I sit up to bail, the water collects under me where I can't get to it. So I let Sim do it.

A red sky lingers at sunset. I'm up, watching the ever changing cumulus on the western horizon. I call out: "Sim, look. There's Alf."

"And over there, there's Mara." Mara was our schnauzer. Cloud watching has always been one of our favorite pastimes while at sea. Layers of orange and red clouds rising above the calm sea leads to sunset. Sim reads from her now very damp assortment of cards. We watch as the last remaining light plays with the clouds overhead. And we pray harder tonight as our little vessel, no longer sturdy, floats gently towards the east...

"Bill, are you awake?"

"Yes."

"I just heard the news from the Voice of America. The tax people got Leona. There's a big protest in Hiroshima on the 44th anniversary of the bomb. I'm glad we're not there. They haven't found the ten people on the oil rig that fell off Texas. Big summit in Honduras of Central American leaders. That's it."

"Better than the Miami Herald. Is there any mention of two ding dongs missing in the Pacific Ocean? Isn't anyone worried? We go off the scope for two months, and the world goes on. Is no one looking for us? What must one do to call on a search?"

I can't believe no one has notified ships in this area to be on the look out for us. More than thirty ships have passed so far within a mile or less. These are the ones we have seen. How many more passed while we weren't looking?

Sim turns onto her knees and looks out the window. I wrap my hand easily around her upper thighs.

"I see a ship. It's far away. No running lights, only two white masthead lights. The lower light is in front. It's coming this way."

Sim has learned how to read ships like a pro. Large ocean going ships have two bright lights visible when the ship is heading in our direction. The lower of the two lights in near the bow of the ship. The angle between the two lights and their location tell us whether the ship is coming our way or not. In this case, the lower light facing us confirms it is heading in our direction. If the two white lights don't line up, Sim can tell it is not going to pass close by. I dig the compass out from under the covers.

"Sim, where is it?"

"Let's see. Look, it's there."

I follow Sim's hand and flash the light at the compass for a second. Three hundred and forty degrees. That means he's heading away from the Canal. The ships we have seen in the last two days have passed to the east or inshore. This ship is inshore but not as far as the others. Soon one must come close, heading our way. We can alert him with our last remaining flare.

I take another look. "He's still heading for us but far away."

"Shall we use the lantern? Shine an SOS?"

"Not yet. Still too far."

Sim lies down, worn out after her fifteen minutes as lookout. In a few minutes, I row the raft around to face the ship. Swells are ten feet, and the ship is out of sight most of the time. It will pass about a mile and a half towards shore.

A mile and a half. We drift at a rate of ten to fifteen miles a day. Let's call it twelve miles a day or one half knot. In three hours or four, we will be in that ship's line of travel. Perhaps the next ship that comes by...

"That ship is gone. What time is it?"

"Two twenty."

"Over five hours to dawn. I have to bail."

Every time I sit up, my cushions slide towards the middle of the raft. We must move them back before Sim can bail, then arch my body with my head on the air tube and my feet on the end of the raft. Sim pushes my cushions back up against the side of the raft. She fills the bailing cup, and I throw it over the side. Six or seven dips and the bilge is dry. I plug in the air pump and start to fill the chamber with air.

WHACK.

The sound of the air must excite the sharks. We never fail to be punched. I've tried to pump air quietly, but the sharks still hear the noise and attack. Luckily, there is no moon tonight, and when I sit up, I can see several large shapes under the raft. I remain ready. Sim's side receives several bumps. More hits on Sim's side. Then a hard whack spins the raft around. I thrust the pole in the water and use it as an oar. We come back on course and I wait.

"Bill, you have to pump. The raft is limp."

I still haven't seen the shark. This one is smart. It hasn't hit my side of the raft yet. I lie down and resort to splashing. It's quiet. The shark has left. I pump the raft up and nap. When I awaken, dawn approaches. Sim still dozes. I turn on my side and begin to bail. I can't get much at a time but at least enough to keep it from soaking Sim.

That's a laugh. Soaking Sim. She's so saturated I could wring a quart of salt water out of her. She sleeps, hair in a tangle, blue trash from the canopy spots her face. I look her over. She has lost a lot of weight. Her thighs were the last to slim down. She's lost her bottom and belly and sadly her pretty bosom. Three weeks ago, she was at her perfect weight. What a shame, we were not saved then. Now her body consumes what little fat remains. When I wrap both hands around my thighs, I now have a six inch overlap though I eat more than a pound of fish a day. Sim stirs.

We kiss and hug without a word. Nights take their toll on us. The invisible, lurking death that surrounds us is so oppressive that, even if we do nap, we awaken exhausted. The gurgle from the escaping bubbles constantly remind us of the raft's bad leak. Yesterday, I lost another of my precious rotten rags. I have tied each of the remaining rags with several strings. We pump air every twenty minutes and the raft is always limp. The floor collapses under our weight and doubles in two whenever a wave rolls by. Two or three times a day, I rearrange the rags. Nothing stops the leaks.

Over the past week, I have gone over why I failed to fix the leak. I simply lost my nerve. I hesitated to open a 1/4 inch hole in the fabric for my backing plate to enter. I should have forced the entire assembly through the hole and let the air leak out for a few seconds. That's what I'll do next time. No, not next time. Now. Right now!

It will take every trick I learned in 40 years as a salesman to get Sim to go along with the new patch project. I have new parts ready. I assemble them, test them, then take them apart. Sim has been watching me.

"What are you doing?"

"What?"

"Don't try to fool me. You're making another patch."

"I'm just keeping busy. Using my hands. I'm the nervous

type."

"You, nervous? You don't have a nerve in your body nor a brain in your head. Bill Butler, I know you. You can't leave anything alone. You're going to screw things up again. Last time you fooled with the leak, you made it worse."

"You always exaggerate."

"Butler, the Lord is watching everything you do. And so am I."

"Sim, I am only trying to make the raft safer. That hole is leaking more and more."

"That's because a fool fooled with it instead of leaving it alone."

"This time, I know I can do it. Look at this patch. Mod II. So much better than the original model. It's going to work. Our pumping days will be easier."

"I don't believe a word you say."

"Ok. Go ahead and pump air every twenty minutes. Bail every 15. Baby, I can fix it. This time it will work."

"That's a laugh."

"We've got to fix that hole. I pumped every twenty minutes last night."

"And what do you think I was doing? Dancing in Chiriqui? I bailed every 15 minutes. I didn't sleep at all. I am dead, worn out, finished, and tired of your tricks."

"I push the washer and gasket inside the tube. With the wing nut, I'll tighten the outside gasket and washer against the inside. Guaranteed."

"Guaranteed? Where do I collect the guarantee after you sink the raft and all those beasts eat us up?"

"There's a guy down at the bottom called Davy Jones. He takes care of all payoffs."

"Ok, ok...go down to your buddy Davy with your patch and leave me alone. You tried the same exact method last time, and it didn't work. What's new?"

"OK, forget it. I won't do it. Let's pump and bail ourselves to death." She's getting on my nerves....but suppose it doesn't work?

I fiddle all day with the patch. The washer I made for my first try was the core of my problem. It was too big to push through the small hole in the plastic. When I started, there wasn't a real hole. The air leaked from an abrasion. I must open a hole in the air chamber first.

This patch should go on tomorrow. Now it's late and I'm tired. If I screw it up again, Sim will never forgive me. That is, if she survives her heart attack.

"Sim, look. I have the patch all figured out." I show it to Sim and explain how I plan to stop the leak.

She listens intently and then says reluctantly. "I'm not sure. I'm at the point where I panic when you bring up a new idea. If we have to do it, let's do it. We can't go on like this. This is hell."

"Why don't you read for now? Start with the one about foot steps in the sand."

Tonight I ask Sim to read the psalms twice. While she reads, I bail. We no longer settle down for the night. We have to bail and pump and fight sharks without stop. The beasts buffet the raft all night. We fight, pray, and splash the pole in the water. I don't bother to sit up any longer. I tie the pole to my wrist, dangle it in the water, and go about my chores..

I fall asleep with the pole in the water. A sharp shark whack awakens me and I find the pole gone. I grope in the dark in real panic. Minutes pass before I recall it's attached to my wrist and floats alongside.

Morning is so slow in arriving. We perch on our cushions, naked. The black striped comforter is a wet, lumpy mass good only for use as a pillow. Simonne sleeps on her life jacket. Buckles and hard foam press into her bony body as she fidgets to get body and cushion into synch. By then, she has to bail again.

I can't ever get comfortable. Sometimes I try to sleep on the bare cushion which is smooth but hard. Then I spread the soggy foul weather gear under me, but the creases tear into my sores. Edges in the foul weather jacket feel like barbed wire. Our semi-comfort is completely gone. Bare survival has taken its place.

Once the sun is up and the day portends to be calm, I gather up my courage and announce: "The time has come for the patch job." I don't know what else to say; the words sound hollow even to me.

"OK, as long as you're sure of what you're doing."

"I screwed up last time. I lost my nerve. I got scared when I heard the air hissing out and didn't push the screw in all the way. This time I will do it right. Don't worry."

"I'm worried to death."

"Relax, baby. Here, look over the patch. Inspect it. Check it out. It will do the trick. It's better than pumping every twenty minutes."

"Twenty minutes is better than sinking or pumping every ten minutes if you botch it again."

"Ok. Let's forget it. Let's keep pumping. I'm through arguing. End of subject."

I turn over and extend my back to Sim. I feign disinterest and sleep. A half hour passes.

"Bill, time to pump air."

"I'm through pumping air. Let it sink. What the hell, it's going to sink sooner or later. Or the sharks will get us. Why suffer any longer? Let's get it over with."

Sim grabs the pump and fills the air chamber.

A half hour passes. The leak gets worse. She pumps again. Then out of the blue, Sim says, "Bill, are you positive it'll work?"

" I was going to say guaranteed, but.."

"Ok. Be very careful."

"I'm always careful."

"Baloney. If you're going to do it, get it over with."

"That's a girl. What a raft mate. I'll have it fixed in a jif."

"Be careful."

Sim pumps air into the chamber until it's tight. I get on my knees and lean over the side. Sim has the screw with the gaskets all assembled and ready to go. I remove the rags and unlace the flaps. I feel for the hole. The slit is so small I can barely feel it. Only the bubbles tells me where it is.

"Sim, hand me your nail file. Then put the pump on and get ready to pump."

"What are you going to do with the nail file?"

"I'm only going to clear some threads away." I keep lying to Sim. If I tell her I plan to shove the file into the air chamber to open the hole, she'll scream. She hands me the file. I open the hole. Masses of larger bubbles escape. I hand the file back to Sim with a trembling hand.

"Pump up the raft and hand me the patch."

The screw has the two washers and the two gaskets and the wing nut in the proper order. Just as I start to push the patch into the hole, I notice the wing nut is missing. I look around in desperation. All I see is blue ocean and loads of trigger fish eager to snack on my fingers. The wing nut fell off. I've done it again. The frothy burble has never been worse.

I lost the other wing nut yesterday under the cushions but didn't bother to find it. The heavy line of bubbles pours out of the hole I call out: "Sim, pump!"

Sim screams. "What happened? What are you doing? What's that noise? The raft is getting limp. I can't keep up. Oh, God, not again, not again."

"I'm only adjusting the patch. Be quiet." If Sim finds out I've lost the wing nut, it'll be the big casino. I'll lose my last strands of credibility. I'll probably lose something worse.

I lift the cushion and try to remain and act calm. Inside I'm frantic. I dig through the accumulation of trash....tiny bits of paper, fish scales, threads, hair...I'll never find it. Why did I start this project anyway? We could have pumped every twenty minutes. All of a sudden, pumping doesn't seem a major chore. If I can't find the wing nut...I don't dare think of the consequences.

I turn the top cushion over, and my heart jumps when I see the wing nut on top of the bottom cushion. I quickly screw it on to the patch, this time with threads to spare. I feel for the hole with my finger, then push the head of the screw inside the air chamber. The washer will not go through. Bubbles increase ten fold when I lean on the screw. The hole is still too narrow. I push harder but can't see what I'm doing for all the bubbles. I push with all my remaining strength. With a pop, the washer slides in, and the flexible leather gasket slides in easily after it.

The squeal of air lessens as I tighten up on the wing nut. In seconds, it's over. The leak is plugged. I lean back slowly. Sim has been pumping wildly and praying aloud. The sudden increase in pressure takes her by surprise. She knows not what to expect. "How did it go? Did you fix it?" She appears stunned. She would like to believe it's fixed but remains unconvinced.

We pump again and plug the air valve and wait. A half hour passes. I lean over. Some bubbles still escape although at a much slower rate. An hour passes.

Sim is overjoyed. "You did it. Baby, you did it." She embraces and kisses me.

"I didn't think you kissed murderers and terrorists, particularly unshaven, unbathed ones. Here, look for a spot without fish scales."

She hugs me.

"You are wonderful. What would I do without you?

"Well, let's see. You could marry a guy who likes dry land. Or someone who takes you around the world on the QE2 with all your finery. Instead you marry a sailor with a sunken boat and a leaky raft who forgot to bring along your clothes. You are really not all that bright."

Two more ships pass to the East. One heads north, the other south. They are less than a mile away. We don't bother to hail. Sim tunes in new stations from San Jose and one from Punta Arenas, both in Costa Rica and both come in strong. There's also a country station from a town called David, in Panama, advertising a barbecue for the weekend...will we make it...?

We're ready for shore. Two pairs of shorts stored under us in a plastic bag haven't been inspected in a month. Will they fall apart like the two T-shirts we bought in Balboa? Those rotted to the point I couldn't even use them as rags to stuff into the leak.

The first day of our ninth week aboard "Last Chance" dawns clear, bright. A tinge of orange tints all horizons. What sort of an omen is that? The patch has improved our life style. We now only pump air every hour and a quarter. One less burden. Sim bails every fifteen minutes, day and night.

How can I improve the fix on the hole in the floor of the raft? I should've put a gasket between the edges when we first sewed the hole together. What can I do to slow the leak?

Shark attacks are down from eighty whacks a day to forty. I expected more sharks as we neared the coast, but it's turned out the other way. I've heard hordes of sharks roam the coasts of Nicaragua and El Salvador. Do we have another great white visiting? Will shark activity get worse as we close with shore?

I fish, make water; Sim bails and looks out; in between, we try our best to find a position that affords a few moments of comfort. Whenever I move, the top cushion slides towards the middle and chokes off the space Sim needs to bail. Then I must move again as Sim pushes my cushions back into their place.

Sim reads as night engulfs our little world. Though the radio tells us we're moving closer, why haven't we seen a fishing boat? When will the current change? At some point, many miles off shore, the easterly current has to turn either north or south. Or will it turn 180 degrees and flow back out to sea? I sleep with my head full of unknowns.

Three ships pass between two and three in the morning, all inside of us, that is, towards shore. Two were bound for Panama and the other headed north. All were too far away to bother signalling. Sim maintains an hourly lookout. She rarely sleeps, for she's afraid that I will also sleep and the raft will fill with water or sink from lack of air or that a freighter will run us down. When I've taken over the bailing chores, I fall asleep after an hour or so, and the water rises over the cushions. Sim awakens from a few moments asleep, her face in the water, sputtering and furious.

Morning opens up on a grey note. A threat of rain is to the north. Simonne looks out the window towards the east and northeast for signs of land. During the past several days, I have often gotten a feeling that she has seen something. Like the island we passed, she will not call "Land-ho" until she is sure it is land. When she first spied the island, I, the incurable optimist, hoped it was mainland. As we approached it and until the very last, I had hoped to see land attached to it. That island had to be Isla de Cocos, for no other island is that far from shore.

Sim has been studying the horizon for an entire day. She looks in one direction more than in others. I keep my eye on her for a telltale sign. She maintains her concentration which, in itself, is heartening.

Curiosity gets the best of me. "Sim, what do you see?"

"I'm not sure. Behind all those clouds, I think I see land. A high line of mountains. When I see it, clouds cover what I'm looking at, and it's there no more. It looks dark blue, darker than the clouds."

How many times in the past weeks have I and Sim too stared at a low lying black line on the horizon? The line remained unchanged for a long while until we were sure it was land. It always turned out to be a cloud.

Simonne rests. I take advantage of the interlude to make two liters of water and catch six trigger fish. Afterwards, I am about asleep when several sharp slaps announce the arrival of the shark pack. Three pokes later and they leave. Their interest in us is not as intense as weeks ago.

I remove my T-shirt to dry the sores on my back and nap. When I awaken, Sim is again scanning the eastern horizon. I pull the binoculars out from under my head where they have been part of my pillow for at least six weeks. One eye piece is full of water. The other, although opaque, passes some light. I disassemble them using the knife as a screw driver and wash the eyepieces, then the mirrors and prisms in fresh water. The sun quickly dries the parts which I reassemble. With the prisms aligned and the eye pieces replaced, I take a look and still see nothing. Water is trapped inside the eyepiece which cannot be taken apart. I remove the strap and toss the binoculars over the side.

Sim's is ecstatic and cries out: "I can see land! There's no question about it. The same mountain peak is there. Low clouds cover the horizon, but above those clouds, I count three peaks. The mountains are high. It has to be mainland. We cannot be far."

I lean up and look at gentle valleys leading up to dark blue peaks hovering in the sky, three or four thousand feet high. "It could be thirty to fifty miles," I tell her. "We could be closer."

As sunset begins its inevitable retreat, Sim reads our daily psalms. The sun sets, and as soon as night takes over from day, we notice lightning in the distance. Soon we hear our first thunder.

"Bill, that storm is coming closer. A while ago, I counted to sixty, but the latest thunder came 40 seconds after the flash."

"Bath time. Get the soap. I hope it misses us because it's chilly tonight."

"Thirty."

"Twenty." Both of us count and compare.

"Wow, that was a big bolt. Bill, do you think we could get hit by lighting? What would it do to us?"

"I'd hate to say it couldn't hit us, the way my luck has been running, but it's extremely unlikely. There's nothing to attract it to us except the water maker. Besides the swells are still fifteen to twenty feet, and we're under the surface level more than half the time. I wouldn't worry about it."

Sim jumps up. "What's that? Listen. A ship!" She looks out and cries out: "No! Look! Oh, my God, it's rain. It's coming this way."

A flash of lightning lights up the ocean and the white wall of rain roaring in from the north. I can see it in the darkness, accompanied by a deafening roar...a white wall...the worst type of squall. We zip up and tighten the windows. I pull my blanket out from under my cushion, soaked and cold, and, without hesitation, pull it over my semi-naked body. Sim covers up with her usual trash bag.

The first gusts of forty knots quickly increase to fifty. Rain hits the raft horizontally and with the wind rushes through the windows and canopy. I push the canopy up with the fishing rod as water sprays into the raft; the cold wind and rain sends shivers through us. I pull my blanket up higher. It's almost warm now. This Andean wool blanket has kept me warm many a night. Sim screams every time an edge rubs against her.

Sheets of rain with hurricane force winds propel the raft to the southwest. We time a lightning bolt at ten seconds, a mile away. I hold Sim's hand and hang on with the other. Gusts of sixty to seventy knots threaten to blow the canopy off. Our fragile raft, without main ballast bags, hugs the sea. We tie the watermaker and pump.

Wind and rain pummel us. Thunder and lightning spend themselves in a powerful show of bravado. The wind decreases and the rain eases. Soon we hear but a distant rumble. We have survived one more trial. What's next?

We slumber, numbed with cold. Sim bails for the balance of the night at the usual fifteen minute intervals. I pump air every forty five. The need to bail every fifteen minutes consumes what little energy we still have. When she starts, Sim can quickly remove four or five cans of water. To get the rest, I have again to suspend myself from head and feet to get the water to trickle slowly from under my cushion into the well created by the ball of Sim's hand as she pushes down on the floor of the raft.

Weeks ago, she used the sponges supplied with the raft to remove the last dribbles of water. When the sponges thoroughly rotted, she sopped water with pieces of the rotting T-shirts and strips of the cotton blanket. Now we have nothing left with which to remove these last drops. Anyway, the tear in the bottom of the raft has left us with a sense of resignation we have been unable to shake. At one time, we busied ourselves drying our covers...Sim was always busy housekeeping. Now we languish in our rotting raft too exhausted to care how we live.

My wool blanket lives in the bilge, thoroughly soaked, under my feet, for there is no other place for it. Sim's irritated and chaffed skin screams if the rough saltwater soaked wool touches her. I try to keep it as far away from her as a raft three feet wide will permit. If I can see that the night is going to be cold and rainy, I wring the blanket out before dark and pull it over me, wet and cold. Fifteen minutes later, I am warm as toast. Sim shivers under her plastic garbage bag.

Toast...food...since Sim mentioned "blini," the word has bounced around inside my head louder and louder. It's Blini-Blini-Blini-hundreds of blinis. I've asked Sim never to mention food of any kind again. It's bad enough to put on the wool gloves with Haagen Daz emblazoned on the back every time I fish. When I get to shore, I'm going to swim in ice cream.

Incredible luck continues to follow us. The three inch rip in the bottom of the raft could easily have been six inches or ten or the full length of the raft. I shudder at the scene; our water making machine could have dropped through the hole; water would have flooded the raft instantly. There is no way we could have contained the water as we did with our four inch hole.

I look to the heavens. Lord, You are merciful. You teach with force and vigor, all metered, never to excess. But enough is enough, Lord. Give us a break....

We continue to bail, day and night, through calm and storm. Lack of sleep tells on us, particularly Sim, who needs a long time to fall asleep. I don't make a move to bail while Sim is awake. And she barely sleeps. She hasn't slept for at least two days. I may bail for an hour around dawn which is the only time Sim naps. While I sleep, she bails and tosses the water out on her own. She over-bails. I am unable to convince her there's nothing wrong with a little extra water in the raft. She refuses to listen.

She is as hard headed as a mule, yet, were she not hard-headed, stubborn, ingenious, and resourceful, we would not have made it this far. She's cursed me, humiliated me, screamed and yelled and carried on, but at the same time, she has helped and sustained me; we've prayed and laughed and cried together, and through it all, she's loved me. A warm feeling flows through me with the certainty of my love for her. We could not have survived this long without each other's help. We belong together. We will be saved together, and our life will be even better than before now that we have found God....

chapter thirteen

0745 SATURDAY AUGUST 12, 1989, DAY 59

Shafts of golden light overcome the dreariness of dawn. Another endless night is over. As if in pity for our plight, wind and waves fade away. The new day radiates hope and promise. Sim looks to the east and cries out with excitement: "Bill, look! Land! Land! Mainland. Mountains. It's so beautiful. It's so clear I can see one, two, no, three mountain peaks. And valleys. I can see the entire coast all the way from north to east. It's spectacular! We are getting closer. God, how could I have doubted you so?"

I pull myself up to the window. Sim gives me a final lift. Pale blue mountains float high above the morning mist. Below the peaks, valleys cascade into the sea. We feast upon the ridge of high mountains that extend far to the north. This is true mainland...mainland Central America...of that there is no doubt.

Sim asks the one question that's been on my mind. "How far away do you think it is? It looks so near and, at the time, so far away."

"It's hard to tell. The peak, the high one in the middle, could be thirty, forty, even fifty miles away. In Manila, on a clear day, we could see the peak on Bataan, fifty miles away. And it looked about the same. The shoreline is much closer than the peaks that we see, but we won't see it for several days."

We marvel at our vista. As the sun rises, light strikes promontory after promontory. Between the dark expanses of forests, rectangular fields of cultivation dot the mountains. We cannot believe that the goal of our voyage is actually in sight...a sight that will not fade into the shape of distant clouds.

Is our voyage really almost over? We have traversed more than a thousand miles of open ocean. Our fragile vessel has fallen victim to giant seas, violent storms, and a multitude of vicious monsters of the sea. By a series of miracles, we have survived their onslaught. Overwhelming gratitude brings us to prayer and to tears of joy.

Sim's spirits turn as bright as our skyline. She's been a remarkable crew. She fought to live and has suffered deeply because of it. I see in her but a shadow of the woman who sailed with me on *Siboney*. She has lived long in the shadow of death. Many weeks ago, she had made peace with the Maker and accepted His will. Now she knows that she will live to tell her story.

Sim's radio picks up signals from San Jose, the capital of Costa Rica and from a town called Carthago. Last night, she again heard a station out of David, a small town in northern Panama, advertising a dancing, drinking, and eating place with many girls. Back to civilization. The direction of the radio signals tell us our drift is to the south. If we had a map to locate the cities. If I had paid a little more attention in high school to the geography of this part of the world. The good news is that we approach the coast, slowly yet steadily.

We should come upon a fishing boat, for the calm weather should bring them out, commercial and sport. This is Saturday; the sports fishing crowd will be out either today or tomorrow. Or don't they bother to fish these waters because of all the sharks? Or is it not the marlin season? Tomorrow, Sunday, could bring out a couple of boats.

Land is a blessing, our salvation, an end to the life and death drama we have lived for more than nine long weeks. Yet land can be jagged rocks leading to even more jagged and sharp cliffs. A rocky shore would quickly destroy our raft. Will we have the strength to swim? Our raft, leaking water and air and structurally weak, may be safer at sea than at many landfalls.

Sim reads. Then we pray, full of hope. God wants to save us. He has watched over us through 1000 miles of open ocean. He has tested our faith in one of the world's most perilous seas. He has shown us His power and His mercy in heavy doses. We have passed His test...so far.

Death knocked thousands of times. Sharks have battered the raft more than eighty times a day, at least 4000 times in the past fifty days. Any of the twelve foot hammerhead or mako or white tipped sharks that circled the raft at dusk could easily have attacked us. Or the great white...but they didn't. Why? The two ships that missed us by mere feet could have ground us into oblivion. Thank you, dear Lord, for your helping hand.

The hours of night are endless hours of toil. We bail and pump. Every night that passes, we feel fewer sharks. In the past days, we have seen but one turtle. We try to nap on our wet, slippery, too narrow, hard as rock cushions. We don't care. Soon, we'll be safe.

Sim prods me and asks, "Are you awake? There's a massive air search going on." I jump. These are the words I have been awaiting. Sim senses my reaction. "No, they're looking for a Congressman lost in Africa. Dozens of planes search for him. Can you imagine? We've been off the scope sixty five days, and we haven't seen a single search plane."

She's right. We left Balboa eighty two days ago. We have not seen a single person in eighty two days. More than twenty five ships have passed close by, and none have seen us. But, if they search for us now, it will be near Hawaii.

We approach shore and we will save ourselves. To hell with the Coast Guard and air searches and ships. We got ourselves into this mess, and we will get ourselves out of it. We'll be on shore and safe in a few days. Besides, as we get within a few miles of the coast, a fishermen is bound to come by. A smaller boat can spot us easier than a freighter. If no one sees us, we will drift onto shore.

That is, if the wind blows from the west. Yesterday, after the squall, an offshore breeze pushed us away from land. We fought hard to remain patient. We knew the onshore wind would return; we had to wait for the forces of nature to again balance out. At first, weak, mere ripples on the mirrored sea, the west breeze increased until once again we were on the move towards land.

Waves will also take us to shore. All debris in the oceans end up on shore propelled by waves and current, sooner or later. Relentless, endless rollers, in tireless succession, head to shore. They hit natural barriers, then bend to face their end head on with a mighty roar.

The night is dense and black. The moon which glowed earlier through a heavy layer of clouds has set. A ship inshore is too far away to bother telling Sim; though she no longer gets depressed with ship sightings. The first dozen that steamed up and passed without seeing our raft drove her to tears. Now we see a dozen lights around us on any given night, all too far to risk our last flare.

I try to nap; Sim bails. The cushion arrangement is abominable, yet I can think of no better solution. Sim wants to go back to the original one high configuration, but I continue to argue that it will only put us constantly under water. The flak will continue, but there'll be no change.

When I open my eyes again, our new day, day sixty, is on us. Sim prays. Dense clouds cover all.

"Morning, sweetie. Are we on shore yet?"

"There's no land. Low clouds cover everything. I've looked and looked while you snored, but it's hopeless. I'm so depressed. I dreamed last night of trees, big, beautiful green trees, with the wind rustling the leaves and little birds hopping from branch to branch, gleefully chirping. How long have I thought I would never sense the feeling of land again? And now that we are so close, land continues to elude us."

Sim bails then retrieves the water making machine. I no longer have the comforter to pad the machine. I put it on my chest to pump. A small rag on my chest and another on my pelvic bone helps cut down abrasion. I pump more slowly now. Two liters will take me an hour. We keep all of our containers full. One never knows....

I'm all bone. Actually, one of my bones gave me a real scare a week ago. Weeks ago, as I ran my hand over my chest, I felt a new bump. As days passed, the growth became larger. A bone was growing right in the middle of my chest. I continued to check. Desperate, I had Sim feel it. She burst out laughing.

"You, dummy," she had said, "Bone doesn't grow. You've lost all your fat. That's some damage you did when you were young. That bump is usually hidden by fat."

She was right. We eat, pump, bail, then nap. As evening approaches, Sim reads, her task each evening made more difficult as the cards stick together. The sun sets allowing us but a quick glimpse of land. Will it vanish like the island? Will our trial never end?

When Monday dawns, land is nowhere in sight. Storms ring the shoreline, dense, dark, and ominous. Menacing masses of grey and black clouds layer the eastern and northern horizons. Bitter disappointment overwhelms Sim.

"I knew it. Every time I get my hopes up, something happens to smash them. I know we have been going backwards. The current turned and we're being taken out to sea. The radio stations from Costa Rica I heard so clearly days ago are no longer there. I hear more Panama and Colombia. Even Radio Sandina from Nicaragua has disappeared. We're no longer going in to shore. What a cruel joke God is playing on us. He puts hope in our hearts, then takes it away. We're headed out to sea, caught in a circular current, forever adrift, until we slowly die."

"Calm down, baby. Land is still there except that the clouds are hiding it. Visibility is under five miles and the hills are thirty miles away. As soon as the clouds lift, you'll be in for the surprise of your life."

"I'm going to be in for the surprise of my life if your prediction turns out like all your others. We're probably off of Hong Kong for all I know. Butler, you can't prove we drift towards shore. You can't tell. Your only reference points are black ugly clouds. I'm starting to think my seeing land was nothing but a dream."

"Impossible. Your dreams only have monsters or dead men sprawled on the beach or monster sharks munching rafts. Besides check the wind direction. See, it's from the west. It pushes us east. East is where the land is. Keep your pants on; we'll be there soon enough."

"Speaking of pants, I've got bad news. I have my period again. Is this a curse or what. I'm 51. How long will this go on? Forever?"

"Again? That's three times in less than sixty days. That's a record for Guiness. Does that mean you're going to tear up the rest of my pillow?"

"Stupid. What do I have to do to get a little sympathy on this dumb raft?"

Sim sits up and looks out. She turns around, excited. A ship approaches. I take a look. She's right, and it's heading to pass close by. Sim turns on her knees, and I pass her the fishing pole with her

T-shirt tied onto the end. She lifts the pole high and waves it back and forth. I wave the red bag.

As I watch Sim, I have to chuckle. Naked, she waves the pole with a battered shirt at the end. This is exactly the way castaways do it in the movies and in the Sunday comic strips. The ship passes four hundred feet away as it steams towards the Panama Canal. We hear the thump of the engine as it spins the propeller. Each turn pushes it farther away. Sim blows the whistle but gets no more than a low squeak. She lets it go without a fuss convinced as I am that merchant ships do not post lookouts.

Before we sailed, I asked a friend, a merchant seaman, about bridge routines on long sea hauls. He confirmed my fears. Most ships sail short-handed. Men on watch keep busy with navigation, instrument readings, and radar, and keep the many Logs. They may glance out a window but a few seconds every hour. The small windows on the bridge provide a poor view of the surrounding waters. It's hardly worthwhile for anyone to look. Besides the radar will sound an alarm if another ship approaches. Our best hope is at night. We have to make good use of our last flare.

As we rest, I notice Sim cock her head. A look of concentration is on her face. She cries out. "Bill, I hear an airplane! Listen. It sounds as if it's taking off."

I hear the faint sound now. It's a propeller plane and it strains to climb. Clouds are higher and the look of them less menacing than they were yesterday. The sound quickly fades away...yet another promising omen.

Afternoon turns into evening. Simonne gathers up her prayer cards she has been drying on the air chamber and reads. The pictures of her family have faded away completely. At last light, she cleans my back, a nighty routine by pouring a little fresh water on my open sores. How we have gone this long without infection, I will never know. Sim says the sores on my back are but abrasions. They are open and ugly but without infection.

Our night is uneventful. Three or four sharks kept us from falling into boredom. The two A.M. monster did not show. At first light, Sim assumes her usual position by the window. Clouds cover most of the coastline. I see her smile as she looks over to me.

"I see land. Just a little piece of it. Thank goodness, it's still close. I was so afraid it wouldn't be there. Thank you, God. Forgive me for doubting. I'm so depressed and so very tired. Only the nearness of the coast keeps me going. It's just days before we make it to a beach on our own or someone finds us. Even the welcome land, to my distorted eyes, appears hostile and unwilling to receive us. Are we tempted with false hopes only to be bitterly disappointed once again? How will this story end? Is the sea ready to release us? Enraged that we have survived its cruelty and about to escape, what new hazards and trials will it throw at us?"

Sim stares off into the distance. "It looks like we're heading for Panama. If we land in the north, the people shouldn't be as worked up as those in Panama City. I heard Noriega closed the airport in Panama City and tossed out all the tourists. We may have to go to Costa Rica to get out."

I agree. Sim bails; I pump. No naps. We talk. We're too excited by the proximity of land. As evening creeps up on us, Simonne reads. Today's sunset evolves into a mass of grey and pale, sickly yellows. Night falls quickly.

Rain begins after midnight. Large drops seep through the canopy. We await the new day with real fear. Memories of how close we came to the island play before us. Are we to drift towards land one day and back out the next, like the tides? We may not reach shore for weeks. Time stands still as day 62 on the raft begins.

Tuesday, August 15th, dawns on two forlorn castaways. Today is Sim's mother's Saint's day. We are so sure she has followed us daily in her thoughts. Sim wanted so much to be on land today, to call her mother and reassure her...to tell her we are safe...alive...

Land is barely visible below the low clouds and through the drizzle. It looks closer, but we must wait until it clears to really tell. I have visions of a sandy beach. Once ashore, will we be able to walk? We have been off our legs since the *Siboney* sank, nine weeks ago. What will happen when we try to get out? We tore the raft getting in. So many questions crowd my mind.

Sim is as happy as I have seen her since we left the Panama Canal. "Morning, my sweet," she says. "I have the local news. My foreign press service couldn't get through. Most of the stations are

Panamanian. I'm afraid we're headed to Noriegaville. I heard there was an incident with American troops and Noriega's police. There's talk about an international commission taking care of the Canal. That situation can't last long."

I nod. "We didn't meet a person when we were passing through Panama that wasn't ready to grab a gun and go hunting for Noriega. Even that quiet taxi driver with the three children wanted to put four big round holes into "Pineapple face" as you call him. When the tables turn down there, Noriega's behind isn't worth a cent. I hope the excitement holds until we get out of here."

Rain falls most of the day, and as night approaches, we face another cold, wet night. Our excellent health is a constant source of amazement. Cold, wet, naked, dirty, and undernourished, mere bones with a layer of skin, we've had not a sniffle. Even Sim's headaches are part of the past. The rain has helped the sores on my back by washing out the salt.

Sim's third period is almost behind us. Three in sixty days. Sim takes it like a trooper, her naked behind chafing on salten bedding. I can tell she is now convinced we will be saved and it's only a matter of time.

We can't get over the absence of sharks. I was sure attacks would increase as we neared shore. Today, so far, we've only had one shark bump the raft. We approach nightfall more relaxed. If the sharks will allow us peace, our dilapidated raft will make it. It'll last another week or until we're on shore.

As weeks passed, we find it more and more incredible that no one has been out looking for us. To hell with everyone. We'll save ourselves. Soon we'll be on shore and need no further help from anyone. That is, if we can walk. Every time Sim tunes the radio, I pray she comes up with the news of an air search for two missing sailors. Or did we miss that broadcast?

Rain falls well into Wednesday morning. The dampness has made my warts grow even more black and spongy. Two are as big as a dime. I scratch one and pieces fall of. The sores on my back itch less after last night's rain. I would like to sit up and look out but don't have the ambition. Sim will wake up soon.

Sim dozes. Bedraggled, emaciated, her hair matted, blue flakes from the canopy litter her face. She rests with an air of peace, her mind momentarily at rest from her daily trauma. I turn onto my left side, take the bailing cup, and with my left hand push the floor of the raft down. Water rushes up to my wrist. I push the cup down, let it fill partially, then pour the water over the side.

I quietly repeat the process. Sim so needs her sleep. She hasn't had a good sleep for a week. She stirs, opens her eyes, senses I am awake and bailing, and lapses again into one of her special sleeps.

When I dry the bilge, I lean back, rest my body, and close my eyes, heavy with sleep. Yes, shore must be in sight. The wind has been out of the west all night. The current also pushes us east. We should be making almost eight miles a day. Land is 20 to 30 miles off. In three or four days, we will be on a beach.

I close my eyes and see a wide beach with a long shallow approach. It's ideal. The raft drifts in slowly, edged on by a gentle breeze. The day is bright. We're in a foot of water. I look down. The bottom is sandy. I jump over and pull the raft onto the beach. I help Sim out. We topple into the warm, rich, cleansing water, naked. We roll over and over as we work the grime from our deepest pores. We pull the raft onto the beach, dress, then embrace. We're safe; we're on land. Nothing can hurt us now.

We rest on the beach for a day then look for a road. At the far end of the beach, there is a young couple in street clothes, walking along the shore. We walk up to meet them, to tell our story and ask for help. They have a car parked near the beach on the road. They are happy to help us. We go back to the raft to pick up the life jacket with our passports and money. When we return, the couple has left. We walk towards the road.

The path away from the beach is even and without the usual thorns. Barefoot, we make good time. We help each other. The path takes us into a forest. It winds around in darkness until it delivers us to a highway. We hear a radio at a small neighborhood store. They have bananas and mangoes. They accept our dollars. I ask them where we are, but they are unable to tell me. We tell them we need help. A young man assures us he will call the local police. We wait, and wait, and I sleep. I am shaken awake. I open my eyes.

It's Sim....

"Bill, land is very close. I can see details on shore. The peaks I saw two days ago are farther away and to the north. I see new land to the east. We have been blown to the south. I heard many Panamanian stations last night. That big party with the music and girls is on in David this weekend."

"Let's go, baby, break out the oars. Can you still do the cha-cha? Any other news?"

"No. Soccer is the main news event in this part of the world. They report soccer scores, and every night there are several soccer games. I like the way the announcer calls out a score as 'goaaaaallllll.' The people go wild."

I smile and we hold hands.

"Can you distinguish any objects on land, like a tree or a house?"

"No, not yet. What a shame we will miss a landfall in Costa Rica. I so much wanted to visit the shrine of Nuestra Senora de Los Angeles in Carthago. She is the patron saint of Costa Rica. I heard on the radio they have an annual pilgrimage on the second of August. They still talk about it. If we make it, we will go to Carthago, a pilgrimage on our own to say thanks." I nod and smile. Yes, of course, we'll go.

By now, it's well after one and time for lunch. I rely on my now standard technique. I have nine trigger fish on board and cleaned in less than an hour. I stuff myself as usual while Simonne barely eats three filets. We nap through the remainder of the afternoon. Sim reads. As the sun sets without fanfare, we prepare for the night. The flashlight and our last flare are in their nighttime place next to my head.

Sim scans the horizon for signs of lights on shore but sees none. Sim bails the raft dry, and I give it an extra heavy pump. We push our cushions against the side of the raft, and we talk. Or I should say, I nod off while Sim continues to talk. She is too excited to sleep.

She jerks up to a sitting position.

"A ship. I hear engine noise. Listen."

The faint hum of a diesel engine becomes louder. Both of us look out at once. We see nothing. I pull out the oar and row the raft around. The hum turns into the heavy thumping of a large diesel engine. I row the raft in a full circle. We see no lights.

The groan from the engine grows louder. We look at each other in silent amazement and again scan the waters around us. The ship approaches completely blacked out. It's invisible.

Sim pulls out the flashlight and says: "Should we signal? He's coming closer? Bill, I'm afraid."

"Let's wait. Honest seamen don't travel at night in a darkened ship. I don't like the looks of it. We may be safer where we are than to get mixed up with some bad guys." The heavy pounding of the diesel is upon us. The horizon is as black as the night, so there's no hope to see any sort of a silhouette. Will they run us down?

Then Sim spots it.

"There it is, and it's not too far away. It's a small freighter or a big fishing boat. Pass me the compass. They are going almost east or towards shore. What a shame. We could have signalled, but, I agree with you, there's something fishy about this fisherman."

The throbbing engines grow fainter, then die out. We are again alone; our hearts pump furiously. This latest alert has frazzled our nerves. We begin our tenth week on the raft. Ten weeks. I can remember back when we considered one week impossible. How did this raft ever last this long?

My thoughts over the past two nights kept returning to *Siboney* as she lies on her side on a flat silt bottom. There is no current to move her sails; new dwellers now well established within her protective crannies. Her hull remains in one piece, of that I am sure for the pressure of the deep equalized as she slowly settled during her two mile decent.

Her water and fuel tanks are certainly crushed unless the vents kept the pressure balanced. The three batteries surely exploded when salt water arced across their terminals. Did the propane tanks burst? When I get home, I'll have to work that one out.

The mainsail surely remains set as do the two jibs. They should last many years. The rigging will keep the mast standing for fifty years or more. The engine is no doubt a mass of rust. My old engine lies in a Miami warehouse; all I have left from my beloved *Siboney*.

There will be a host of hardware on board *Siboney* that will last for centuries. I struggled with rusty chain through fifty years of anchor hauling, and for this trip, I bought fifty feet of three eights inch stainless chain. That chain and the three anchors will be intact hundreds of years from now. I can't believe that I didn't throw the Bruce anchor over the side when I plucked it out of the lazerette. Water covered the decks; nothing could have saved *Siboney* from going to the deep, but years of habit made me set it down easily on the deck as if I would use it again sometime.

At Isla de Aves, near Venezuela, we dove for years on a three hundred year old French shipwreck. We found anchor chain, chain plates, and spikes in excellent condition. Can we raise *Siboney*? My crazy heart says yes, but I know it cannot be.

Siboney would float. The wood hull, inside the fiberglass hull, would have expanded and sealed the crack. A miniature sub could place several heavy duty air bags inside *Siboney*, fill them with compressed air, and *Siboney* would rise on its own. On the surface, we could pump out the remainder of the water then sail her home. The trick will be to find her.

Enough dreaming. It's time to fish and make water. I want all the water bottles full and a load of fish aboard when we hit shore. We must prepare for any eventuality. We eat, relax, and try to nap.

The weather clears, and Sim returns to her position as lookout. The details we saw this morning on shore vanish in the haze. We are more than twenty miles off. Every hour brings us closer to salvation...spiritual and physical salvation...we're so close...Lord, bring us to a safe haven...

⮞chapter fourteen⮜

2100 THURSDAY AUGUST 17, 1989, DAY 64

"There, Bill, more to the left."

I see it. A halo of light, a loom, ever so faint. It's a small town. On the other hand, small towns normally don't make a loom. It's a medium size city. The direction of the radio signals tells us it's in southern Costa Rica.

Though faint and far away, this is our first visual sign of life on shore. We see no lights, but there are surely people. Eighty four days have now passed since we have seen another person. We saw no one on any of the three dozen ships that so far have passed alongside.

Sim again echoes the queries I ponder. "What do you think it is? How far?"

"I can't see the horizon, but I sense it is up high in the hills. It could be thirty or so miles away. It has to be a fair sized city with mercury street lighting; otherwise, the light would not create a loom."

"I see the horizon. The city is way above it." Sim's keen eyesight starts her thinking. "Can you imagine, if it is a city, all those people sleeping in their homes, secure and dry and warm while we are out here fighting for our lives. Oh, Bill, it's time this trip ended. It's time for a shower and a cafe con leche and bread. Yes, bread."

"Soon, baby, soon. We're drifting onto shore. In two or three days, we'll be on shore and safe and sound. I don't feel a single muscle in my legs. When we reach the beach, we may have to crawl after we find we can't walk."

"That's great news but don't try standing again. You almost tore the raft apart last time."

Five or six weeks ago, in a fit of anxiety, my legs cramping and aching, I had tried to get up on my feet. The exercise almost turned into a disaster. My right foot slipped off the cushion and onto the floor of the raft. The tape that holds the floor of the raft to the air chamber ripped off, and for a moment, I thought I'd done it again. After closer inspection, we found another tape under the floor maintained the seal. That was the last time I moved off my rear end.

A light breeze blows out of the northwest. We should move five or more miles closer to shore tonight. That will put us inside the twenty mile mark. Local fishermen surely come out this far. We could be found and on shore tomorrow.

Friday dawns on a day made in heaven. At first light, Simonne searches for land. When I awaken, I find her starry eyed. She helps me up. The sky is cloudless. Land, reflected on a mirrored sea, reaches far to the north and to the south. High mountains to the east cast dark shadows on farm land that rush out to meet us. High, forbidding bluffs lie ahead. Behind it, blue-green forests gently rise towards the high land.

Sim calls out excited. "Bill, look, a cruise ship, coming this way. Wow, just like in the ads. It's so large and so white and clean. It heads north. Oh, Lord, bring him to us. Look! There!"

The magnificent white liner cruises slowly near shore, its passengers surely on deck enjoying the same magnificent view. Will no one look our way? The ship comes closer. It's one of the larger ones, almost as big as the QE2, but higher off the water. Sim waves her shirt at the end of the fishing rod. As the ship approaches, Sim sees people walking on deck. She screams and I blow the whistle. It heads north, away from the Canal, its hold full of the comfort and safety we so badly need. It's probably one of the trips that start on the west coast, cruises half way through the Panama Canal, turns around, and returns. Passengers are no longer allowed ashore in Panama because of vandalism and the threat of revolution.

Sim hands over the mirror. This is the first time a ship has been in line with the sun with the sun bright. I line up the mirror as Sim waves her shirt. I chuckle every time I see her wave a white T-shirt on the end of the pole, naked...exactly like the cartoons. The ship nears, now less than a half mile away. The sea is perfectly calm and the visibility as clear as it has ever been.

Cruise ships have a better lookout system than merchant vessels, and besides hundreds of passengers have nothing better to do than look out. Except, on this ship, they surely all look the other way at the bright green shoreline and the stately mountains. We wave frantically. The sun feels good as we bob on gentle swells. Sim hasn't stopped swinging the pole and yelling the entire time the ship passes. We wait in vain for the telltale change in course or a difference in the propellers. The ship continues on its course, and within minutes, it is but a dot on the northern horizon.

We fall back, exhausted from the exertion and once again deeply disappointed, to pump and bail. More than forty ships have now passed close at hand. Not included are the lights of ships we see far off at night. Last night, Sim counted seventeen ships. So far, none has seen us. That is except for the small white ship that sped by early that rainy morning several weeks ago. We wasted two flares that day. They saw us but didn't stop. We have one last flare although a shortage of flares hasn't made that much difference. So far. We haven't had a ship approach close enough at night that we've seen in time.

I catch nine triggers for lunch, filet all nine, and serve them up. We postpone water making until evening. The sun makes it too hot for any heavy work. Besides we must conserve our energy, for the big test may still lie ahead. Sim eats four of the eighteen filets. I eat until I can stuff no more down, and I still lose weight. Neither of us has had a bowel movement for seven weeks. That might be another record for the books. I wonder what happens to the two pounds of fish I eat every day? I do cut the fish in minute pieces and chew them well. Our bodies must absorb it all.

The sun has worked its way to the west which makes the shore easier to see. Sim spots trees and several white objects that look like buildings. High rock bluffs rise vertically at the water's edge, but we're still too far away to see the actual shoreline. As the height of the bluffs is unknown, we cannot judge how far away we are.

Individual landmarks are clear. We must be within twenty miles. We drift at seven to ten miles a day. In two days, we'll be on shore, three at most. Will we arrive on a dark night in a squall? Will jagged reefs extending from shore wait to extinguish "Last Chance" as breakers roar and waves expend their power? Will we row off until morning.

The thought runs a cold chill through me, but sooner or later, we will have to face up to a landfall whatever it might bring. Is the sea really ready to release us? Is the land hostile and unwilling to receive us? Are we tempted by false hopes only to be again bitterly disappointed? Our real test still lies ahead.

I fish again at five and catch six triggers. Sim doesn't eat at night, so I eat everything but two filets. I save more than I need but better waste a trigger or two than run short now that we're this close. Besides they are such ugly, mean fish. If I fell in the water, they'd clean my bones off in ten minutes. Hundreds circle under the raft waiting. A couple of days back, I caught one too many. When I threw it back in, the other trigger fish thought it another carcass and started after it. Terrible beasts, the piranhas appear docile in comparison.

I make two liters of water now that it's cooler. A fiery sky lingers as we look first at the setting sun, then east to land as it slowly vanishes. Evening prayers have more meaning tonight, and we are drawn together as never before. We have suffered so much side by side that we are now one of body. Our differences, whether small or large, arising from our different characters, disappear. We now know we are meant to be saved.

As the sun sets, we see lights high on the hills and the loom of a large town. Sim jumps and calls out: "Bill, a ship!"

I look to where Sim points and see two white lights in a line and below them bright red and green running lights are clearly visible. The ship cannot be a half mile away.

'He's coming this way" I cry out. "Let's get the flare ready."

"Wait. Remember our agreement. This is the last flare, and you're not going to waste it like you did with the first two."

"This is different. Look, the ship is heading straight for us. The two white lights are right in line. He's going to run us over. Let's get the flare ready."

"No, no, no. Wait. I'm not sure. Let's not waste the last flare."

"Ok. You hold the flare. I'll signal an SOS with the flashlight."

I flash SOS repeatedly.

Sim shakes me excitedly: "Bill, look. On the bridge. There's a man. He flashed a light twice."

"Dammit, let's fire off the bloody flare."

"Ok, do it."

"Thanks, boss." I turn over on my knees, lean outside the raft, and remove the wax wrapper on the end of the flare. I take the wooden end cap in my left hand and rub the abrasive on the cap against the end of the flare. The flare fails to ignite. I rub it again. Nothing happens.

It fires on my third try. A bright purple flame erupts from the tip of the flare. Slag spurts in all directions. Sim grabs me as I press out of the window to hold the wooden shaft of the flare as far as my arm can take it from the raft. The smallest drop of slag on the air chamber and our voyage would be over in seconds. As the flame heats up, the light turns a bright reddish purple.

The ship steams towards us at a perfect angle. If they hold course, they'll miss us by no more than a hundred feet. The person on the bridge with the lantern shines it our way. A light comes on on a lower deck, and several shapes move about. Sim jumps with excitement: "Bill, they've seen us. They're getting ready to throw a line."

"No question they've seen us. The lantern is still shining on the bridge. Can you see the man holding it?"

"Yes. Are they stopping?"

"I don't know." The flare burns brightly. It burns my fingers, but I hold on as I thrust it towards the ship. In seconds, as soon as the captain can get the order down to the engine room, the ship should be slowing down to pick us up. I can't believe our incredible luck. Tonight we'll sleep away from predation and death, in a dry, clean bed.

Sim screams. "Bill, they're not stopping. They see us but they're not stopping. HELP. AUXILIO."

I scream. The ship is abreast, much less than one hundred feet away. We can see its every detail. It's six or seven thousand tons, a small freighter. A man on the lower deck has a big moustache. We scream for help in Spanish, certain they have given the order to stop. The speed of the engines change. Are they going into reverse? Or are they pulling away? They are surely turning. Or are they? What in the hell is going on?

"Bill, they aren't stopping. What's the matter with those guys? That's impossible. We've wasted our last flare! How can they not stop? Can't they see we're in distress." Devastated, we continue to yell and flash the light, but the ship continues on its course, and it's stern drops quickly away. The flare burns my fingers, and I drop it into the sea where it sizzles and sinks. When I look out again, the ship has vanished in the darkness.

I try to encourage Sim: "Forget them, baby. We'll be on shore soon. We don't need anyone to help us. Besides they're headed the wrong way. That ship just left land. Suppose their destination is Korea or who knows where. We would be taken out to sea on another ocean journey after we've worked our way towards land for so long. Forget him. Let him go."

Sim blasts back at me: "If they had stopped, I would have jumped on board even if they're off to the moon. I want to get off this raft no matter how I do it. If I thought I could swim it, I'd be over the side this minute."

"Sweetie, relax. It'll soon be over. And get the swimming scene out of your head. The trigger fish would pick your bones clean before you get ten feet away." She shrugs my words away.

The anxiety of the near miss lingers with us well into the night. What was that all about? They saw us and took off! What did they think we were? I've never heard of castaways being abandoned on the high seas. May the miserable bastards fry in hell.

On the other hand, land is truly at hand and we're moving in the right direction. We'll be ashore in a day or two. We must shrug off this latest setback and replace it with a strong current of anticipation, for soon we'll be ashore. Thoroughly excited, we fail to sleep. What will the new day bring?

The wind blows out of the west, exactly what we need. Come on, current, take us to land. Come on, raft, keep afloat...we're almost there...don't let us down now. Another day, two or three at the most...

chapter fifteen

0100 SATURDAY AUGUST 19, 1989, DAY 66 ADRIFT

Simonne is up and leans against the arch. She paddles gently as she scours the shoreline for sign of life. Lights seen nights past are hidden by the light overcast that threatens to envelop the raft. Safety is so near at hand and yet so far. If we could only paddle this raft..or come across a fisherman.

Fishermen....where in the hell are they? The sea is alive with every conceivable variety of fish, but we've traversed 1200 miles of ocean, and we have seen not one fishing boat. Sim thinks she saw one off the island we passed, but I still think it was a rock. We'll never know for sure.

Sim continues her vigil by the window. I thought for a while she was on to something, but now I'm sure it's just anxiety to reach shore and safety. In either case, I'll watch her out of the corner of my eye for any change in expression. How I hope she'll see something. Even a single light bulb. A fire. Any sign of life.

Now more than ever before, I am confident our trip will end well. We should drift onto shore in a day and a half, and if the weather remains calm, our landing shouldn't be too bad. If we arrive at night, we'll paddle off until dawn. We can do that without too much trouble. We'll take turns like we did so many days ago when the dolphin tore the hole in the bottom or paddle together if need be.

A light overcast delays the arrival of Saturday, the 19th of August, our sixty sixth day as castaways. Our day really arrives when it dawns, for the pitch of night somehow belongs to the day past. Neither of us sleeps as the skies grow lighter. I pray for a deep sandy beach. As soon as we can touch, we'll jump over the side and wash off two months of dirt. I'll rub sand into my crotch to get rid of the blood and guts of hundreds of trigger fish. The blue waterproofing which penetrates every pore will float away in the refreshing water.

The specter of a rough landing at night though is all too real a possibility. Sharp black heads of coral break the waves as the wind and waves push us ever closer. Frantic, we paddle, then push off submerged rocks in a last effort to stay off. A larger wave pushes us up and over the reef. The raft, rented, deflates. We stay with LAST CHANCE. Shore is far. We pray for daylight...and swim...dear Lord, protect us.

The sky clears as six hundred and sixty minutes of darkness begins to yield to the power of the sun. My engineering training keeps my mind busy calculating trivia; we have lived through forty three thousand minutes of deadly blackness on this voyage, more than 95,000 minutes of total terror. Will these odious nights soon be over? Or does our ultimate test yet lie ahead?

The sky turns dirty grey. Sim sits up with the compass in her lap and paddles the raft until she faces east. Low clouds heavy with moisture obliterate the coastline. Will it be there, or are we to live through yet another disappointment? Will the wind blow fiercely out of the east and push us back out to sea?

The power of the sun eats away at the cloud cover, and soon land is clearly in sight to the east. Yesterday's cliffs rise black and rugged out of the sea to end abruptly at a cape several miles to the south. Low hills rise in the haze beyond the cape indicating a bay twenty or more miles deep running to the east. If we miss a landfall to the north of the cape, we will face another three or four days adrift. Yet, inside the cape, we have a better chance to be seen by fishermen.

To the north, the high cliffs turn into a long, even headland. As the day grows lighter, the clouds lift to reveal several peaks far inland. Rolling hills lead up to a large mountain or volcano. High brownish green mountains rise to embrace the clouds all the way to true north.

I need two reference marks on shore to plot our drift. If I can align two points, one closer to us than the other, I can tell whether we are drifting east towards the bluffs or if we will miss them by falling too far to the south, so far, I find not a single distinguishing feature on the landscape.

The wind shifts to the northwest after mid morning, an unfavorable twist which will tend to move us south. I have no way to measure the effect of current and can see nothing on shore to line up as a range marker. If this wind continues, we'll miss the cape to the south. Our only chance is to sail the raft. If I row it around so the bow heads north, the wind against the side might help us move to the northeast. It's worth a try.

I prop my head up with a life preserver so I can see out the window and row the raft around with the paddle tied to one end of the fishing rod until the headland lines up with the edge of the canopy. When I stop rowing, the end of the raft that heads north drifts slowly to the south. When the headland is out of sight, I row until it again appears in the window. I continue to row for the next two hours. I can't tell if I'm doing any good, but at least it does no harm. If we miss the cape, we'll get to shore a few days later.

Why are there no landmarks on shore? The bluffs to the east have not a single distinguishing feature, and even if they had, I see nothing in the highlands behind that could serve as a range mark. As noon approaches, I have my paddling down to an easy routine. Three strokes puts us on course. In four minutes, the raft drifts until I can no longer see the headland. I then pull three times on the oar which I leave hanging over the side when I'm back on line.

The hot sun forces both of us to strip. Hope radiates towards us from ashore and from above. We will live...of that we are now sure...our ordeal is almost over...the hazards of the sea are behind us...or are they?

We have water and food. We're healthy and feel good. When I think back over our trials of the past two months, I fill with wonder at how fortunate we have been. We've sailed 1200 miles in a torn plastic raft. Tempests and beasts have fought to subdue and destroy us. Every time, with the hand of God upon us, we managed to escape from the jaws of death. Twenty miles remain to be safely ashore. Only the thought of seeing our families again buoys our emaciated, tired bodies.

Sim calls out: "Bill, I can see trees clearly, palm trees. The rocky cliffs are about fifty feet high. I see a house towards the north. How far away do you think we are?"

I look out and guess we're fifteen to twenty miles off. I reply, "We'll be on shore in 48 hours if not sooner. The four hours of rowing have made me hungry. How about lunch? Trigger?"

"Sounds terrific," Sim banters back, her spirits buoyed by the proximity of shore. "Shall we try a little soy sauce on it today?"

"That's my joke. I think I'd rather have a dab of lime juice. I'm tired of the same old soy sauce every day. If you have nothing better to do, pray for a wind shift. We need the wind to shift from north of west to the south or as close to it as possible."

I join Sim in prayer. Help us, dear Lord. Just a little shift in wind towards the south. Please. If that's not possible, that's OK too. Thank you for all Your help during the past ten weeks. To be alive today, here and now, is nothing less than a miracle.

My spiritual conversion has been another miracle. Throughout our first days on the raft, I was convinced that my strength and knowledge of the sea would suffice to see us through to safety. The sharks, more than the violent tempests, brought me ever so slowly to understand that, without the hand of God, we would never make it to shore. As I look back, each smash by a shark inched me closer to the Lord. At first, I struggled with the Lord's Prayer, first to remember the words, then to fully fathom the meaning of each. Our Father...what a powerful beginning...He looked after us faithfully through thousands of frightening hours, leading ever closer into His fold...never pushing or shoving...always tenderly leading me closer to Him...until my faith in Him totally dominates my day.

Simonne has prayed non-stop since the first day and has recited two to three full rosaries daily. Her faith led me to find mine, at first by assisting me in prayer, later through spiritual discussions. In recent days, since Simonne heard of Nuestra Senora de Los Angeles, I have been praying she help get God's attention to our plight and somehow guide a ship towards us. My prayers to la Virgin de la Caridad del Cobre worked miraculously warding off attacks by the most violent of our predators. My new found faith has given me comfort and solace through interminable nights of terror and will forever change my life. Why, oh why, did I not find it earlier in my life?

The skies have cleared, and the green vegetation so near invites us to run up to it and embrace it. The sun is overhead which means it's time for lunch. I don my gloves backwards on opposite hands as the trigger fish have worn out the palm of the right glove. More than forty trigger stings cover my fingers.

Yesterday's leftover fish spent the night spread on the paddle which I have found keeps it fresher than stashed in a can. I cut the bait into one inch blocks and run it through my hook. The fabulous panorama distracts me. Days ago, it was but empty ocean. Now we are near heaven. I feel like that first man so long ago beholding his enchanted garden.

With the baited hook in my left hand, I lean over the side of the raft to check what's swimming around. Many times, I've had to postpone fishing until the sharks have left, but today only triggers surround the raft at a depth of two to three feet. I dip the bait in the water and right away the triggers surface with their grunting, sucking sound. In a splash of boiling water, my hook is bare. I bait it again and again. The triggers are now wild, hovering inches below the water, each fighting for position. They look up and watch my every move. I move my hand quickly six inches off the water, and a dozen leap at it. They're ready.

I check my glove and touch my bait to the water. My right hand flies out and around a trigger. I grab it too close to the tail, and it wiggles free. I re-bait and try again. The second one is too large and I can't get my hand around it. I must shoot out and grab them before they activate their trigger, a one inch spine with a barb at the end.

I hold my first trigger tightly against the camcorder-case filleting board and quickly remove both filets. Gripped by its tail, I lower it into the water. The sea boils with eager trigger fish. I grasp a second trigger as I throw the first ten feet out. Dozens of triggers dart to the sinking carcass, tearing it apart until seconds before a large shark dispatches the remains. I repeat the process until I have ten triggers cleaned.

We eat lunch and nap. When we stir and look out, the wind has shifted to the south. Once again, our prayers are answered. If this breeze can only blow all night tonight, we will be very close to shore by tomorrow afternoon. As the day wears on, the southeast wind continues to pick up. We couldn't ask for more. There is no need to row.

At four, I prepare to catch our evening meal. I sit up, paddle in my lap full of bait when a loud roar out of nowhere startles me. Sim jumps up and cries out: "Bill, a large white boat is going to run us down." It slaloms down six foot seas, one second heading to run us down, the other to miss us.

"Bill, he's going to run us down. Is it a fishing boat?"

"It looks like a sports fisherman, as in my dream. He's seen us. He's coming right to us."

Sim cries with joy. "Baby, we are saved. Oh, my God, my God. They have seen us. They're slowing down. Oh, it's real. It's not a dream." She cries and laughs at the same time. Tears run down her cheeks."

"Quick, get the pants out," I cry out as the launch slows and turns.

Sim digs a soggy plastic bag out from under the cushions and pulls out pants that have not left the bag for sixty six days. Sim puts on a small, dirty, sleeveless shirt and her life jacket.

The boat is now alongside. A half dozen men are on the rail looking down. We cry without shame and wave. We can't stop. I see the Coast Guard stripe on the side of the boat. I think it's the U.S. Coast Guard."

I look up, hands cupped, and call to the men on deck in English. "Thank you! Thank You!" I cannot find words. My head reels.

One of the men throws a line which I fasten to the raft. They hold the raft a few feet off the patrol boat which rises ten feet above us and bobs wildly in the waves. The stern rises and falls six or more feet.

Steps that lead to the deck are three feet off the water, a hopeless leap. The crew looks down at us in amazement, for we must be a sight, unbathed for ten weeks and nothing but skin and bones. My beard has grown almost three inches. When I boarded the raft, all I had was a slight moustache.

I turn and drink in the expression of sheer joy in Sim's face. I turn to her: "Sim, remember what we have been talking about. Getting out of the raft is dangerous. We haven't been on our feet for ten weeks. I'm not sure we can stand."

"Oh, Bill. I'm going to see my babies again and my mother."
Tears stream down her dirty face. I try to calm her.

"Sim, be careful. Sit tight. Let's get the canopy off so we can
stand."

I struggle with the zipper of the canopy. It jams, half open.

"Sim, hand me the knife." With it, I slash the remaining half
of the canopy. One man, on the bottom rung, hangs out, hand
extended. A crew member pulls on the painter.

"Ok, Sim, you're first. Careful. Go!"

Sim turns on one knee. She cannot stand. I hold her as she
tries to kneel. The patrol boat heaves in the heavy seas. Sim waits
for the bottom rung to drop and lunges for it. I give her a push as a
sailor takes her hand. Seconds pass as she dangles in space, I ready
to catch her if she falls. He pulls her to safety with a single hand.
She weighs nothing. On deck, another crewman takes her in his arms
and carries her towards the main deck.

I load the sailbag with items I want to save: the Log Book,
work book, knife, compass, our psalms, and hand it up to the
waiting crew. It's time for me to go. I look up at the wildly gyrating
boat, not sure I can make it up on my legs. Suppose I can't stand?
The crew beckons. I stand up and lunge for the ladder in one motion.
I hang on and struggle for a foot hold. My feet touch the sea. I can't
find the rung. And I didn't put on my life vest. My strength ebbs as
my hands slip from the rung. As I begin to fall, two men grab my
arms and pull me up. With a jerk, I too am safely on deck.

Sim and I crawl to a hot air vent amidships and sit on the
deck. We embrace. And cry. We are safe. The voyage is over...after
sixty six days at sea. We have drifted more than 1150 Nautical miles.
We each have lost more than fifty pounds...but by the grace of God,
we are alive....thank you, dear Lord, for saving these two
undeserving castaways...

⟶ chapter sixteen ⟶

1800 SATURDAY AUGUST 19, 1989
ABOARD THE COSTA RICAN COAST GUARD
VESSEL *PUNTA BURICA*

I huddle next to Sim against a hot air vent. The ship's crew stares at us, too awed by the two near-skeletons plucked from the sea to speak. Simonne pulls her life vest tighter for warmth. Thankfully, one of the men slips a cushion under us. The cold steel deck pressing through a thin layer of skin against my bones felt like a bed of nails. I speak to a crew member in Spanish. The reaction is immediate. Spanish speaking castaways?

One of the men jumps from the stern ladder into the raft. I feel for the seaman, for the stench of rot permeates all. I'm glad we dropped the soggy, rotten comforter over the side as they came along side. He passes up the water machine, the radio, the flashlight, and the cushions.

The crew of the patrol has two lines around the raft and prepare to lift it. I passed up the sailbag sure they would abandon our faithful little vessel. The raft is jerked up to the deck. Hundreds of trigger fish swim aimlessly around the spot where the raft floated. They lost their home, their habitat, their umbrella of protection. Surely, many have been with us a good part of our thousand mile entire voyage. Tough luck, gang. So long. Though they kept us alive, I am happy to see them no more.

The patrol boat comes to life with a roar. Two men join us, and we tell them pieces of our story, then ask them who they are. We find we're aboard a Costa Rican Coast Guard Patrol boat, the *Punta Burica*, stationed at the port of Golfito, Costa Rica. They had been out since dawn in search of a shrimper that had disappeared several days earlier. They found us instead.

They had sailed a random course all day. On the way back to shore, the helmsman spotted what he thought was a buoy. With the captain's permission, he changed course and headed for it. Of a sudden, they are upon us. My prayers were truly answered. We cannot stop thanking them enough. They smile, happy for us.

Captain Nunez joins us as the patrol boat picks up speed. Engines roar. Spray flies. The warm air from the vent keeps us warm. Sim, with her shredded shirt, looks like someone straight out of Tobacco Road. Her life jacket still tightly tied, she leans against a bulwark, starry eyed, unmoving, ecstasy radiating from her face, still unable to grasp all that has happened in such short time. The entire rescue operation lasted less than fifteen minutes. From the moment when we first heard the engines until we were both aboard took less than five.

Crewmen surround us and ask dozens of questions. They stand amazed with our answers. The Captain gives Sim a new T-shirt. All crew members vanish as Sim changes. I sit shirtless for my shirt, tied earlier in the day to the top of the raft canopy, has disappeared. I didn't see the shirt when the raft came aboard, so it may be back with the trigger fish.

The *Punta Burica*, now at top speed, heads north. The Captain tells us we are 13 miles from the coast according to his radar, and we are heading for Golfito, their home port. He says we will be taken to a hospital. We assure the Captain a hotel would be fine. There's really no need for a hospital. A couple days of rest and we'll be ready to travel home. After all, we have been stuffing ourselves with fish and drinking all the water our bodies called for.

He smiles, agrees, and turns away. I call him back. Sim unbuttons a pocket in her life jacket and removes our passports. I take them and, with the Log Book, hand them to the Captain. How many times did I rehearse this scene on the raft.

We remain on deck and chat with the crew. The helmsman who spotted us stops by. This man's sharp eyes and attention made all the difference. It turns out the *Punta Burica* had sailed earlier in the day and had headed West, into the Pacific Ocean. The Captain ordered a random search pattern. After a long leg to the west, the boat motored south, then east, then north, back west, later south. They were on their return trip east when they came across our raft.

The joy of being granted new life overwhelms us. We remain speechless. We give all of our belongings to the crew. The helmsman gets my watch. Sim gives her radio to another young man. The blanket goes to another. We keep the sailbag nearby with the knife, the compass, and other memorabilia. The raft is the center of attention. They cannot imagine how we lived 66 days in that flimsy raft. It is now but a heap of trash.

A crewman brings out two glasses of warm milk. He asks if we would like dinner. Yes! I could eat anything. He returns below. As we speed along at nearly 20 knots, low black squall clouds form in our path. The Captain suggests we go to the pilot house. We help each other walk the two dozen steps. Each step is a shaky, painful trial. They usher us in and close the door behind us. The first big drops hit the deck.

The pilot house is freezing cold. The helmsman offers me one of his shirts to wear. They bring Sim a blanket. We sit on the floor and try to stay out of the way. The Captain is on the radio. Another man scans the radar. A crew member arrives with a plate of food. Captain Nunez stops him cold. He has just spoken to a doctor at the hospital; we are to have nothing to eat except milk.

My heart, not to mention my stomach, collapses. I had seen the plate of red beans and rice and had smelled its aroma. The Captain is adamant and the plates return below. Who cares? We're alive and well. Nothing else really matters.

Heavy sheets of rain block our way. A blinding glare of lightning and a clap of thunder shake the very keel of our vessel. The helm slows the engines. Two men study the radar. The Captain is on the radio in hurried communication until flashes of lighting force the Captain to shut down the radio.

Visibility is zero until lighting lights up the ocean around us. With the boat slowed and in calmer waters, I struggle to my feet. I hold on to the hand rails tightly and find I can stand. I test my legs and balance. I'm not quite sure I can walk on my own.

The aroma of red beans beckons from below. Steep stairs lead to the galley and dining area. Everything is compact but neat and clean. On the stove, there is a pot with rice and another with the beans. Saliva fills my mouth. I'd forgotten what real food was like.

The stairs down to the galley are almost vertical. Can I negotiate them? I ask a crew member if I can go below and sit. He says that would be no problem. I study the stairs and hand rails again and decide to go for it. I take one step at a time until I reach the bottom. When I sit at the mess table, the crew gathers around. I tell a couple of sea stories. They offer crackers. I send some up to Sim.

The smell from the pot of beans drives me wild. When I ask a crew member to serve me a plate, he reminds me the Captain said no. But, I argue, the Captain is on deck piloting the boat in the storm. Please, por favor. He breaks down. I eat two plates and know I have gone straight to heaven. My first hot meal in 66 days.

I work my way back up the stairs with a few more crackers to where Sim sits crouched alongside the wheel. I don't tell her I had two plates of beans; her stomach isn't as tough as mine. The storm is a bad one. Two men stare into the radar, an older model and not easy to read, as they try to steer a course into a channel between many rocks. Another patrol boat ended up on the rocks earlier. Captain Nunez holds the boat at dead slow. When the rain eases, he increases speed. Soon we pass an entrance marker and approach a pier. An ambulance waits nearby. Several dozen people stand on the dock in the steady drizzle. The launch eases in and the crew quickly secures it.

The Captain helps Sim ashore. The pier gyrates wildly; it's a floating pier. The waves must be monstrous. We cannot walk from all the bouncing around. We greet villagers who stand in the rain, joke about not walking too well, then enter the rear of the ambulance. Two wooden benches in the rear seem rock hard as we head away with a cough and a roar.

We reach the hospital in minutes. I insist the driver take us to a hotel, but Sim insists we go the hospital route for a day or two. I can barely walk from the ambulance to the hospital as the hospital gyrates as badly as the pier. This entire town must be afloat.

We are taken to the emergency room where a nurse offers us a brownish, sweet drink. We try it and find it fabulous, God's last gift to us. It turns out to be agua dulce, sweet water, made of sugar cane juice. We each drink three large glasses.

One of the nurses leads us to a pay phone where Sim calls her mother in France. Joy overwhelms both. Her mother just knew we were lost and near death and had prayed constantly. Her candles had burned eight weeks. I next call my daughter Susan in Texas who I shocked with the true extent of our odyssey. We try to call the boys in Miami without luck.

A hospital staff worker summons me into a little office to complete the usual hospital paperwork. With two fingers, he pecks away at a typewriter. He enters name and address. Then he asks my occupation. Without a second thought, I reply, "Naufrago", shipwrecked or castaway in Spanish. At the moment, I feel like nothing else and so content to be one, a live one at that.

I mention to the young man that someone should do something with that pier where we landed. He asked why. I explain how it bounced around in the waves. He assured me that the Americans had driven those piles forty years ago and the pier is as solid today as it was then.

A nurse draws blood which surely smells of trigger fish. Then we proceed to shower. Sim is first, for there is only one shower with no door and open to the public. A nurse turns on the water as Sim cringes at the cold and shies away. Sim waits, then asks when the hot water is going to start. "Senora, she says, there is no hot water." Poor Sim suffers through an icy shower. Back in bed under the covers, she feels better than any queen between silk sheets.

While Sim showers, I tell sea stories in the emergency room. I am so happy to be alive that I am unable to contain my exuberance. When Sim appears from the shower, I jump in. I revel in the cold water and use a bar of soap to wash off juices of 400 trigger fish from my crotch. I feel new.

Sim is given one of three beds in the ladies ward. I end up in the men's ward, also with three beds. We are the only patients. We learn the United Fruit Company built the hospital dozens of years ago. Built of wood and two stories high, it has room for dozens of patients, a complete operating area, and a large outpatient building.

The facilities, though slightly primitive by modern standards, are clean and staffed with nurses and doctors who take a genuine interest in us. Instantly, we make friends with all. By the time we finish bathing, the time is past eleven in the evening. My bed rests against a window which stretches up to the ceiling, its glass jalousies long gone. A cool breeze flows over me as I prop up on my pillow and look out at the full moon. The garden outside glows soft yellow. Royal palms stand majestically, reminding me of a lighthouse. How great to be alive. This is paradise.

I cannot sleep, and I really don't want to sleep. Why sleep at a moment like this? For all purposes, I have been born again. Fleecy clouds slip by between the moon and the palm trees. The gentle breeze carries the sweet scent of life...a truly enchanted evening...

Hours slip by. My IV is almost empty and my bladder is full, so I drag the three legged stand to the bathroom. On my way back, I peek in at Sim. She holds court; the staff is entranced with her sea stories; she too to excited to sleep.

When I awaken next, daylight floods the room. I hear a cough, turn, and notice both beds are full. When I get up and start to walk, the pain in my legs make me flinch. Forgotten muscles complain. It's a good sign...I'm alive.

I peek in at Sim. She's asleep. She didn't get six hours sleep total during the last week on the raft. An entirely new staff is in place. In no time, I make new friends. Sim awakens for breakfast. She had nightmares, and a gentle nurse sat in the room with her until she was again asleep.

I looked at the breakfast roster while hobbling around and found that there was one cardiac breakfast, whatever that is, two dietetic breakfasts, and 6 regulars. The dietetics must be for us. To our surprise, we get regular breakfasts.

I join Sim on her bed, and we both clean our plates of gallo pinto or red beans and rice, a good piece of fresh cheese, two pieces of bread, and coffee. We surprise the doctor with our good health. Sim is anemic, and we will each receive several bottles of various IV solutions during the next three days. They'll check our blood again then.

The doctor tells us the press called and will arrive soon. Will we meet with them? We are so happy to be alive we agree to anything. The excitement starts before eleven Sunday morning. Several local reporters and photographers drop in for stories.

On Monday, the entire Press Corps bursts into the emergency room at the little El Golfito Hospital. At dawn, Channel 7 from San Jose sets up their cameras in one of the examining rooms. Crews from the four major U.S. networks arrive with full equipment. They take over the other examining room and an office. Sim talks on the phone to correspondents in Paris and Melbourne, her interviews bubbling with newfound life.

The hospital has two telephone lines and a pay phone in the lobby that accepts overseas collect calls. Calls come in non-stop over both lines. Why all the fuss? Is our adventure a hot story? When rescued, our main preoccupation was getting through to our family and friends to tell them we are alive and well.

I take a call from the National Enquirer. The man is insistent. He offers $1000 for an exclusive. Instinct tells me to refuse. I'll talk without a tie down. At that moment, my body sends a strong signal that a bowel movement is imminent; I ask him to call back, and he says he will hold.

I hobble to the toilet trailing the tripod with the IV. Cramps bring sweat but no luck. I hobble back to the phone. The man from the Enquirer is still there. I reply to other questions about the trip until cramps again interrupt. He will stay on the line; I go back to the bathroom, nothing again.

I return to the phone, answer two more questions, then rush back to the bathroom. This goes on for a half hour. I haven't had a movement for seven weeks. Sim hasn't either. The man from the Enquirer stays on the line; I return and complete the interview.

Agence France Presse calls from Paris and Sim tells our story. All four US networks have set up in the emergency room. We are so happy to be alive we follow their orders gladly. We're in utopia; we're alive, and we will see our family again. The excitement continues all day.

Lunch and dinner again consists of gallo pinto, red beans and rice, surrounded with either a small piece of meat or vegetable. Famished, we devour everything served though we know this is not what we should be eating. The press leaves. Calls continue from friends and family until late into the night.

The children arrive in San Jose tonight and should be here tomorrow. The U.S. Embassy called saying they will meet the children at the airport and transport them to Golfito. The U.S. Coast Guard has called twice from somewhere near San Francisco. They want the name of the boat, its size, and our destination. At eleven, the nurses disconnect the phones.

We soon learn that emergency rooms are noisy. Monday night turns out to be asthma night. Half a dozen people come in with varying asthmatic ailments. Both wards are full with coughing men and women. Every time I walk to the bathroom, I pass people in the lobby with oxygen. The noise continues but we sleep.

Mid morning Tuesday, daughter Sally and granddaughter Cody arrive by air followed by my son Bill, Jr. and Sim's eldest Cris, who drove the tortuous six hours with a representative from the U.S. embassy. Of the people who knew us before, the children are the first to see us. Our physical condition alarms them. They say we look like two people out of a concentration camp. They insist we move to a better hospital, but we refuse. We are happy in the Golfito Hospital where everyone has been so great; besides it's the only hospital within miles.

The embassy representative, Steve Groh, offers the services of the U.S. embassy. We appreciate the offer, but we have everything we need; passports, travelers checks, cash, and credit cards are intact. He can't believe it. Part of his job is to help U.S. tourists, who, with mere hours in the country, have lost their passports, money, and everything else. Lost at sea for 66 days, we haven't lost a thing.

I'm alive and everything else can wait. My trips to the bathroom turn to the desperate. Many times, I almost faint. My pleas to the doctor yield two tiny suppositories. I plead for something more substantial, but the doc says to let nature take its course. Two hours go by with no results. I tell Sim that I feel like I'm in labor. She insists labor is much worse, but I doubt it. My trips to the bathroom are down to every ten minutes...almost like Sim's bailing routine. When I pass, the entire staff laughs with me.

At long last, it's over. I feel like a new man. I bathe in the delightful fresh water and return to my clean bed. I give Sim the good news; I'm 100% alive again.

Simonne faces a problem with a lady roommate. Sim awoke last night to find her sitting on a little stool by her bed, mumbling. When Sim opened her eyes, the lady gave a disoriented religious dissertation. She kept Sim awake most of the night.

The bright moon, swaying palms, lush trees, and puffy clouds confirm I am in paradise. I spend a good part of the night looking out or on my way to the bathroom. I now have diarrhea caused by too much chocolate and the wrong food. I should have brought a few trigger fish with me. Most of my trips end up with a shower and clean clothes. While I run to the head, Sim sleeps soundly.

Wednesday arrives. Nurses remove the IV's in the morning. It's time to bust out of the hospital. Yesterday, we talked to the head doctor concerning our departure today. We received neither a yea nor a nay. Today when he arrives, we will try again.

Sim made friends with a French couple who live in Golfito. They want us to spend a night at their home before flying to San Jose. The doctor arrives; he wants us to stay until we're stronger. We insist on leaving. He realizes we are anxious to fly back home and reluctantly approves our release. We leave the hospital amidst tears and farewells.

We move nearby to the home of the French couple who has a hot water and bubble bath for Sim. A chicken dinner around a family sized dinner table makes us feel on top of the world.

On Wednesday noon, we fly to San Jose in a small airplane chartered by Cedrik, a high school buddy of my son Jim. We're met by TV cameras and the press. Channel 7 of San Jose, Costa Rica and the newspaper, La Nacion, almost adopt us. They cover our every move and their representatives become close friends. We drive to the Sheraton, which has a family room where all six of us fit comfortably...Sim and I, Cris, Sally and Cody, and Bill, Jr.

The phone continues to ring while we try to relax. A prayer group of ladies, devoted to the patron Saint of Costa Rica, visit. I'm in bed under the covers and decide to stay there to rest a bit. My legs ache as any newly used set of muscles normally ache. Next comes a priest from a small town in northern Costa Rica who operates a small old people's home. He gives Sim prayer books and religious medals.

Cedrik picks us up after dark to join him in a little get together with friends at his house. After hellos and a few sea stories, out bursts Cedrik with a large plate of sushi. Everyone joins in laughter and banter. I surprise them all by eating the entire tray. His guests can't believe their eyes. Perhaps I should have left a few pieces for someone else.

On Saturday, we fly back to Miami on Pan Am. Customs, who had arranged for the press to stage at a side door so as not to interrupt the normal flow of passengers, suggested we slip out the main door. We refuse; we've had a good rapport with the press, so why avoid them now?

We head for the exit. Sim follows in a wheel chair, her legs too weak for the long walk down the airport corridors. The door opens. Ten TV camera crews and our family reach out to greet us. Kisses, hugs, tears, and interviews follow. The English speaking press on the right catch our attention first, and I banter with them for several minutes.

A voice in Spanish from my left cries, "Give us a chance too." We turn to the Spanish speaking media and run through their queries. I'm having a great time.

We're home. We're alive. Dear Lord, thank You. You are infinitely generous. You gave us new lives to live. You taught us all so much. Thank you, thank you for your love. We shall follow in Your footsteps. Forever.

survival

A story such as ours would be incomplete without a few words on the subject of survival. Several books in print address most topics on survival at sea. Michael Greenwald, who appeared with us on the Oprah Show, has authored as complete a treatise as I've seen entitled "Survival." We see no need to repeat much of what he has so concisely presented. We will stick to the main lessons we learned from our experience.

Allan Villiers has stated that "All loss of ships at sea is due to error." My error was to sail in a vessel that did not withstand the demands of the sea. In our case, this included a battering by maddened two ton whales. I sail next in either a heavy metal hull or a fiberglass bottom with a solid layup of at least an inch. Whales are but one of the hazards mariners face. Ship containers, reefs, rocks, other vessels await unwary sailors. Next time, I want to come out a winner...or at least afloat.

Anyone who ventures offshore today should not leave without a 406 MH EPIRB. The 406 satellite system, now fully operable, will pick up a distress signal in hours, pinpoint its location in less than a day, and have rescue craft alongside in under 48 hours. Prices for this survival tool have plunged. It's the best way to counter the main menace to survival...time.

The will to survive is essential. Throughout our sixty six day odyssey, both Simonne and I desperately yearned to continue living. No matter how many times Sim screamed that she wanted to die and have it over with, these were but passing fits of frustration and fear. They had nothing to do with giving up. In every crisis, such as when we almost sank or when the dolphins tore a hole in the floor of the raft, Sim responded in seconds with the vision and energy needed to salvage the situation. She wanted to continue living and I did too. Battered incessantly by man-eating sharks, death always present, we both knew we would fight furiously until the very end. We would struggle for life, back to back, until our last iota of energy gave way to eternal darkness. Never give up no matter what the odds are.

Before we left Miami, we should have left a better system for our family to track our progress and detect emergencies. Because of its source of propulsion, it is not always easy to predict the exact position of a sailboat on the face of the earth. Long before we left, I generated a computer spreadsheet with a four year detailed plan of our circumnavigation. It showed ports of call, dates, distances, routing, and expected weather. Most of our family saw it at one point or another. We kept to our program all the way to Panama. When we arrived in the Pacific later than planned, we opted for an alternate course to Hawaii to avoid hurricanes.

Under way, we regularly radioed new coordinates to the children. They knew where we were but had no way of visualizing our possible options, a difficult subject to master. I know of but one or two friends, high seas sailors, who could have accurately followed our progress and predicted our moves. Someone on shore needs to be fully briefed, knowledgeable, and capable of following the progress of a boat. To find us, our rescuers needed to get raw data from a dozen different sources, find professionals who could accurately analyze the information, conclude we had sunk, establish the time and probable location of the disaster, the direction of drift of the raft, and mobilize a private air search to the forecast area. Add to the above bad weather, thirty foot seas, and a small raft, its colors fading daily, and the task proves hopeless. In our case, a rescue operation would certainly have centered near Hawaiian waters. Who would have guessed, after eighty seven days at sea, that we were drifting three hundred miles from our starting point? The truth of the matter is: without an EPIRB, don't count on rescue.

Our Mayday messages were hamstrung with the wrong equipment and by time; although as shipwrecks go, we had lots of time to get off: twenty minutes. My radio, an amateur radio Kenwood TS-440AT, had the tuner built in and was not as versatile as a larger external tuner. I didn't buy a marine type, single side-band transceiver because of economics and versatility. Marine sets don't work the amateur bands easily nor completely. I couldn't tune to the Coast Guard emergency frequency, 2182 KHZ, because I would have had to change the resonator, a five minute job. Anyway,

2182 KHZ doesn't carry all that far. I had less than five minutes to enter a frequency, tune the set, and get on the air on three different channels. All the time, water rose steadily over my waist. Another near-fatal mistake, I did not post on the door to my radio locker a list of frequencies to use in an emergency. I couldn't find my frequency crib sheet among the trash floating in the cabin.

A hand held VHF radio would have shortened our trip considerably. I made the mistake of buying a cheap VHF. In the storm we experienced several days before we sank, a minor leak from a new deck fitting soaked the radio. When we sank, it was drying and uncharged. Buy good equipment, fully waterproof. Spend the money.

A "Panic Bag" is the answer. Critically placed and easy to grab, it contains most of the items needed in an emergency. All well and good. To be of any use, the kit must be constantly maintained; that is, batteries changed or charged, food inspected and rotated, tools cleaned and oiled, cannibalized items returned, etc. Would I have had my "Panic Bag" 100% up and ready to go at 0430 A.M. June 15, 1989...at this one instant in all of the days, more than 800 in all, spread over twenty-two years, that I have been at sea aboard *Siboney*? I doubt it. But we didn't do badly when it came to grabbing stores. Appendix 1 lists the gear that made the raft. Any more stuff and the ex-captain may have had to stay behind.

Many ask to what we attribute our survival. There are several factors. If the raft hadn't held up, what good would the watermaker have been? The unlimited supply of fresh water and trigger fish made a major difference in our health while adrift and through our recovery period. The knowledge that we could drink any quantity of fresh water we wished gave us peace of mind with which to cope with the many other facets of survival. Our Survivor 35 worked flawlesly. Efficient rain catchment could make the difference between life and death for a castaway without the ability to produce his liquid needs. Coast Guard approved rafts have provisions for catching rain, but then for it to work, it needs to rain. We had many rainy days. I spent many hours struggling to fill various containers with little success. I found it much easier to use the desalinator. Without it, I would have been hard pressed to maintain an adequate supply of fresh water. Ingenuity is vital, but we didn't see rain for two weeks. I attribute our good health to our unlimited supply of drinking water.

Castaway in the wrong raft from the very first minute made life extremely uncomfortable and hazardous. It didn't help to find out later that a similar raft, a six man, cost but a hundred dollars more. A better raft, rated "Coast Guard Approved," would have had two air chambers, one above the other giving us an added margin of safety and comfort. The Switlik Coastal raft proved its exceptional durability and design beyond all expectations. Its large ballast bags maintained stability in heavy going, a lot of force 6, and a couple of gales. It proved 100% stable in high seas. It sure would've been nice to have had the extra buoyancy.

A raft owner should witness its periodic inspection and inflation to insure all work is done correctly: new batteries for the flashlight, the patches are lubricated, all the accessories you need are included, there are varied fish hooks, etc. An extra air pump and means to inflate the raft orally are important. If a water maker is part of the raft package, it would preclude use in non-emergencies. A bright colored flag mounted on a telescopic device might help for signalling. Include a strong police-type whistle; those supplied with our life preservers were trash. Extra patches in various sizes are a must. The two patches supplied with our raft were an inch and a half at their smallest dimension. The hole we found towards the end of the trip was but a pinpoint. If I had to cut a one inch hole in the air chamber to insert the patch, we'd again have lost all our buoyancy and risked our lives. A better solution is a patch as used on tubeless tire repairs. Important too: watch them inflate the raft. When I pulled the inflation lanyard, with *Siboney* ready to drop out from under me, I knew not what to expect.

I am down on flares and high on signalling with a firearm. With a few rounds for the gun, I could have signaled the "Ter Eriksen" when it passed close by on day two. The bullets in the locker next to the gun or the large package of flares on top of the bag with comforters may have helped lop weeks off the trip. The Lord had other plans for us. He decided we needed time to find Him.

Still I'm not happy with the thought of again trying to survive at sea in a plastic "deflatable" raft. On land and at sea, most of us are accustomed to direct and manage our destiny. For sixty six days, we could neither propel nor direct the raft. We drifted towards Isla de Cocos for a week only to miss it by a couple of miles. We rowed, tried to sail, prayed, all for aught. Manufacturers of marine equipment need to design a life saving device that is stable in heavy weather, slightly maneuverable under wind propulsion compact, and quickly deployable. Tinker has come close, yet rough seas, coupled with powerful, fast moving waves as we experienced in our first month at sea, would have capsized it repeatedly.

Flares are on the top of my list of the least needed items for a raft. Don't go to sea without a varied assortment but don't expect spectacular results. Modern ships are fully automated and a lookout is an exception. A gun with bullets is better or the VHF radio. All ships are expected to monitor VHF channel 16. Why doesn't someone market an old fashioned "May West" crank type radio with the new emergency frequencies?

Would three dozen flares instead of just three have made a difference? My reason for saying this is purely mathematical. Flares fire for a minute or perhaps a few seconds longer. The watch aboard merchant ships on the high seas may look out for a total of five minutes out of every half hour. Factor in the average twenty foot ocean swell and the odds of catching the crew's attention boils down to luck.

No two people are the same. Everyone must understand the chemical balance and needs of their body. My body does not store salt. When I perspire and do not take salt tablets, I immediately get dizzy, have stomach cramps and a headache. That's why I drank salt water. Sim didn't need salt and felt fine without it. The stress and effort of abandoning ship and adjusting to raft life depleted my salt reserves. On day 3, I was too dizzy to move. I drank two cups of salt water daily followed with a fresh water rinse. On arrival at the hospital, blood analysis proved I had a much higher mineral count than Simonne. The bottom line is: know your body and react to the signals it sends before it's too late.

The right companion is vital. I could not have made the voyage alone. Sim says she would not have made it alone, but I dispute that. She is resourceful and has a strong will to live. She's a survivor and could have made it without me. We both are grateful we had no babies or small children to contend with. Sailors who travel with children must take extreme precautions. They should not place themselves in a position where they may be adrift for a long period. Stay close to shore, buy a larger than needed raft, and follow the above.

The art of signalling a passing ship is directly dependent on early detection. An enclosed raft seriously limits visibility. We missed most ships because we didn't spot them until they were nearly abreast. Then it's too late to shoot a flare. We heard every ship that passed close by before we saw them. A stethoscope type device, glued on to an air chamber and connected to ear phones similar to those used on commercial aircraft, would increase early detection of approaching shipping.

Incredible as it may seem, one of man's earliest methods of signalling worked for us while the EPIRB and single side-band radio failed. The message cast off in an ampty Perrier bottle on July 6 washed up on the shores of Punta Burica, our projected landfall, and was found by a beach patrol officer on the fourth of September, 1989. The officer had seen us on Costa Rican television and in the local newspapers but called us nevertheless in Miami to report his find and wish us well. He later turned the note over to the press which carried it in their dailies. This helped us to reproduce it accurately in Chapter 8.

Other than satisfying natural curiosity, navigation on a liferaft serves little useful purpose. I kept my dead reckoning going out of habit and boredom. The radio told us more about our progress than stars or sun which were more often than not hidden behind clouds. Yet every factor helped dissuade our perpetual fear that we were drifting west into the empty wastes of the Pacific Ocean. I know how the Bailey's felt as they drifted farther and farther from land.

We kept up our daily routines such as position estimates, three meals a day, happy hour, and prayers throughout the entire voyage. Though we tried to maintain this link with our previous life, our experience wrought drastic changes upon both of us; the most significant is in the way we moved close to God and now closely follow His principles in our daily life. Life has become all the more meaningful for us because of this. We know not what He has in store for us but our senses and heart will stay tuned to His messages.

life in the world of
sharks

Simonne and I agree without reservation on one point: were it not for the shark population in the Pacific Ocean, our 66 day, 1200 mile voyage in a six foot plastic raft would have been a breeze. Except for the first five and the last six days, sharks menaced us continuously with instant death. Sharks battered the raft at all hours, day and night. One pack travelled along with us while we drifted 600 miles. We could tell they were the same sharks by their time of arrival and pattern of attack. And two had tags.

I labeled the bunch of sharks that paid us a daily visit "SHARK PACK." They called on us every day for five weeks at between ten and eleven in the morning. They may have attacked at night as well, but it was impossible to tell. It was easy to spot "SHARK PACK." One five footer had a white one inch round tag just ahead of its dorsal fin. The other, a six foot lemon shark, wore a two inch long tag alongside the dorsal fin. Sim's good Franco-Italian blood exploded during their visits. "I would like to meet the 'PEEG' who tagged these monsters instead of blasting them!" she would exclaim again and again. As time passed, our relationship with "SHARK PACK" evolved from sheer terror at their very first call to deja' vu towards the end of our voyage.

We still remember vividly the first time a shark hit our raft. It happened on day 5 after two in the morning. Up to that moment, our nights had been more or less pleasant. We'd sleep four to six hours at a time if the seas were not pounding and the raft did not need air. We had nothing more to worry about than a turtle or two a day, getting found, and deciding what to use for bait when our food ran out. That first bash completely changed our life style.

Seas at that time were four to six feet on 25 foot swells, relatively easy going. Once every hour or so, a wave bigger than average would come boiling towards us and give the raft a good wash. After two nights, we were growing accustomed to the roar of breaking waves and the crash splash that followed. We even napped between soakings. Then of a sudden, the raft is struck so violently both of us jump. I thought a fifty foot breaker had washed over us. Sim leaned over and whispered "Shark!." We embraced tightly. I shushed needlessly for the only sound around came from two pounding hearts.

The next crash spun the raft around 180 degrees. My side was now to leeward, not good since I was using my extra weight to windward for stability. Five more slaps in a row put us into a real panic. Neither of us moved. Not a word was said. I held Simonne tightly, my mind wildly trying to sort out this new situation. Whack. Whack. Whack again. Sim whispered, "Pray." We prayed. The shark left. Too tense to sleep, we held each other tightly until dawn.

During the following three days, sharks battered the raft regularly, day and night. Our reaction was always the same. Panic. We embraced and prayed. Over the next 50 days, sharks whacked our raft more than 3500 times. As days passed, we observed how they approached and slapped our tiny vessel. This led us to the why behind their behavior.

Sharks, as we know them now, have been around for a long time, over 25,000,000 years. Their roots go back even further, to the Middle Devonian Period, 375,000,000 years ago. Twenty seven species of sharks attack man and boats. Most sharks are scavengers and carnivorous. We saw several hammerhead sharks. They eat everything from a wide variety of fish including other sharks to turtles, birds, seals, squid, garbage (including plastic), and carrion. Fortunately, a particular plastic raft was not on its menu du jour. All sharks love warm water except the Great White, which will go anywhere for a meal. The water temperature during our entire voyage ranged between 24 to 26 degrees C (78 to 82 F), a perfect habitat for sharks. From day ten onwards, we were surrounded continuously by these predators.

Whenever I started to fish, I would first take a look around to determine what was around. The sharks were always there. On calm and sunny days, our giant underwater aquarium held hundreds of fish of various varieties at different levels with sharks intermixed at all depths with fish of all sizes. The fish did not appear at all concerned with the presence of the sharks, and the sharks never made a move against a member of our growing "family." Whenever the fish population disappeared, I started to worry.

Smaller sharks remained close to the surface and near the raft. Large sharks approached from below and would circle the raft in ever shallower orbits. "SHARK PACK" was an exception. Often they came surfing in, fins out of the water much like dolphins and, at the last second, ducked under the raft. Some had a great time zipping between our ballast bags. One devil got his daily kicks by whacking inside the ballast bags. Sharks segregate according to size which protects the smaller individuals from predation by the larger ones. There was a regular "nipping" order, with the leader demanding and receiving plenty of space.

Mature sharks segregate by sex and come together only during the mating season. When parturition is imminent, the female moves to a nursery area, gives birth, and leaves her offspring with other newborn. Floating slowly along, we picked up increasing numbers of small sharks that looked to us for protection.

Sharks have a slow rate of growth, one to three inches per year. Males of the same age stick together because, if they mix with larger sharks, they will become part of the day's menu. The twenty to thirty sharks in "SHARK PACK" were all five to six feet long.

Although we couldn't tell a male shark from a female as it zipped by, I feel all sharks that whacked the raft were males fulfilling a mating ritual etched eons ago. We had over two months to view and take note of their behavior, and the conclusions we have reached are based on hundreds of observations. A shark marks its territory or presence by spraying as do many species in the animal kingdom. With a virtually empty ocean, our raft, travelling at a top speed over the bottom of one knot, became a favorite outlet for the sex drive of all the local male shark population.

A typical day would begin at ten in the morning with a whack or two by immature sharks of less than two feet. As the day progressed, larger and larger sharks would swim by, and we got the impression each was driven to remove the scent left by our earlier admirers. At 1030, "SHARK PACK" would arrive and keep us entertained with an hour of punishment. When the "PACK" left, we would relax, meditate, and prepare for lunch. Sim would grasp the opportunity to chew me out for the 912th time for getting her into this horrible situation from which she would never get out alive and thus never see her babies again, who would never know what happened, etc, etc. I lost count of the times I prayed for a shark.

After noon, I usually started fishing. Though our raft was always surrounded by sharks, none came close while I fished. When fishing, I had always to be on the lookout. To keep from losing my only hook, I would use small pieces of bait and hold it never more than six inches below the surface. Occasionally, two to three foor sharks went for the bait, but it was never seriously approached by a mature shark. During our voyage, I landed more than 330 fish and disposed of each carcass over the side. The trigger fish would move in first, then hurriedly give space to the first shark. In a flash, it gulped the remains.

Right around four in the afternoon, sharks would pummel the raft again a couple of times, never too intensely. Usually, it was a member of the runt pack that resided full time under the raft. Dusk was normally one of our quieter moments. Simonne would read the psalms; then we'd pray, watch the sunset if any, and prepare our sleeping quarters for the evening. As the sky slowly changed from day to night, the immatures were replaced by the BIG ONES. I spotted them first around sundown during our third week. At least twice as long as the raft, several monster sharks circled ten feet away. At first, I couldn't tell what it was. Later I saw the unmistakable shape of a hammerhead. Others were mature silkies. Obviously, a BIG ONE never touched us.

Some sharks circled the raft in one direction to strike all four sides progressively. Others would whack one side, skip two sides, and appear from below to whack the fourth side. Many times, a shark shot from under the raft, went out ten feet, and turned back. As it shot towards the raft, it would turn belly up at the last moment.

When even with the raft, it would spray it with an oily substance. Still belly up, the shark would deal the raft a violent whack with its tail. Often the raft would spin from the blow. The shark continued to circle and whack the raft again and again to punish us without mercy.

We had to fight back or risk losing the raft. One morning, a three foot lemon shark tried my patience by whacking all four sides of the raft over and over again. I prepared the heavy half of our fishing rod and lay in wait with rod poised harpoon fashion. As the shark approached and turned bottom side up, I gave it a good zonk on the belly. It flipped its tail, soaking me. I declared WAR! Its next pass was a swim-by to check out what had happened. I caught the shark between the eyes. It left the area. We weren't bothered by sharks during the next three hours. Success.

From this moment on, our approach to sharks changed to that of aggressor. No longer were we going to placidly await obvious disaster. Experience taught us that a lone shark would first approach the raft from the depths and slowly circle towards the surface. On its first close approach, it would merely brush the sides of the raft. This became our signal to get ready. Simonne was much more sensitive to sharks than I, and often times I would ask her, "Was that a wave or a shark?" If a shark, I would sit up, get the pole ready, and wait.

Sometimes the shark vanished, but more often it would circle under the raft and come back for another try. I had to remain alert and nail it before it got excited and increased speed. This approach considerably reduced damage to the raft and to our nervous systems. Unfortunately, there were a bunch of non-conforming sharks that remained unimpressed by my bonking skills. They whacked the raft no matter what we did.

Darkness enveloped the raft minutes after sunset. No lingering tropical cornucopia of colors in the deep Pacific. Just shades of grey. The shark population normally gave us a break until after 10 at night. We would get a hit or two just before midnight but nothing very scary. All hell would break loose sometime around two in the morning. The first time it happened, I was sure we had been run over by a freighter. This shark appeared nightly during more than forty nights. Besides arriving at the same time every night, the attack pattern was always the same.

Faster than a destroyer at flank speed, it would zoom past all four sides of the raft, spraying and whacking, spraying and whacking. I would splash, bonk, and even yell at it. I hit it many times. None of my tactics worked. During all the shark attacks, Simonne prayed intensely. After days trying to subdue our 2 A.M. fiend physically without success, I gave up. Lying down with the raft receiving incredible punishment, I prayed. Our prayers seldom failed to be acted on at once.

Many sharks attacked at night or during the day during violent rain storms. Some storms lasted 36 hours. In this case, our only defense against sharks was prayer. We would pray and the sharks would leave. I never ceased to be amazed. Often, after I had prayed and the sharks had backed off, my mind would wander. Whack, and the raft would spin. Just a reminder to keep praying. Once our two AM shark left, life quieted down until mid-morning.

TAKEN ON RAFT UPON THE SINKING OF *SIBONEY*

* INDICATES ITEMS TOSSED OVER THE SIDE

GEAR SUPPLIED IN SWITLIK RAFT PACKAGE

2-PADDLES
1-PUMP
2-PATCHES
1-SMALL BAILING BUCKET
1-LARGE ORANGE BAG
3-SOLAS FLARES
1-RUBBER TOSS RING

1-FLASHLIGHT
2-PACKS SEA SICK PILLS
3-SPONGES
1-ROLL YELLOW ROPE
1-ROLE CORD
1-KNIFE
1-SEA ANCHOR

SHIP'S GEAR

1-CHRONOMETER *
1-BAROMETER *
1-SHIP'S COMPASS
1-LOG BOOK
1-38 cal. REVOLVER *
4-LARGE COCKPIT CUSHIONS
1-SURVIVOR 35 DESALINATOR
2-SMALL COCKPIT CUSHIONS
1-MINI-B EPIRB * (DAY 25)
2-SETS FOUL WEATHER GEAR
1-SAILBAG, LARGE
1-KNIFE
2-PAIRS SAILING GLOVES

1-SMALL FLASHLIGHT
1-LARGE BUCKET
1-ELECTRONIC COMPASS
1-NAVIGATION WORKBOOK
2-WHISTLES
2-BOXES MATCHES
1-FISHING REEL/ HOOK
1-FISHING ROD,
1-BINOCULARS * (DAY 50)
2-LIFE PRESERVERS
1-CAN OPENER
1-PAIR COTTON GLOVES
1-HAND LANTERN (DAY 30)

FOOD AND LIQUIDS

2-2.5 GALLON WATER JUGS +
1-ONE GALLON WATER JUG +
7-EVIAN, ONE LITER
2-PERRIER, LARGE +
1-LARGE COKE +
1-SMALL 7-UP + (MESSAGE)
5-CANS BEER
3-CARTONS JUICE, SMALL
1/2-JAR PEANUT BUTTER
1-CAN PEARS

2-CANS SALTINES, +
1-CAN SPANISH MUSSELS
2-CANS DIET VEG-ALL
1-CAN JUICE
1-CAN MUSHROOM SOUP
1-CAN HEARTS OF PALM
1/2-BOTTLE HENNESSY +
1-CAN CHICK PEAS
3-SMALL PCK. RAISINS

NOTE: ALL CANS USED FOR BAILING UNTIL RUSTED
+ THESE WATER & FOOD CONTAINERS DISCARDED WHEN
EMPTY

CLOTHING

2-BALBOA YC T-SHIRTS *
2-PAIRS SHORTS
1-DARK BLUE T-SHIRT
1-LADIES SLEEVELESS SHIRT

1-BALBOAYC SWEAT SHIRT*
2-T-SHIRTS WHITE *
1-RED T-SHIRT *
1-BATHING TRUNKS, MENS

NOTE: * INDICATES CLOTHING ROTTED

BEDDING

1-BLANKET, WOOL,SINGLE
1-COMFORTER, KING, POLY * (WET-DAY 50)
1-COVER, COTTON,TWIN * (DAY 55)
2-COMFORTERS, TWIN, COTTON *

TOILETRY

1-MIRROR
1-DARNING NEEDLE
2-TWEEZERS
1-BRUSH
2-TOOTHBRUSHES *
1-NAIL BRUSH
1-SET SAMPLE PERFUMES *

2-LARGE SCISSORS
6-JARS LOTIONS *
1-COMB, LARGE
1-STEEL NAIL FILE
1-TOOTHPASTE
1-KUKIDENT
1-ROLL KITCHEN TOWELS

MISCELLANEOUS

14-BALL POINT PENS
1-SET OF 20 FELT POINT PENS *
2-LARGE TRASH BAGS
5-CARDS WITH PSALMS
1-MEDAL ST. MICHAEL
1-NAIL SCISSORS
1-SET PINCHITOS PLASTIC
6-CASSETTES *
1-SKETCH BOOK *
1-LOT CREDIT CARDS
2-PASSPORTS
1-MEDAL, VIRGEN MILAGROSA
1-FRAME WITH ST MICHAEL
1-EYEGLASSES, READING, BILL
1-EYEGLASSES, SUN, BILL
1-WATCH, DIGITAL, BILL'S
1-MEDAL, VIRGIN OF LOURDES
1-EYEGLASSES, SUN, SIM
1-WATCH, RAYMOND WEIL, SIM'S
1-CAMCORDER, SONY* & CASE
2-JAPANESE LANGUAGE BOOKS *
1-EYEGLASSES, CLEAR , SIM

1-FELT POINT PEN
2-ZIP LOCK BAGS
1-ROSARY
1-SET PHOTOS, FAMILY
1-NAIL CLIPPER
2-INDIAN MOLAS
1-WALKMAN RADIO
1-CAMERA, MINOLTA
1-WALLET-SIM'S
1-TRAVELLERS CHECKS
1-LOT CASH
1-SET DOMINOES
2-COMPACTOR BAGS

readings

Simonne read each evening at last light, most often in the order as listed below. When shark attacks were at their worst or when the sea most threatened to swallow us, she read again during the day. Towards the end of our voyage, with the cards soaked and dissolving or when incessant rain made it impractical to remove them from their plastic bag, we recited the prayers from memory, one filling in for memory lapses of the other.

The following prayers appear on a Prayer Card given to us by a member of the Gospel Ship Ministry in the mid 80's while at anchor in Green Turtle Cay in the Bahama Islands. The card has two leaves, the cover carrying an image of a tall ship sailing in heavy weather with text on the remaining three pages.

They that go down to the sea in ships, that do business in great water; these see the works of the Lord, and His wonders in the deep.
For He commands, and raises the stormy wind, which lifts up the waves of the sea.
They mount up to the heavens, they go down again to the depths: their soul is melted because of trouble.
They reel to and fro, and stagger like a drunken man, and are at their wits end.
Then they cry unto the Lord in their trouble, and He brings them out of their distresses.
He makes the storm a calm, so that the waves are still. Then are they glad because they are quiet; so He brings them unto their desired haven. Oh, that men would praise the Lord for His goodness, and for His wonderful works to the children of men....

Shipmate, God's gift of everlasting life is a FREE gift.
*"For god so loved the world that He gave His one and only Son
(Jesus), that whoever believes in Him should not perish, but
have everlasting life."*   John

Jesus also says, *"Truly, Truly, I say to you, He that belives in
me has everlasting life."*   John

I pray that if you have never trusted Him, just the best you
know how, talk with God and tell Him that are accepting this
Free Gift of Eternal Life by trusting in Jesus Christ as your
Personal Savior. When you have done this, you can know that
your Salvation is Secure by what Jesus says, *"And I give to
them eternal life; and they shall never perish, neither shall any
man snatch them out of my hand."*   John

**This well known parable from the gospel according to Luke
was printed on a card Simonne received in the mail in the
early '80's.**

What man of you, having a hundred sheep, if he has lost one
of them, does not leave the ninety and nine in the wilderness,
and go after the one which is lost, until he finds it? And when
he comes home, he calls together his friends and neighbors,
saying to them, "Rejoice with me, for I have found my sheep
which was lost."
And when he comes home, he calls together his friends and his
neighbors, saying to them, "Rejoice with me, for I have found
my sheep which was lost." Just so, I tell you, there will be
more joy in heaven over one sinner who repents than over
ninety-nine righteous persons who need no repentance.

The following parable taken from Mathew was printed on another card received by Simonne in the early 1980's in response to a donation:

9 Or what man is there of you, whom if his asks bread, will give him a stone?

10 Or if he ask a fish, will he give him a serpent?

11 If ye then, being evil, know how to give good gifts unto your children, how much more shall your Father which is in heaven give good things to them that ask him?

12 Therefore all things whatsoever ye would that men should do to you, do ye even so to them; for this is the law and the prophets.

The following Parable, "Footprints," was printed on a card given to us in December, 1985, at the funeral of a good friend in New York City. Its author is unknown. The reverse side of the card has an image of the Virgin Mary.

One night a man had a dream. He dreamed he was walking along the beach with the LORD. Across the sky flashed scenes from his life. For each scene, he noticed two sets of footprints in the sand; one belonging to him, and the other to the LORD.

When the last scene of his life flashed before him, he looked back at the footprints in the sand. He noticed that many times along the path of his life there was only one set of footprints. He also noticed that it happened at the very lowest and saddest times in his life.

This really bothered him and he questioned the LORD about it. "LORD, you said that once I decided to follow you, you'd walk with me all the way. But I have noticed that during the most troublesome times in my life, there is one set of footprints, I don't understand why when I needed you most you would leave me."

The LORD replied, "My precious, precious child, I love you and I would never leave you. During your times of trial and suffering, when you see only one set of footprints, it was then that I carried you."

Lastly, Simonne would read a prayer in Italian urging Jesus to intercede in the beautification of Pope John XXIII:

PER LA BEATIFICAZIONE DI PAPA GIOVANNI

Signore Gesù, che Ti sei degnato di scegliere come Vicario in tera il Tuo servo Giovanni XXIII, perchè con la sua vita ricordasse al mondo la Tua bontà, Ti prego, **degnati di glorificarlo** con lo splendore dei Santi **e concedermi,** per la sua intercessione, la grazia di cui ho tanto bisogno.

Non guardare alla mia miseria, che è tanto grande, ma ai meriti del Tuo servo, che visse di Te e per Te.

Arricchiscimi, o Gesù, della sua bontà e fa che io venga a lodarti in Cielo con la Vergine Tua Madre e con tutti i Santi. - Amen!

   Pater, Ave e Gloria

The reverse side of the card carries an image of Pope John XXIII.

⊖log⊖

OF

"LAST CHANCE"

This is a verbatim copy of the LOG written while adrift aboard our raft, *Last Chance*. We include several pages reproduced from the original to provide the reader with its flavor. We scored results of our domino games on the top of the third page. Though soaked for over two weeks the Log remains fully readable but not of the quality required for reproduction herein. Please contact the publisher for details on how to order a full-sized copy of the actual handwritten LOG.

TIME	LOG	CHART COURSE	COURSE STEERED	WIND	BAR.	THER.	SEA	WEA.	CLDS.	REMARKS
1700										JUST LOST 2ND DORADO OF DAY-FIRST A SHACKLE THEN AN + NOW A RIG BUCKLE - STEER SCREWED UP ON BOTH - BOTH TO BOAT - 1ST CRAW IN 14 ins - 2 + 3RD IN SELF STEERING - COW BROK 1007
1300										3 BEANS FOR SUP + BACON THAT BEEN HANGING IN COCKPIT FOR A WEEK! 15 June THURSDAY DAY 22
0300										SURROUNDED BY WHALES - 10/15 FT LONG - BLACK - RAIN - RAIN 1007 -
0400										BUMPED TWICE BY WHALES -
0530										GOT HIT BY WHALE - HARD - OPENED SEAM - BILGE PUMP NOT MANUDING
0545										ABANDONING SHIP - LIFE RAFT INFLATED - LOADING WITH FOOD/WATER - PUNCTURED RAFT!
0600										ABANDONED - SIBONEY DECKS AWASH - 5°30'N 99°104
0615										SIBONEY SANK - AFLOAT ON RAFT 15 June THURSDAY DAY!
0800										ORGANIZED RAFT - PUT CUSHIONS UNDER US - PURGED BOAT - MAKING INVENTORY - PATCHED HOLE - PUMPED UP - HOLDING
1500										9 HRS IN RAFT - SPENT IN SELF ANALYSIS - CRYING - ANALYSIS OF OUR CHANCES OF BEING FOUND - DIP

FUEL IN TANKS AT START _____   TOOK ABOARD _____ AT FINISH _____ USED _____
FRESH WATER IN TANKS AT START _____   TOOK ABOARD _____ AT FINISH _____ USED _____
DAYS RUN _____ MILES   TOTAL CRUISE RUN _____   M11.201x

TIME	LOG	CHART COURSE	COURSE STEERED	WIND	BAR.	THER.	SEA	WEATHER	CLDS.	REMARKS
										THE ANNY DAY MESSAGE ON B13.2 GOT OUT - CRYING - IS THE GARB WORKING WHEN WILL THE KIDS LOOK FOR US - HOPE THE 10 MILES DON'T RETURN - OUR PROSPECTS - HOW MUCH WE LOVE EACH OTHER - WHAT A BUMP WHY TAKE FINE BOAT TO GO -
1700										ABLE 1/2 DAY - RAINY - PLAYED DOMINOES - SIM CHEAP -
2300										TRYING TO SLEEP - CAN'T - REMINISCED - MADE PROMISES
										16 JUNE FRIDAY DAY 2
0300										TURTUG FELL IN LOVE WITH RAFT - BUMPED FOR LONG TIME - SKIP FINALLY BEAT HIM WITH PADDLE ON HEAD & HE GOT HINT
0400										POURING
0800										FINALLY SLEPT - DAY DAWNED RAINY - WET IF WE GET OUT OFF THIS ONE WE'LL BE BETTER PEOPLE FOR US FOR OTHERS, FOR LIFE WHICH IS WHAT WE PRAY GOD FOR.
1200										FIGURE 25 MI SET EAST + 6MI SET N - RAINING - PLAYED DOMINOES - SKIP WON 6-5.
1430 100										WAVES HIGH - BREAKING ON US - TAKING WATER SLOW BAILING WIND DOWN - WAVES DYING AT LAST BAR 2500B - ??

FUEL IN TANKS AT START _____   TOOK ABOARD _____ AT FINISH _____ USED _____

FRESH WATER IN TANKS AT START _____   TOOK ABOARD _____ AT FINISH _____ USED _____

DAYS RUN _____ MILES   TOTAL CRUISE RUN _____ MILES

TIME	LOG	CHART COURSE	COURSE STEERED	WIND	BAR.	THER.	SEA	WEA. THER.	CLDS.	REMARKS
		DOMINO CHAMPIONSHIP								
June 15	SM 5	June 16	Mi	818.44	June 18	June 17	05 27 53 261⁄2 (11)		June 18	June 20 / June 21
28 #1	BLL	1	Mi						153.44	560 / 2935
	SM	4	MH	817.19		04788.86.65	5⁄2 8⁄1105		8.38 76 45 Mi M⁴157	9158867 / 7856 7904 8.80 Mi 20 50⁴ 31
2030				Tonight TER ERIKSEN passed by 200 yards to the N &						
				did not STOP! nearly ran us down! God help us!						
2045				INCREDIBLE - HE DIDN'T STOP- OUR HOPES SHATTERED -						
				NEVER AGAIN WILL A SHIP COME THAT CLOSE - I hope						
June 17				SATURDAY DAY 3						
0800 -				WHAT A NIGHT - RAINY - GETTING ROUGH - STORMY.						
				WE'RE STILL IN SHOCK OVER LAST NIGHTS MISS						
				EST MTG 20 MI SE TO EAST 5 MI JU - SIM ITEM @ ALMA LMR						
1030				LUCK IS NOT WITH US - VALVE IN DUE OF THE FLOTATION TANK						
				IS STUCK OPEN - AIR LEAKING - WE HAVE TO KEEP PUMPING -						
				WIND S 12-15 KNOTS - SEAS TEN FEET - OVERCAST- NOTHING						
				IN SIGHT - WE PRAY TO JOSE GREGORIO HERNANDEZ & JUAN XXIII						
				WEAVES BREAKING - WE HAVE TO MAKE 17. GOD WILLING!						
1200				IN INVENTORY - HAVE 6 GAL WATER, 1 WATER MAKER, 2 CAPS CRAYGOR						
				8 TINS VEGETABLES, 5 BEERS, 1⁄2 JUG BRANDY - COMPASS - BAR.						

FUEL IN TANKS AT START _____ TOOK ABOARD _____ AT FINISH _____ USED _____

FRESH WATER IN TANKS AT START _____ TOOK ABOARD _____ AT FINISH _____ USED _____

DAYS RUN _____ MILES   TOTAL CRUISE RUN _____ MILES

15 JUNE DAY 22 OUT OF BALBOA
0300-SURROUNDED BY WHALES-10/15 FEET LONG-BLACK-
RAIN-BAR 1009
0400-BUMPED TWICE BY WHALES
0530-GOT HIT BY WHALE HARD-OPENED SEAM-BILGE
PUMP NOT HANDLING
0545-ABANDONING SHIP-LIFE RAFT INFLATED-LOADING
WITH FOOD/WATER,PUNCTURED RAFT 0600 ABANDONED
BOAT-SIBONEY DECKS AWASH-LIGHTS BLAZING-5 DEG
30'N, 99 DEG 0615-SIBONEY SANK-ADRIFT ON RAFT

15 JUNE THURSDAY-DAY 1
0800-ORGANIZED RAFT-PUT CUSHIONS UNDER US-
PURGED BOAT-MAKING INVENTORY-PATCHED HOLE-
PUMPED UP-HOLDING
1500-9 HRS IN RAFT-SPENT IN SELF ANALYSIS-CRYING-
ANALYSIS OF OUR CHANCES OF BEING FOUND-DID THE
MAYDAY MESSAGE ON 13113.2 GET OUT-CRYING-IS THE
EPIRB WORKING-WHEN WILL THE KIDS LOAD FOR US-
HOPE THE WHALES DON'T RETURN-OUR PROSPECTS-HOW
MUCH WE LOVE EACH OTHER-WHAT A DUMB WAY FOR A
FINE BOAT TO GO
1800=ADRIFT 1/2 DAY-RAINY-PLAYED DOMINOES-SIM
CHAMP-
2300-TRYING TO SLEEP-CAN'T-REMINISCE-MADE
PROMISES

16 JUNE FRIDAY   DAY 2
0300-TURTLE FELL IN LOVE WITH RAFT-BUMPED FOR
LONG TIME-SKIP FINALLY BEAT HIM WITH PADDLE ON
HEAD AND HE GOT HINT
0400-POURING
0900-FINALLY SLEPT-DAY DAWNED RAINY-WET-IF WE
GET OUT OF THIS ONE WE'LL BE BETTER PEOPLE, FOR US
FOR OTHERS, FOR LIFE WHICH IS WHAT WE PRAY GOD
FOR
1200-FIGURE 25 MILE SET EAST AND 6 MI SET N-RAINING-
PLAYED DOMINOES-SKIP WON 6-5

1430-WAVES HIGH-BREAKING ON US-TAKING WATER-SIM BAILING
1600-WIND DOWN-WAVES DYING AT LAST-BAR 950 MB ???
2030-TANKER TER ERIKSEN FROM OSLO PASSED BY 200 YARDS TO THE NORTH AND DID NOT STOP! NEARLY RAN US DOWN! GOD HELP US!
2045-INCREDIBLE-HE DIDN'T STOP-OUR HOPES SHATTERED-NEVER AGAIN WILL A SHIP COME THAT CLOSE-I HOPE

JUNE 17 SATURDAY DAY 3
0800-WHAT A NIGHT-RAINY-GETTING ROUGH-STORMY-WE'RE STILL IN SHOCK OVER LAST NIGHTS MISS-ESTIMATE 20 MILE SET TO EAST 5 MI N-SIM HEARD ALMA LLANERA
1030-LUCK IS NOT WITH US-VALVE IN ONE OF THE FLOTATION TANKS IS STUCK OPEN-AIR LEAKING-WE HAVE TO KEEP PUMPING-WIND S 12-15 KNOTS-SEAS 10 FEET-OVERCAST-NOTHING IN SIGHT-WE PRAY TO JOSE GREGORIO HERNANDEZ & JUAN XXIII-WAVES BREAKING-WE HAVE TO MAKE IT! GOD WILLING!
1200-INVENTORY-HAVE 5 GAL WATER, WATER MAKER, 2 CANS CRACKERS, 8 TINS VEGETABLES, 5 BEERS, 1/2 JUG BRANDY-COMPASS-BAR, CLOCK, WATCH, CAMERA, CAMCORDER, 2 LIFE PRESERVERS, FULL SET COCKPIT CUSHIONS, CAN OPENER, BUCKET, SPONGES, FOUL WEATHER GEAR, 3 COVERS, RADIO RECEIVER, EPIRB (STILL ON-BUT NO ONE LISTENING!)-3 FLASHLIGHTS-WRITING MATERIALS-3 FLARES, 5 JUGS JUICE, 2 PAIRS SHORTS AND 4 T-SHIRTS, WHAT WE MISSED-SET OF FLARES, CHART, HORN, PILLOWS, SHOES (LITTLE USE NOW)-CLOTHING-MEDICINE-TOOLS-ON THURSDAY ATE NOTHING BUT 2 CRACKERS, FRIDAY OPENED CAN OF VEGALL-1/2 LUNCH-1/2 FOR SUP-TODAY HAD 2 CRACKERS SO FAR..LOST SEA ANCHOR-HAVE HAD TO MAINTAIN VALVE IN RAFT-LOSING AIR-RAFT CHRISTENED "LAST CHANCE"
1641-WE HAVE PROBLEMS WITH 2ND PUMP-WE WILL

HAVE TO PUMP EVERY 1/2 HOUR-WE THREW AWAY GUN, CAMCORDER, HEAVY BOTTLE OF WATER, CLOCK, BAROMETER. WE TRY TO KEEP OUR SPIRITS. WE ATE 3 CRACKERS TODAY. SALLY, JOE,CRIS,ALEX WE ARE SENDING YOU MENTAL MESSAGE. PLEASE CALL THE COAST GUARD! LORD JESUS HELP US!
1716-SEAS GETTING ROUGHER-RAFT VERY UNCOMFORTABLE-DOES NOT KEEP AIR INSIDE-SIM STARTED PERIOD-WORRIED ABOUT SHARKS-NO TAMPAX OR ANYTHING

JUNE 18 SUNDAY DAY 4
1430-VERY BLACK NIGHT-HUGE WAVES-WIND,RAIN-RAFT NOT HOLDING AIR-SKIPPER DIZZY-DRANK SEA WATER-OPENED A CAN OF GARBANZOS-ATE HALF-RAINING AGAIN AT THIS HOUR-WAVES 15 FEET AND MORE-3RD DAY RUN EST. 20 MILES EAST 8 MILES NORTH-OUR LADY OF LAGHET YOU DID A MIRACLE FOR MY MOTHER WE NEED ONE NOW-GOD HAVE MERCY ON US! SIM BLEEDING PRETTY BAD-DIZZY TOO.

19 JUNE MONDAY DAY 5
0820 RATHER PEACEFUL NIGHT-RAFT LOST AIR-HOLE IN BOW-TURTLES BOTHERED AGAIN-DAY CLOUDY AS USUAL-SEA BUILDING-DRINKING SALT WATER TO REPLACE SALT
1145 FIXED LEAK IN RAFT-HOLDING AIR BETTER-WINDS 12 KN-SEAS MIXED-ESTIMATE NOON POSITION 102 HRS FROM LAUNCH-90 MI EAST 60 MI NORTH-97 DEGREES   40 MIN NORTH AND 6 DEGREES 30 MINUTES NORTH
1330 WIND/WAVES UP-DOMINO GAME
1400 RUF-VICIOUS SEAS-FAST WAVES-WHAT A BEATING

20 JUNE TUESDAY DAY 6
0930 TERRIBLY RUF NIGHT-BUT SURVIVED-SIM SLEPT A LITTLE NO TURTLES AT LAST-BUT HAVE RESIDENT DORADO-BRKFST-GLASS SALT WATER AND CRACKER-FILLING

1899 JUST FINISHED SUP-2 CRACKERS ONE COOKY, 1
GLASS SALT WATER AND ONE SWIG COKE-SUPER
SPREAD-LUNCH WAS ONE PEANUT BUTTER CRACKER
AND WATER-NEED RAIN-3 LITER BOTTLES EMPTY-WIND
DIED FOR MOST OF PM SO WAVES DOWN-NOW WIND UP
FROM S-WAVES 10/14 FEET FROM S/SW/W/SE-VERY
CONFUSED AND VICIOUS-DORADOS UNDER BOAT MOST
OF DAY-ALSO MIDSIZE TURTLE-HAD TO BONK IT 4 TIMES-
TOMORROW WE FISH-ALSO MAKE WATER-SKIES
OVERCAST-GOOD VISIBILITY-KIDDIES SHOULD BE
WORRIED-WE PRAY-SENDING MANY MENTAL MESSAGES

21 JUNE WEDNESDAY DAY 7
0900 QUIET NIGHT AT LAST! ONLY MODERATE WAVES
BREAKING-WE BOTH SLEPT BASTANTE-MADE 1 LITER OF
WATER IN 25 MIN-GOOD DAY CLEAR S WIND BUILDING-
EST 2 DAY RUN-40 M E 15 M N POSITION 0600 97 DEG W 6
DEG 45' N TODAY IS BIRD DAY
1100 INVENTORY-1 CAN VEGALL, 1 CAN ?, 1 CAN SOUP, 1
CAN JUICE, 2 BEERS, 1 CLAM, 1 CAN ?. 1 LGE APPLE
JUICE, 2 PERRIER, 1/2 L COKE, 1 SPRITE, 2 EVIAN, 1 CAN
CRACKER, 8 L WATER, RAISINS, 1/2 JUG COGNAC
1340 EVERYTIME WE REORGANIZE WE END UP WITH LESS
ROOM!-DAY SUNNY, LT S BREEZE-SEAS LIGHT (STILL 6/8
FT)-BOTH LOSING WEIGHT!-KIDS MUST BE GETTING
WORRIED-WE'VE MISSED CALLS TO JOE-CONGRATS TO
CRIS-FATHERS DAY-ETC-HAVE SENT MANY SIGNALS TO
SAL AND JOE AND CRIS-HOPE THEY CALL MR. VAZQUEZ-
GET GUSTAVO INVOLVED-COAST GUARD-WE SENT
MAYDAY ON 13113.2-NO LUCK-WE PRAY FAMILY IS IN
GEAR-HELP!

22 JUNE THURSDAY DAY 8
1000 GREAT NIGHTS SLEEP-SEAS FLATTENED OUT-
PUMPED AIR IN AT 12 & 3 AND 6-BREAKFAST-2 CRACKERS
AND WATER-SKIES CLEAR-GREAT DAY FOR AIR SEARCH-
COME ON GANG-GO! JIM-DALE-OUR "FAMILY" STILL
WITH US-VARIOUS DORADOS, SEA BIRDS THAT ARE

HANKERING TO LAND-TURTLES THAT BUMP OUR BUTS-
BUNCH 10-12 " FISH?? WE WANT TO FISH-DON'T DARE-
FEAR HOLE RAFT
1530 BALMY DAY-PLAYED NAME GAMES-SIM WON AND
BATTLESHIP-SKIP WON-STILL GOING E-HARDLY ANY
DRIFT N-HAD PEANUT BUTTER COOKIE LUNCH-MANY
DORADO UNDER BOAT-STILL HAVEN'T FIGURED HOW TO
SNAG-BEEN LOOKING FOR PLANES/BOATS-NOTHING FOR
FIVE DAYS-
1830 NO WIND AND CURRENT APPEARS LESS-WE SWING-
BEEN PLAYING 20 QUESTIONS, DOMINOES NOW
2100 FIRST REAL SUNSET-SIM WON DOMINO GAME-TRIED
TO FISH WITH HOOK MADE OF PIECE OF WIRE-NO LUCK

23 JUNE FRIDAY DAY 9
0900 WE HAD IT ALL LAST NIGHT-FIRST SHARKS WHICH
KEPT SIM FROM SLEEPING-TOOK ONE FULL ROSARY-
THEN HEAVY RAIN-THEN SLEEP-AT 0600 WIND SHIFT TO
WEST-RAFT HEADING N (OR S??)-SO SET IS SE-GUESS-JUST
FINISHED BRKFST-CRACKER CRUMBS-5 RAISINS-1 COOKY-
STUFFED-MUST MAKE WATER-MADE 2 LITERS IN 45
MINUTES-NOT BAD
1320 WIND LIGHT FROM WEST-RAFT HEADING SE-LUNCH
1 PEANUT BUTTER CRACKER
2020 RAINED-MADE 1 MORE LITER WATER-DINNER 2
CRACKERS AND WATER-YUM

24 JUNE SATURDAY DAY 10
0945 POURED ABOUT MIDNIGHT FOR 1 HOUR PLUS-NOW
HEAVY OVERCAST MUCHO RAIN AROUND-HEADING E-
WIND SW 12-SEAS MIXED EST SET 150 DEG AT 1 KN AND
DRIFT NE AT 1/2-THUNDER-BRKFST 1 CRACKER
1230 RODE OUT HARD SQUALL-30 KNOTS-WAVES
BREAKING-RUF-GOT 1/2 LITER RAIN WATER-WIND W-
HEADING S
1800 RAINED ALL PM-WIND STRONG 4 HRS FROM W-
FORGOT-AT NOON WE OPENED MYSTERY
CAN AS RATION FOR THE WEEK--PALMITOS!

JUNE 25 SUNDAY DAY 11
1100 BEEN RAINING STEADILY FOR 24 HOURS SKY
LEADED-BREAKFAST 2 CRACKERS WIND W 7/10 KN-SEAS
FAIRLY CALM-HEADED SOUTH-RAFT SWINGING TO SE-
RAINING

JUNE 26 DAY 12
0900 POURED ALL DAY YESTERDAY-LET UP AT NIGHT-
SUN IS OUT
1800 RUF RUF DAY-15 TO 30 FOOT ROLLERS-MANY
BREAKING ON RAFT-ALL WET AGAIN-WIND S 15/20 SET
EASTERLY-MADE THREE L WATER ANIMALS ALL OVER-30
SEA BIRDS SPENT NIGHT WITH US-SOME WANT TO PERCH
ABOARD-TURTLES-SHARKS-DORADO-A GROUPER
(LUNCH?)

JUNE 27 TUESDAY DAY 13
0930 SEAS ROUGH ALL NIGHT-WIND S 15-TOUGH TO
SLEEP-DAY CLEAR-WHERE ARE THE PLANES???
1110 BIG WHALE JUST BLEW S WARDS FROM RAFT
1800 WIND SW ALL DAY-ABATING-WAVES 12/16 FEET-A
FEW BREAK-SWINGING 80-120

JUNE 28 WED DAY 14
0900 CALM NIGHT NO WIND CURRENT LIGHT SWINGING-
SLEPT
1400 CLEAR SKIES WIND 5/7 SW CURRENT LIGHT COURSE
SWINGING 90-140 RIGGED FISHING SPEAR BY CUTTING
FISHING POLE IN TWO AND STRAIGHTENING HOOK-WE
HAVE LOST A LOT OF WEIGHT-GOD IS HELPING US.
1640 SPENT AFTERNOON FIGHTING OFF TURTLES
(BROKEN BACK AND BARNACLES) "THE ENDANGERED
SPECIES" CAUGHT ATTENTION OF SHARKY JR UNDER THE
RAFT

JUNE 29 THURSDAY DAY 15
0600 CALM NIGHT SIM SLEPT WELL SKIP SO SO-MUCH
LESS LIFE AROUND-BUMPED

0900 SLOW MOVING NIGHT-CLEAR DAWN
1000 WIND WAVES PICKING UP-OVERCAST-LOOKS LIKE
BLOW-CURRENT SLOW-SWINGING 90-120 WIND 330-
TRYING TO FISH-NO LUCK
1230 BACK IN CURRENT 90/110- WAVES 10 KN 330 DEG
CLOUDY-LIGHT SHOWERS-ABOUT 50 BIRDS WHO WERE
WITH US LEFT THIS MORNING
1700 TOUGH DAY-SHARKS WHACKING RAFT TRYING TO
REMOVE REMORAS.-RAINED MADE 2 LITERS WATER-
FOUGHT OFF TURTLES/BIRDS WIND SW-COURSE 120-80

JUNE 30 FRIDAY DAY 16
0900 TERRIBLE NIGHT-SHARKS BATTERING RAFT-WAVES-
RAIN-LIGHTNING-DAY GRAY-MORE RAIN WIND 260 DEG
10 KN COURSE 150

JULY 1 SATURDAY DAY 17
0900 ANOTHER GREAT NIGHT BOBBING AROUND THE
PACIFIC-WIND 240 DEG-SHARK HARASSING RAFT ALL
NIGHT-BIRD SLEEPING ON CANOPY. RAIN SEEPING
THROUGH HOLES IN CANOPY AT 7 AM TWO TURTLES
PRETENDING TO DO IT UNDER THE RAFT
1300 MADE THREE LITERS OF WATER BETWEEN SHOWERS-
STILL RAINING HEAVY-CURRENT VERY LIGHT SWINGING
HEADING? SOUTH-WAVES/SWELLS OUT OF 240 DEG-STILL
BELIEVE BEING PUSHED EAST ABOUT 1/2 KNOT
2000 RAINED ALL DAY-SOAKED-ROOF LEAKS! TURTLES,
BIRDS, SHARKS-WHAT'S NEW-CURRENT UP-WIND 240 DEG

JULY 2 SUNDAY DAY 18
1000 RAINED ALL NIGHT-DAWN DRY -QUIET-16 DAYS
WITHOUT SIGHTING A BOAT-22 DAYS SINCE OUR LAST
CALL-HELP GANG!! TODAY IS SUNDAY THE LORD'S DAY-
WE PRAY-ONLY HE CAN SAVE US BODY AND SOUL-NO
BIRDS-A WATERY DESERT, DESOLATE, INFINITELY SAD-
GOD BE MISERICORDIOUS TO US SINNERS. HELP US!
1600 CURRENT FAIRLY STRONG-HOLDING 0900-WIND
WAVES 220 DEG 7/10 KNOTS-FISHING UNSUCCESSFUL-

SUNNY WITH INTERMITTENT LIGHT SHOWERS-TIME IS
MOVING AT TURTLE PACE.

JULY 3 MONDAY DAY 19
1000 MADE GOOD TIME ALL NIGHT-HELD 90-120-RAINED-
SHARKS WHACKING RAFT HARD-WIND NOW LIGHT-
COURSE 90 + - WIND 230 DEG SKIES BLACK-HEAVY WITH
RAIN
1220 CURRENT STRONG WIND 220 DEG COURSE 090 DEG
PARTLY CLOUDY RAIN BEHIND US BLUE SKY IN FRONT E
MADE 2 LITERS OF WATER-SHARK KEPT BUMPING

JULY 4 TUESDAY DAY 20
POURED SUPER HEAVY LAST NIGHT-WE SOAKED-
MIDNIGHT FINALLY CLAM-WE SLEPT-DAWN A BEAUT-
HAPPY FOURTH-CELEBRATED WITH 1/4 CAN JUICE 1/2
COOKY MARIA EACH-NO WIND-NO CURRENT ALL NIGHT-
ADRIFT
1800 EXCITING 4TH-MADE 2 1/2 L WATER-LUNCHED
CRACKER WITH PEANUT BUTTER + 3 DROPS COGNAC-AT
2 SMALL TURTLE CAME OUR WAY-SNAGGED IT AND GOT
SUPPLY OF MEAT-DUMPED BLOOD ETC AND ROWED
AWAY-GREAT MEAT-SUPER TASTE-ALSO MAJOR DRYING-
BEAUT OF DAY-DRIFTED TILL 1300 THEN WIND 230 CAME
UP-GOING 60 DEG-1 KNOT
2030 SEAS CALM-SHARKY STILL WITH US COURSE 150
STEADY-SEAS UP-230 DEG WIND

**JULY 5 WEDNESDAY DAY 21 GLORIA AL BRAVO
PUEBLO!**
0800 NIGHTMARE NIGHT SHARKS CONSTANTLY
WHACKING RAFT-HUGE TURTLE SCRATCHING RAFT FOR
HOURS-LIGHT RAIN-BEAUTIFUL STARRY SKY UNTIL 2 AM-
WIND PUSHING 1 KN TOWARDS 060-CURRENT LIGHT-
AFTER 2 AM WIND LIGHTER-DRIFTED 1/2 KNOT OR SO
0940 NOW BOAT HEADING 120 DEGREES WIND 210
CURRENT LIGHT-WIND PUSHING US TOWARDS 045 DEG AT
1/2 KNOT-HAD BREAKFAST 1/2 MARIA COOKIE AND 4

RAISINS-WE PRAYED ALL NIGHT-KIDS WAKE UP!! HELP
US-O GOD LET US SEE A BOAT!
1345 WIND STILL LIGHT 250 DEG BREEZE 7/10-COURSE 150
DEG-SEAS LIGHT-DAYS VERY BEAUTIFUL-CAUGHT FISH 3
LB-THOUGHT WAS GROUPER BUT LOOKS LIKE A CARP
LARGE SCALES DARKISH BROWN-ATE 1/2 KEPT OTHER
HALF FOR SUPPER. HAVE HAD USUAL SHARK, TURTLE
AND BIRDS VISIT-3 NEW BIRDS LOOK LIKE SEAGULLS
SPLIT TAIL-GORGEOUS DAY-GOD IS THE GREATEST-WE
ARE GRATEFUL FOR LIFE AND DIVINE HELP. HAD SIP
COGNAC AND SANG GLORIA AL BRAVO PUEBLO.
1820 HOLDING STEADY ALL AFTERNOON ON 120 DEG-
MODERATE CURRENT-WIND SHIFTED TO WEST-RAIN
WEST WIND PICKING UP TO 15 KN-BEING PUSHED EAST 1
KNOT-SHARKS ALREADY HERE-HAD PERRIER FOR HAPPY
HOUR-FIXED TWO SCRATCHES ON RAFT WITH TAPE-LET'S
HOPE IT LASTS.
2040 WIND FROM WEST SQUALLING-10/15 KN-DOING AT
LEAST 1 KN-COURSE EAST

JULY 6 DAY 22 THURSDAY
0800 HORRIBLE NIGHT-STORM AND RAIN-BUMPY SEAS-
UNRELENTLESS SHARK ATTACKS-NO SLEEP-PRAYED ALL
NIGHT-THANK THE LORD DAWN IS HERE-GOD IS TOO
GENEROUS-COURSE 090 ALL NIGHT AT 1 KNOT + WIND
SW PUSHING US TOO
1440 WIND 210 DEG HAVE BEEN ON 090 DEG ALL
MORNING TRIED TO FISH NO LUCK PARTLY CLOUDY DAY
WAVES 4 TO 6 FEET-HAD 1 CRACKER WITH PEANUT
BUTTER FOR LUNCH-4 RAISINS EACH-WE WILL TRY NOW
TO SLEEP A LITTLE-PRAY MORE

JULY 7   FRIDAY DAY 23
0900 WIND WELL ALL YESTERDAY PM WITH SAILBAG
SPINNAKER-COURSE 090 DEG WITH WIND 210 DEG-AT 2100
RAIN SHOWERS BROKE-CURRENT STEADY ALL NIGHT-
POURED 4 TO 5 HOURS WIND DIED-TOWARDS 5 AM SKIES
CLEARED SUNRISE AT 0800 BRIGHT RED SKIES PARTLY

CLOUDY SEAS LIGHT WIND 190 DEG CURRENT
MAINTAINING COURSE 090-BILL ROWED ALL NIGHT WITH
HOMEMADE PADDLE KEPT THE SHARKS QUIETER-LET'S
HOPE IT WORKS-VIRGEN DE LA CARIDAD TOLD BILL A
BOAT WILL COME TODAY-WE'LL KEEP LOOKING-SENT
YESTERDAY A BOTTLE WITH A MESSAGE-THANKS GOD
FOR A RESTFUL NIGHT-LES ANGLAIS ONT DEBARQUE..
1430 TJIF EXCEPT HERE IT'S TSBF TURTLES PESTERING
ALL MORNING, SHARKS CIRCLING THE RAFT, BIRDS
PERCHING ON THE RAFT AND CAUGHT SMALL BAIT FISH
WITH VERY LAST PIECE OF TURTLE BAIT (VERY STINKY)
THEN CAUGHT 2 SEMI GROUPERS WHICH WERE
DEVOURED A LA SASHIMI. NO WIND, CLEAR DAY DRYING
COVERS FROM LAST NIGHT SOAKING-COURSE 090
CURRENT LIGHT 1/2 KNOT +/- RESIDENT SHARK ATE FISH
CARCASS
1800 WIND SW 5 KN ALL AFTERNOON-SET TO E VERY
LIGHT BUT STEADY-SKIES STILL CLEAR-SHARKS
KNOCKED FOR DINNER-UPSET DORADOS-AMAZING NO
SOUNDS OUT HERE FOR BREEZE, WAVES, FISH SLAPPING
WATER, OCCASIONAL THUNDER. WHERE IS EVERYBODY?
WHEN WILL THE SEARCH START? WE ARE 46 DAYS OUT
OF PANAMA-28 DAYS WITHOUT RADIO CONTACT.
2030 NO WIND NO CURRENT SINCE 1800-LIGHT BREEZE
FROM SOUTH-GORGEOUS SUNSET HOPEFULLY NO RAIN-
BILL WHACKED BABY SHARK TRYING TO WHACK THE
RAFT-SOME NEW SEA GULLS-WE ATE REST OF FISH FOR
DINNER
2400 BREEZE DID NOT MATERIALIZE AFTER ALL-NO WIND
NO RAIN NOTHING BUT BEAUTIFUL STARRY NIGHT

**JULY 8 SATURDAY DAY 24 ON RAFT (28 DAYS) 46 DAYS
OUT OF BALBOA**
NO WIND NO CURRENT ALL NIGHT-LIGHT LIGHT BREEZE
NOW FROM SW-LIGHT CURRENT SWINGING 090/120 +/-
DAY CLEAR-GREAT VISIBILITY-SHARKS WHACKED RAFT
ALL NIGHT-WE HAD TO ROW TO HELP KEEP THEM AT
BAY-BILL WHACKED THE BIGGEST WITH PADDLE THIS

MORNING-WE PRAY AND WE PRAY-PLEASE SEND THE
COAST GUARD
1100 HEARD FAINT AIRPLANE SOUND FAR AWAY FOR 2/3
MINUTES
1900 NO WIND/CURRENT ALL DAY-SUNNY-CLEAR-
STARTED BONKING SHARKS AS WELL AS TURTLES-LET'S
SEE IF IT GETS US PEACE-MADE NO PROGRESS-DID NOT
FISH TODAY-TOO MANY SHARKS
2400 NO WIND. SEAS CALM-SHARKS WHACKING RAFT
WITHOUT LETUP

JULY 9-SUNDAY-DAY 25 ON RAFT-47 OUT OF BALBOA
0900 RAIN STARTED AFTER MIDNIGHT AND WIND
INCREASING-LIGHTNING AND THUNDER ALL OUT OF
WEST-BILL FELL ASLEEP EXHAUSTED AND I HEARD A
RUMBLING NOISE-IT WAS A FREIGHTER LESS THAN 100
YARDS AWAY-PASSED US BY SO FAST-BEFORE WE COULD
SIGNAL WITH FLARE WE SIGNAL WITH FLASHLIGHT TO
NO AVAIL-WAS GOING 150 DEGREES-WIND INCREASED
NOW BLOWING 15/20 KNOTS OUTS OF SW-WAVES STRONG,
RAINING, COMPLETELY OVERCAST-THE WAIT GOES ON-
WE PRAY-
1600 WIND STOPPED ABOUT NOON AND E CURRENT
STARTED-WIND NOW PICKING UP AGAIN-SKIES CLEARED
AT 1300 NOW CLOUDING OVER-FISHING EXPEDITION
CANCELLED AFTER CATCHING SHARK-CUT MOUTH TO
GET HOOK OUT-DOZEN SHARKS UNDER BOAT-
2000 CURRENT KEPT US ON E ALL AFTERNOON-WIND SW
AT 10/12 KN-FIGHTING OFF SHARKS AND TURTLES AS
USUAL-SKIES CLEAR-WE PRAY FOR A TRANQUIL NIGHT-
SEAS SUBSIDING

JULY 10-MONDAY, DAY 26 ON RAFT-48 OUT OF BALBOA
0900 CURRENT STRONG ALL NIGHT SLIGHTLY WEAKER
NOW-WIND/WAVES LIGHT FROM SW-RAINED NEARLY ALL
NIGHT-UNRELENTLESS SHARK ATTACK-KEPT SHARP
LOOKOUT UNTIL 0600 WHEN BOTH OF US FELL ASLEEP
EXHAUSTED-DAY VERY CLOUDY, RAIN ALL AROUND.

1800 CURRENT STRONG ALL DAY-WIND/WAVES FROM SW 15 KN-ESTIMATE TODAY RUN WILL BE 30 MILES IN A 070 DEGREES-BEEN BUSY DAY FISHING EXPEDITION STARTED AT 10 AM USING 3 DAY OLD ROTTEN BAIT-WITH THAT CAUGHT SAME SHARK AS YESTERDAY-WITH THAT CAUGHT BAIT FISH-WITH THAT CAUGHT GROUPER FISH-FINALLY FINISHED BY 2 PM-BILL ATE SHARK, SIM THE GROUPER-SKIES CLOUDY-INTERMITTENT RAIN-HUGE WAVES 15/20 FEET-POOR VISIBILITY

JULY 11 TUESDAY-DAY 27 ON RAFT-49 OUT OF BALBOA-I MONTH SINCE LAST CONTACT
0900 FIRST GOOD NIGHTS SLEEP IN DAYS-MIRACULOUSLY THE SHARKS LEFT US ALONE EXCEPT FOR TWO OR 3 LITTLE RUBS. RAINED ALL NIGHT-RAIN SEEPING BADLY THRU CANOPY-US AND COVERS SOAKED-THANKS GOD IT'S NOT TOO COLD-
1300 OUT OF THE GRAY AN APPARITION-A WHITE FREIGHTER-WE SCRAMBLED, WASTED 2 FLARES OUT OF 3-SCREAMED, WAVED, PRAYED, TO NO AVAIL. COURSE OF SHIP 120 DEGREES.
1500 NO CURRENT, SWINGING AROUND ALL DAY-WAVES FROM SOUTH-NO WIND-TRIED FISHING CAUGHT 1 BAIT FISH-THE OTHERS DID NOT BITE-BILL SNAGGED A TURTLE-BIG ONE-HAD TO CUT LOOSE OUTER FLIPPER-RAINING AGAIN
2400 CURRENT CAME UP ABOUT 2 AM AND RAN TILL 5 AM-THEN PICKED UP AGAIN LATER-POURING RAIN-WE WERE ALREADY SOAKED BEFORE IT STARTED NOW WE ARE SOPPED-LARGE QUANTITIES OF WATER IN BILGE-TURTLE HARASSING ALL NIGHT-NO SIGN OF RAIN LETTING DOWN.

JULY 12-WEDNESDAY DAY 28 ON RAFT-DAY 50 OUT OF BALBOA-DAY 31 SINCE LAST CALL
1200 RAINED ALL NIGHT-HAD TURTLES ALL NIGHT-EVERYTHING IS SOAKED AND DRIPPING-NO SIGN OF CLEAR WEATHER-WE PRAY AND HOPE

1800 FISHING CAUGHT ONE BAIT AND 3 EATING FISH
WHICH WE PROMPTLY DEVOURED-SKIES CLEARED IN
MIDDLE OF AFTERNOON AND WE WERE ABLE TO
REMOVE A LITTLE DAMPNESS FROM COMFORTER-
WEATHER APPEARS CLEARING CURRENT STEADY
COURSE 090/120 DEGREES-WIND STILL LIGHT FROM SW-
WAVES/SWELLS ABATING
2400 SHARKS FOUND US AGAIN AFTER 3 DAYS OFF. GOD
HELP US!

**JULY 13 THURSDAY DAY 29 ON RAFT-DAY 51 OUT OF
BALBOA-DAY 32 SINCE LAST CALL**
0900 ANOTHER TERRIBLE NIGHT-REPEATED CONTINUOUS
SHARK ATTACKS ON THE RAFT-TRIED TO WHACK THEM
BUT THEY WHACKED US MORE. FINALLY HIT ONE HARD
THIS MORNING. BESIDES SHARK HAD BIG TURTLE
BOTHERING ALL NIGHT-SENT HIM OFF THIS MORNING
WITH SCISSOR JOB-HOPE WE MADE OUR POINT-CLEAR
DAY-WE'LL TRY TO DRY-RAFT LOOSING AIR FASTER-
CURRENT LIGHT-WIND LIGHT-IF ANYBODY IS LOOKING
FOR US TODAY IS THE DAY. PLEASE HELP! WE NEED IT
SOON. WE PRAY
1900 GOOD CLEAR DAY-DRIED A LOT BOAT HELD 090 ALL
DAY-GOOD CURRENT-WIND SOUTH 7/10 KN-HAD USUAL
TURTLE/SHARK VISITS AND DEALT WITH EACH-NO FISH
AND NOW NO BAIT-RAFT LEAKING AIR BADLY-

**JULY 14 FRIDAY-BASTILLE DAY-VIVE LA FRANCE-DAY
30 ON RAFT**
0900 USUAL NIGHT-SHARKY HIT HOURLY-CLEAR-MOON-
SLEPT SOME-CURRENT STEADY FROM W-NO WIND-RADIO
FIX-SANDINA 030 COSTA RICA 060
1900 CELEBRATED BASTILLE DAY WITH THE SINGING OF
THE MARSEILLAISE BY SIM AND CONSUMPTION OF THE
LAST HEINEKEN-DAY SUNNY-CALM-GOOD CURRENT ALL
DAY-060, 150 AT TIMES-AT 1500 WE CAME ACROSS LOTS
OF TRASH-STILL IN IT-FOUND PUMICE STONE-TRASH LINE
RUNNING SOUTH-HEARD FAINT RADIO TODAY

2400 SHARKS! CURRENT HELD-LITTLE WIND 150 DEG 7 KN-PARTLY CLOUDY

JULY 15 SAT-DAY 31-1 MONTH ON RAFT-DAY 53 OUT OF BALBOA-DAY 34 SINCE LAST CALL
WHERE ARE THE TROOPS???
1900 NO CURRENT-0800-1200-THEN CURRENT UP STRONG-WIND WAVES UP FROM S 12/15 KN-SHARKS ARRIVED ON SCHED-BAD TURTLE ALL DAY-CELEBRATED MONTH WITH OPENING CAN-CREAM OF MUSHROOM SOUP-GREAT-SKIP WON DOMINO GAME TODAY-RAINED-PC-LOOKS LIKE TOUGH NITE AHEAD

JULY 16, SUNDAY-DAY 32 ON RAFT-54 EX BALBOA-35 DAYS SINCE LAST TEL CALL!
1800 WIND 15 KN OUT OF 230 DEG-SEAS 15 FEET-CURRENT STRONG SINCE LAST ENTRY-COURSE 120 STEADY-NIGHT HAD ALL-WIND/WAVES/RAIN/SHARKS/TURTLES BUT WE MANAGED TO REST-TURTLES KEPT SHARKS AWAY-MADE OUR USUAL 2 LITERS WATER-HAD ROUTINE DAY-1 CRACKER FOR BREAKFAST-NAP-1 CRACKER WITH PEANUT BUTTER FOR LUNCH-NAP (ALL THIS TIME BATTING SHARKS AND TURTLES) MADE WATER AT 1700-THEN HAPPY HOUR (3 DROPS HENNESSY)-DOMINOS-SIM WON-AND 1 CRACKER AT 1900-THEN SIM READS PRAYER-AND LET THE NIGHT COME!!-

JULY 17 MONDAY 33RD DAY ON RAFT
1200 WIND 240 DEG 15 KN BLEW ALL NITE AND GOOD CURRENT-A FEW SHARKS/TURTLES-RAINED
1500 WIND CURRENT DOWN-NEW VISITORS TWO DOLPHINS AND MANY SHARKS ALL CHASING SCHOOL OF FISH UNDER BOAT-LOTS OF EXCITEMENT-WE LAID LOW
1830 ADD WHALES AND DAY FULL-SKIP CAUGHT 6 TRIGGER FISH WITH BARE HAND-ATE 4 FOR SUPPER-RAINING-NO WIND AFTER BIG SQUALL OUT OF EAST-CURRENT LIGHT TO EAST

2400 WIND WAVES WAY DOWN-CURRENT LIGHT COURSE
120-150 DEG-FEW VISITS

JULY 18 TUESDAY 34TH DAY ON RAFT!
1200 COURSE STILL 120/150-WIND WAVES LIGHT-SHARK
PACK VISITED-BEAT THEM OFF-ALSO PERSISTENT
TURTLE-NEW WHITE BIRDS
1600 BUSY PM-SHARKS LEFT AND STARTED FISHING-
TOUGH TO GET THROUGH PIRAÑAS TYPE TRIGGER FISH-
WOULD TOSS GUTS ONE WAY TO ATTRACT THEM AND
HOOK OTHER-CAUGHT ONE 5 # GROUPER AND A 2
POUNDER-THEN TOSSED SMALL PIECE OF BAIT DEEP TO
GET BAIT FOR TOMORROW AND CAUGHT 50 POUND BULL
DOLPHIN-LANDED AND ATE-BOTH STUFFED-WIND UP
SINCE 1500 AND WAVES-STILL DOING 120/150-COSTA
RICAN STATIONS GETTING STRONGER-ESTIMATE 100
MILES OFF COAST +/-
2400 HEAVY GOING-RUF-WIND 210-COURSE 120-GOING
FAST-FEW BUMPS

JULY 19 WED 35TH DAY
1200 RAINED ALL NIGHT-HEAVY-RUF-COLD-GOING FAST-
FEW ANIMALS
1600 BLEW ALL DAY 210 DEG 15 KN-15 FT SEAS AND
MANY BREAKING-FINALLY AT 1500 CLEARED- TRIED TO
DRY THINGS-LITTLE LUCK-FISHED-CAUGHT 1 GROUPER
AND 3 BAIT FISH (WITH HANDS)
2400 POURING RAIN WIND WAVES DYING-RAFT SOAKED-
WE BAILED ABOUT 3 CANS OUT OF IT AND IT IS STILL
SLOSHING

**JULY 20 THURSDAY 36 DAY-58 DAY OUT OF BALBOA-40
DAY SINCE LAST CALL**
1200 RAIN STOPPED MIDMORNING-ATTEMPTING TO DRY
THINGS-NO WIND-NO WAVES-NO CURRENT
1800 CAUGHT 2 "GROUPERS"-SEMI DRIED BEDDING-WIND
PICKED UP FROM 240 DEG 7 KN COURSE 180 DEG WHICH
INDICATES NO CURRENT-SUN FINALLY COMING

THROUGH-USUAL SHARKS AND TURTLES VISITS-NO BIRDS-NO LAND-NO PLANES-NO BOAT-IS REALLY NOBODY LOOKING FOR US-OUR ONLY TRUST TO BE SAVED IS IN GOD-WE PRAY A LOT-SOME MOMENTS OF DESPAIR BUT A DEEP FAITH IN GODS HELP

JULY 21 FRIDAY 37TH DAY
1200 CURRENT DUE 160/170 PICKED UP SPEED-ALSO WIND WAVES DURING NIGHT-GOING WELL-WIND 15 KN 210 DEG-DRY!-FEW ANIMALS
1800 SEAS/WIND UP TO 20 KNOTS 15/20 FEET-DRY ALL DAY UNTIL NOW-MANY VISITORS-COURSE 120/150 STRONG-CAUGHT 2 GROUPERS
2400 RAINED-WIND CONTINUED STRONG-COURSE 090/120-BARELY ANY SHARKS DURING NIGHT BUT MANY TURTLES-NO SLEEP FOR SIM-CAPTAIN SNORING-RAFT SOAKED FROM HUGE WAVE AND RAIN ALL NIGHT

JULY 22 SAT DAY 38 HAPPY BIRTHDAY ALEX
0900 POURED ALL NIGHT-COURSE 090/120 ALL NIGHT-POURING RAIN-CALMED SEAS-CAUGHT 2 BAIT FISH AND 1 GROUPER-CELEBRATED ALEX'S BIRTHDAY-SANG
1800 SEAS CONFUSED ALL DAY-AFTER MIDMORNING SQUALL FROM EAST-MID AFTERNOON LIGHT BREEZE WAVES FROM SW-COURSE 150 +/- VERY LIGHT CURRENT-SKIES CLEARED SOME SUN-BEING HARASSED BY 2 DIRTY TURTLES-HUGE-TRYING TO MAKE OUT UNDER THE RAFT. WHERE IS THE COAST GUARD??

JULY 23 DAY 39
1800 LIGHT SW BREEZE-DOING 120/150 IN LIGHT CURRENT-BEAUT OF SUNNY DAY-DRIED ALL
1900 ALMOST SANK RAFT-TRIED TO REARRANGE FRONT PATCH AND LOST ALL AIR-FLOODED RAFT-WET ALL-BIG DRILL
2400-WET RAINY NIGHT-120-150-BAD-BAILED AND BAILED

JULY 24 MONDAY DAY 40
1800 STILL SOAKED-BAILED-TRIED TO DRY-LITTLE SUN-
RAINED ALL NIGHT-WIND SW 12 KN-COURSE 120 IN MOD
CURRENT--OVERCAST-RAFT LEAKING AIR, PUMP
HOURLY-

JULY 25 TUESDAY DAY 41
1200 HEAVY WIND SOUTH AT 15/20 WAVES 20 FEET ALL
DAY RUF-090 COURSE-STILL BLOWING-SOAKED-SHARKS
BAD-PACK IS BACK-HIT AND THEY LEFT
1630 SHIP WENT BY GOING WEST-1/2 MILE TO NORTH-
DIDN'T SEE US-RAINING
2400 STILL RUF-GOOD CURRENT GOING 090-120-WIND 210-
STRONG 15 KN-STILL RAINING

JULY 26 WEDNESDAY-DAY 42-WEEK 6
1600 RUF BLOWING ALL DAY-STILL GOING EAST-RAIN
STOPPED ABOUT 4 AM-RAFT LEAKING AIR-PUMPING
HOURLY-LITTLE SLEEP-EVERYTHING SOAKED-SIM
DEPRESSED-NEED TO GET HELP SOON-DOWN TO 10
CRACKERS AND 1 CAN OF?..FISHING POOR-ONLY
TRIGGER FISH-ATE THEM AND CAUGHT SIM A RABI-
RUBIA

JULY 27 DAY 43-BEGINNING OF 7TH WEEK-DAY 64 OUT OF BALBOA
1700 WIND 210 STRONG ALL NIGHT 15 KN DECREASING
RECENTLY-WAVES 10/15 FEET MOVING FAST
OCCASIONALLY BREAKING ON US-SEVERAL BAD SHARK
ATTACKS LAST NIGHT-LUCKILY NO RAIN LAST NIGHT-
GOOD SUNNY DAY TODAY-FISHED 6 HAND CAUGHT
TRIGGER FISH-NOTHING ELSE THERE-COUPLE OF SHARKS
HIT US DURING THE DAY-RECEIVED COASTAL STATION
DURING DAY FOR FIRST TIME-ESTIMATE POSITION 50 NM
OFF CENTRAL COSTA RICA WITH RAFT SPEED + 1 KN AT
070-RAFT HELD COURSE 090/120 PAST 2 HOURS-NOW
PUMPING RAFT EVERY 45 MINUTES-WE PRAY THE LORD
HAVE MERCY ON US AND BRING US TO A SAFE HAVEN-

SOON

JULY 28 DAY 44 FRIDAY
1400 LAND HO!! SIM SPOTTED MOUNTAIN 120 DEGREES AT 1330 DISTANCE 30 MILES-WIND AND WAVES EASED DURING NIGHT BUT STILL FROM SOUTH-COURSE EAST ALL NIGHT-CLEAR-MANY SHARKS-SHIP PASSED US GOING EAST AT 0400-ASSUME THAT'S PUNTA ARENAS-HEARD MANY LOCAL COSTA RICAN STATIONS-090-INCLUDING PUNTA ARENAS STATION-TODAY ANYHOW WAS THE MOST GORGEOUS DAY EVER-WIND SOUTH 10 KN CURRENT STILL EASTERLY-FISHED ONLY TRIGGER FISH-ATE IT ANYWAY-WILL NOW PRAY AND THANK FOR SO MANY GOD GIVEN GIFTS...

JULY 29 SATURDAY-DAY 45
0700 DAY DAWNED CLEAR AND BRIGHT..ISLAND BIGGER ON HORIZON..BEFORE SUNUP WE DECIDED TO ROW..LOWERED CANOPY AND TIED BALLAST BAGS AND STARTED ROWING..AFTER AN HOUR WE REALIZED FUTILITY OF ROWING..TRIED TO SAIL RAFT WITH 1/2 OF CANOPY UP..DIDN'T WORK..FINALLY GAVE UP AND RE-RIGGED CANOPY
1400 THINGS GOING DOWN HILL FAST-NOW PUMPING RAFT EVERY 20 MINUTES-LAND-AN ISLAND STILL MILES OFF -10/15-WIND CURRENT LIGHT ALL DAY NOW PICKING UP-WIND 225-ISLAND BEARS 105-MADE USUAL WATER-TRIGGER FISH FOR LUNCH AND DINNER-HAND CAUGHT-BEAUT OF DAY SO EVERYTHING DRY-CANNOT FIND AIR LEAK-LORD..PLEASE...

JULY 30 SUNDAY DAY 46
0800 DEPRESSING-ISLAND NOW AT SAME DISTANCE AS DAY BEFORE YESTERDAY..YESTERDAY WE MUST HAVE GONE BACKWARDS 10 OR SO MILES..TERRIBLE..DOESN'T HURT IF NO LAND IN SIGHT BUT WITH VISIBLE PROOF WE ARE NOT GOING EAST IT HURTS..
1200 A REAL MIRACLE-TOWARDS EVENING YESTERDAY

RAFT LOST MORE AND MORE AIR-PUMPED EVERY 45
MINUTES-NOW IT IS EVERY HOUR-A MIRACLE.
1700 WIND CURRENT PUSHING US AWAY FROM ISLAND-
LITTLE WIND AM-PICKED UP TO 10 KN 240 DEGREES IN
PM-FISHED AM AND PM-MADE WATER-BAD MEAN
SHARKS-RAINED-COMES RIGHT THRU-WE PRAY AND
PRAY
2000 BIG SHARKS IN NEIGHBORHOOD..LITTLE ONES
STAYING AWAY..WE STAYING VERY QUIET-ISLAND
BEARS 120 WHICH MEANS WE ARE GOING NORTH OF IT..

31 JULY MONDAY DAY 47
0800 WIND SOUTHWEST LIGHT-STARTED RAINING 0400-
POURED-EVERYTHING SOAKED
1200 ISLAND NOW CLOSER BEARING 160..NOT GOOD..WE
MAKING PLANS ON HOW TO HANDLE LANDING ON THE
ISLAND..WHICH ISLAND CAN IT BE..WE PRAY IT IS AN
ISLAND NEAR THE COAST..WIND BLOWING 12 KNOTS
FROM 240..CURRENT PUSHING US 090..CONFIGURATION
OF THE ISLAND CHANGING..WHEN WE FIRST SAW IT HAD
TWO HUMPS..ONE LARGER..NOW ALL WE CAN SEE IS ONE
LARGE HILL..
1800 RAIN STOPPED AT 1100-GRAY..WIND ALL DAY SW-
GOING 030/040 GOOD-NOW PICKING UP-LARGER WAVES-
BAILED-FISHED-SIM SAW BIG HAMMERHEAD-LOOKS LIKE
RUF NIGHT

NOTE:AT THIS POINT THE PAGES IN THE LOG BOOK TURNED DAMP. WHEN THE BALL POINT PENS REFUSED TO WORK WE USED A FELT POINT THROUGHOUT THE FOLLOWING SEVEN DAYS. ON DAY 53, AFTER DOLPHINS TORE THE RAFT FLOOR,THE LOG ENDED FULLY IMMERSED AND MANY OF THE FELT POINT ENTRIES WASHED AWAY. IN THE FIRST TWO DAYS UPON OUR ARRIVAL IN COSTA RICA WE RECONSTRUCTED THE LOG FOR THE REMAINING DAYS.

1 AUGUST TUESDAY DAY 48
0800 WIND ALL NIGHT 210, 15KN ISLAND 220 AND CLOSE..ESTIMATE 4 TO 5 MILES..BUT UNLESS WE GET VIOLENT WIND SHIFT TO NORTH WE WILL MISS IT
1300 MADE WATER..FOUGHT SHARKS..RAFT STILL LEAKING BADLY..SIM SAW LARGE WHALE SHARK PASS DIRECTLY UNDER RAFT..WE FELT RAFT RISE..

2 AUGUST WEDNESDAY DAY 49
1200 ISLAND NOW 240..RAINY DISMAL DAY..ISLAND ABOUT 15 MILES AWAY..SEAS FAIRLY CALM..CURRENT MODERATE..
1500 MADE WATER AND CAUGHT 12 TRIGGERS FOR LUNCH AND SAVING A FEW FILETS FOR DINNER..WATER LEAKING BOTHERSOME..SORES ON OUR BEHINDS AND BACK WORSE..SIM BAILS EVERY 15 MINUTES DAY AND NIGHT..

3 AUGUST THURSDAY DAY 50
0900 ISLAND NOW 260 AND 20 TO 30 MILES AWAY..WONDER WHAT IT WAS..STILL RAINY..RAINED MOST OF NIGHT..SEAS CALM..WSIND 240 AT 12 KNOTS.

5 AUGUST SATURDAY DAY 52
0900 DAY DAWNED QUIET AND PLEASANT..SHARKS HIT US ALL NIGHT AS WELL AS TURTLES..ONE PAIR OF TURTLES HAVE BEEN FORNICATING ALONGSIDE RAFT

DURING THE PAST 30 DAYS..MUST TAKE ONE SHOT PER
EGG..SOMETIMES FEMALE HIDES UNDER RAFT TO
ESCAPE AND MALE CHASES AND ALL HOLY HELL BREAKS
LOOSE
1300 MADE WATER AND CAUGHT TRIGGERS..HAD A HARD
TIME SINCE TRIGGERS NERVOUS AND WOULD NOT COME
CLOSE TO SURFACE..
1500 FOUND OUT WHY TRIGGERS NERVOUS..FOUR OR
FIVE LARGE DOLPHINS IN AREA FEEDING..SOME COME
RIGHT UNDER RAFT CHASING TRIGGERS AND SCHOOLS
OF OTHER FISH..FISH VERY NERVOUS..SHARK PACK IS
AROUND..ALSO DORADOS SWIMMING FAST..
1600 ALL HELL BREAKING LOOSE..DOLPHINS FEEDING
LIKE CRAZY..SHARKS GETTING STIRRED UP..HOPE THEY
LEAVE BY DARK
2100 FEEDING FRENZY GOING ON AT FULL CHOLA..WE
HAVE BEEN HIT REGULARLY BY SHARKS AND
DOLPHINS..THESE ARE BIG ANIMALS..ABOUT 10 FEET
LONG AND HEAVY GRAYISH WITH SMALL SPOTS ALL
OVER..THEY APPEAR TO BE EATING EVERYTHING IN
SIGHT..
2300 GETTING HIT PRETTY BADLY..HAD A SHARK SWIM
INTO ONE OF THE BALLAST BAGS..HE STRUGGLED
WILDLY FOR WHAT SEEMED LIKE THE LONGEST TIME
BUT MUST HAVE BEEN ONE OR TWO MINUTES..WE
HOLDING ON TO EACH OTHER TIGHTLY..TRYING TO
FIGURE OUT WHAT TO DO IF ANYTHING..FINALLY HE
WORKED HIS WAY OUT..

6 AUGUST SUNDAY DAY 53
0200 BATTLE STILL GOING ON WITH DOLPHINS-SHARKS
AND BAIT FISH ALL ZIPPING AROUND WITH US IN THE
MIDDLE OF THE MELEE..
0230 SOME ANIMAL..FIGURE IT WAS A DOLPHIN WITH HIS
DORSAL FIN..PUNCTURED THE BOTTOM OF THE
RAFT..CANNOT FIND LEAK..SIM BAILING
CONTINUOUSLY..
0500 SKIP TAKES OVER BAILING JOB FROM SIM WHO TRIES

TO SLEEP..ALL ANIMALS LEFT AROUND 0300 AND THINGS
HAVE BEEN QUIETER..
0800 FINALLY LIGHT..WE START LOOKING FOR
LEAK..FIND IT TOWARDS BOW..SIM FINDS ONLY SEWING
NEEDLE..NO POINT TO IT..WE FIRST TRY THREAD IN SIMS
KIT..NO GOOD..MUST RE DO WITH THREAD MADE FROM
NYLON LINE..FINALLY SEW UP TEAR..ABOUT THREE
INCHES LONG..BUT NOT WATER TIGHT..
1200 REARRANGED CUSHIONS FROM ONE DEEP
CROSSWISE ON RAFT TO TWO DEEP LENGTHWISE..THAT
WAY WE CAN KEEP A LITTLE DRIER..RAFT FILLS UP
EVERY 15 MINUTES..SIM TAKES OVER BAILING JOB..SKIP
MAKES ALL THE WATER AND PUMPS AIR..AND
FISHES..MADE TWO LITERS OF WATER..
1900 DARK AND CLOUDY ALL DAY..CAUGHT
TRIGGERS..SHARKS FINALLY CAME BACK AFTER BEING
GONE MOST OF THE DAY AND NOW
HARASSING..THOUGHT THEY WOULD BE TIRED AFTER
YESTERDAYS EVENT..

7 AUGUST MONDAY DAY 54
1200 DOLPHINS ARE BACK..SAME BUNCH..WE PRAY THEY
WILL LEAVE US ALONE..TRIGGERS HAVE ALL TAKEN
OFF..
1300 TRIED TO FISH BUT NOTHING AROUND..WILL WAIT A
WHILE..
1700 FINALLY CAUGHT USUAL 10 TRIGGERS..MADE TWO
LITERS OF WATER..WIND LIGHT FROM 240-260..CURRENT
MODERATE..RAFT HEADING 090..EVERYTHING WET ON
RAFT..CAMERA SOAKED..TOSSED IT OVER SIDE..SHAME
TO LOOSE FILM.

8 AUGUST TUESDAY DAY 55
1700 SIDE OF RAFT LEAKING AIR..HAS BEEN LEAKING
BADLY FOR ABOUT A WEEK..HAVE BEEN STUFFING RAGS
AROUND HOLE AND HOLDING THEM IN PLACE WITH
STRINGS..BUT RAFT LOSING MORE AND MORE
AIR..PUMPING EVERY HALF HOUR..TOUGH TO

SLEEP..ENGINEERING PATCH WITH SCREW FROM FISHING
REEL..RUINED FIRST ONE GETTING IT OUT OF REEL..HAD
TO CUT ALMOST ALL THE LINE OFF THE REEL TO GET IT
OUT..MADE GASKETS OUT OF LEATHER
GLOVES..WASHERS FROM CAMERA CASE..WILL DO IT
TOMORROW

9 AUGUST WEDNESDAY DAY 56
1200 FINALLY FINISHED PATCH AND INSTALLED
IT..HALLELUJAH..IT HOLDS AIR..HAD TO OPEN HOLE IN
RAFT SO INSIDE PART WOULD FIT..LOST A LOT OF AIR
DURING PROCESS..SIM PUMPED FRANTICALLY..BUT NOW
THINGS ARE BETTER..IMAGINE HOLE MADE BY
COMPRESSED AIR CYLINDER WHEN HIT BY SHARKS..
1500 FISHED..MADE WATER..

10 AUGUST THURSDAY DAY 57
1400 WEEK NINE NOW BEGINNING..INCREDIBLE..HAVE
SEEN TWO TO THREE SHIPS EVERY DAY..MOST PASS TO
THE EAST GOING NORTH OR SOUTH TO THE
CANAL..RADIO SIGNALS FROM COSTA RICA STRONG..

11 AUGUST FRIDAY DAY 58
1200 CLOUDY DAY-SIM THOUGHT SHE SAW LAND BUT
COULD NOT BE SURE..DARK LAND LOOKING THINGS ON
HORIZON TO EAST COULD BE CLOUDS..WE HAVE BEEN
FOOLED MANY TIMES
1400 MADE WATER AND FISHED..SHARKS STILL A DAILY
PROBLEM..

12 AUGUST SATURDAY DAY 59
1000 LAND HO..NO QUESTION ABOUT IT..SIM SPOTTED IT
FIRST-LONG AND HIGH ON THE HORIZON..HARD TO
JUDGE DISTANCE..ESTIMATE 20 TO 30 MILES..WIND
WEST..CURRENT ?..WE APPEAR TO BE DRIFTING SOUTH
AND EAST-
1300 MADE WATER THEN FISHED THE USUAL FARE OF
TRIGGERS..DAY CLOUDY BUT HORIZON CLEAR AND CAN

SEE LAND CLEARLY..MUST BE COSTA RICA OR
NORTHERN PANAMA FROM RADIO SIGNALS..
1400 THE MOUNTAIN LOOMS LARGE-A BIG BLUE
WONDERFUL GORGEOUS MORNING BUT SO ARE
MORNINGS SINCE WE SAW THE COAST AND NO DOUBT
"IT IS THE COAST"-LOVELY COSTA RICA-THE NAME SAYS
EVERYTHING-SIM HEARS THE RADIO NOW ALL DAY
CLEARLY: SAN JOSE, CARTHAGO, DAVID IN PANAMA ..
TODAY THEY WERE ADVERTISING FOR A DANCING AND
EATING AND DRINKING PLACE WITH GIRLS AVAILABLE-
WHAT NEXT.

13 AUGUST SUNDAY DAY 60
1700 DAY OVERCAST..DARK..MENACING..SHARKS
ATTACK MUCH LESS WITH ONLY 8 TO 10 HITS A
DAY..ONE OR TWO AT NIGHT..ALMOST BEARABLE..MADE
WATER..COAST BARELY IN SIGHT BETWEEN CLOUDS.
WEATHER IS GETTING WORSE NEAR THE COAST-SIMONNE
DEPRESSED, EXHAUSTED, MENTALLY AND PHYSICALLY
BUT INSIDE SHE HAS HOPE-KEPT ALIVE BY THE
PROXIMITY OF THE COAST THAT IS ONLY A MATTER OF
DAYS AWAY. WE WILL MAKE IT TO THE BEACH ON OUR
OWN OR WE'LL BE FOUND-TODAY WE HEARD AN
AIRPLANE TAKE OFF--IT MUST HAVE BEEN NOON-WE
WERE SO SURPRISED WE DID NOT EVEN CHECK THE
TIME-

14 AUGUST MONDAY DAY 61
1700 GRAY UGLY DAY--WIND LIGHT FROM WEST..STORMS
ON SHORE - SHIP PASSED NOT 400 FEET AWAY-GOING TO
THE PANAMA CANAL--SMALLISH FREIGHTER--WE DID
ALL THE USUAL THINGS-SIM WAVED T-SHIRT TIED TO
THE FISHING ROD WHILE I WAVED THE RED EMERGENCY
KIT WHICH IS STILL BRIGHT ORANGE. TRIED TO USE THE
MIRROR-THE SUN IS ALWAYS IN THE WRONG PLACE..WE
HAVE TWO WHISTLES BUT WE CAN YELL LOUDER THAN
THE WHISTLE-BOAT JUST PASSED-WE COULD HEAR
ENGINE LOUD AND CLEAR.

15 AUGUST TUESDAY DAY 62
1000 CLEAR DAY-LARGE PASSENGER SHIP PASSED TWO
MILES IN TOWARDS SHORE-BRIGHT WHITE-BEAUTIFUL-
GOING NORTH AFTER EXITING THE CANAL..DIDN'T SEE
US
1200 SEVERAL OTHER FREIGHTERS PASS, TWO INSIDE
AND TWO TOWARDS SEA
1700 RAINED MOST OF DAY..LAND IN SIGHT..WE SEEM TO
BE MOVING SOUTHEASTERLY SINCE COSTA RICAN
STATIONS AT CARTHAGO NOW NOT SO STRONG..MADE 2
LITERS OF WATER..SIGHTED SEVERAL SHIPS WITHIN A
MILE..TWO OR THREE TO THE WEST AND A COUPLE
INSHORE TO THE EAST..RADIO WAVES BEAMING MORE
AND MORE ON PANAMA-EVEN HEARD PANAMA CITY-
SOME STUPID INCIDENT WITH AMERICAN TROOPS AND
NORIEGAS POLICE

16 AUGUST WEDNESDAY DAY 63
1700 RAINED ALL DAY-RAFT LEAKING AIR AND
WATER..SIM BAILS EVERY 15 MINUTES DAY AND NIGHT
AND WE PUMP AIR EVERY 45 MINUTES..WE DECIDED NOT
TO TOUCH ANY PATCHES..BETTER LEAVE THINGS BE IF
NOT TOO BAD..
2200 HEAVY SQUALL HITS..WE SUDDENLY HEARD LOUD
ROAR AND WHEN WE LOOKED WE SAW A SOLID WHITE
WALL APPROACHING..BATTENED WINDOWS..WIND 60
KNOTS PLUS..RAIN LIKE BUCKSHOT..BLEW AND POURED
FOR TWO HOURS..SEAS NOT PARTICULARLY BAD..RAFT
BEHAVED WELL..GOT WET BUT EVERYTHING SOAKED
ALREADY
SIM TRYING TO KEEP WARM AT NIGHT COVERED WITH
GARBAGE PLASTIC BAG-BILL WITH SOAKING WET WOOL
BLANKET GIVEN TO US BY FRIENDS IN CAPACHO VIEJO IN
THE ANDES-WE TALK ABOUT THEM-XMAS SPENT WITH
THEM-NY EVES-SITUATION IN VENEZUELA-WORLD
CHANGING FAST-WHAT DO WE DO IF WE ARE SAVED..

17 AUGUST THURSDAY DAY 64

1200 RAINY..MADE WATER THEN FISHED 9 TRIGGERS..
1700 STILL RAINING..RADIO STRONGER..CAN HEAR MORE
PANAMANIAN STATIONS AND FEWER FROM COSTA RICA..
CHIRIQUI RADIO STATION NORTH OF PANAMA-BIG
SOCCER GAME IN DAVID-GOOOOL THE ANNOUNCER
CALLS OUT-THEY TALK ABOUT A RANCH RESTAURANT
AND DANCING AND BAR-B-Q CHICKEN AND STEAKS-
MOUTH WATERING-TALK ABOUT SERVICES AT CHURCH
IN COSTA RICA-CANNOT SAY ANY LONGER WHERE ITS
COMING FROM-REALLY AFRAID WE'RE GOING TO MISS A
LANDING IN COSTA RICA AND BE PUSHED TOWARDS
PANAMA'S COAST WHICH WE KNOW IS FURTHER AWAY.
WHEN GOD?...WHEN???

18 AUGUST FRIDAY DAY 65

1200 DAY CLEAR COAST IN SIGHT-BEAUT OF A DAY-SEAS
CALM-NO WIND-NO CLOUDS-SAW WHALES FEEDING AT A
DISTANCE
1300 FISHED AND CAUGHT USUAL 9 TRIGGERS, FILLETED
AND ATE-SHARKS NO LONGER A PROBLEM..HAD BUT ONE
THIS MORNING
1600 WE'VE SEEN SEVEN SHIPS TODAY
1700 FISHED AGAIN CAUGHT SIX TRIGGERS-MADE TWO
LITERS OF WATER-GETTING PAINFUL SINCE NO LONGER
HAVE BEDDING-MAKING WATER ON BARE CHEST AND
BELLY-ALSO TAKING LONGER AND LONGER BUT CAN
STILL MAKE TWO LITERS IN LITTLE OVER HALF
HOUR..NO RUSH ANYWAY
2100 INCREDIBLE..SAW SHIP APPROACHING.. COMING
STRAIGHT FOR US..HELD OFF USING LAST FLARE UNTIL
SURE HE WOULD COME CLOSE..FLASHED SOS WITH
FLASHLIGHT AND SOMEONE ON BRIDGE FLASHED TWICE
WITH DIM LANTERN--ALSO SAW LIGHT COME ON LOWER
DECK..LIT FLARE AS SHIP PASSED 100 FEET TO THE
SOUTH..FLARE BRIGHT-NO DOUBT SHIP SAW IT..BUT
THEY JUST PUT ON MORE SPEED AND LEFT US..SHIP WAS
HEADING NORTH..

19 AUGUST SATURDAY DAY 66
1200 WIND WEST-SEAS CALM-LAND DUE EAST-ROWED 2
HOURS KEEPING RAFT INTO WIND HOPING TO TACK
NORTH TO OFFSET S CURRENT..ESTIMATE LAND 10 MILES
OFF-PRAYING FOR WIND CHANGE..
1600-ROWED KEEPING RAFT HEADED TOWARDS FAR
POINT OF LAND WITH COAST ALMOST PARALLEL TO
DIRECTION..HOPING TO MAKE POINT..SIM CAN SEE TREES
CLEARLY..SOME HOUSES..CANNOT BE TOO FAR
OFF..EXPECT TO BE ON SHORE WITHIN 48 HOURS..IF GOD
WILLS
1650-WIND SHIFTED MIRACULOUSLY SOUTH TO 220-
GREAT
1900-SAVED-AT 1700 HEARD LOUD ROAR AND LOOKED
OUT TO SEE WHITE LAUNCH BEARING DOWN ON US-
COSTA RICAN COAST GUARD VESSEL "PUNTA BURICA"
UNDER COMMAND OF CAPTAIN ROBERTO NUÑEZ
SALAZAR. HIS HELMSMAN GERMAN SOTO SPOTTED US-
THOUGHT IT WAS BUOY-WITHIN MINUTES THEY PULLED
OVER AND BACKED ON US. CREW THROUGH LINE WHICH
I FASTENED TO RAFT. ANOTHER CREW MEMBER
GRABBED SIM'S HAND WHILE I PUSHED. LOADED
SAILBAG WITH LOG, KNIFE AND PASSED IT UP. CREW
HELPED ME ABOARD THEN ONE MAN JUMPED INTO RAFT
AND RECOVERED EVERYTHING-RAFT LIFTED ONTO
DECK-HUNDREDS OF TRIGGER FISH LEFT HOMELESS-
1930-ENTERING GOLFITO TREMENDOUS LIGHTNING
STORM--BOAT SLOWED WAY DOWN--RADAR PICTURE NOT
TOO GOOD..
2000 ON SHORE-PIER ROCKING WILDLY!!!BUT IT WAS
US..AMBULANCE TOOK US TO HOSPITAL WHERE WE
RECEIVED EXCELLENT CARE..COLD WATER SHOWER-
AGUA DULCE-SOOTHING CREAM FOR SORES-ARE WE IN
HEAVEN?

Mexico

.Lyn & Dougal Robertson
with three children
and friend saved by
crew of *Toka Maru II*.
Sailed 800 Miles in 38 Days.

Maurice & Maralyn Bailey,
Saved by crew of *Weolmi*.
Drifted 1500 NM IN 118 DAYS

Day 2 path of
the *Ter Eriksen*

✕

Day 15
Birds Leave

Siboney Sunk
June 15, 1989
by Pilot Whales.

Day 20, Ship
nearly runs
over the Butlers

Lucette Sinks
June 15, 1972 Sunk
by Killer Whales.